DEVELOPING AGILITY AND QUICKNESS

SECOND EDITION

National Strength and Conditioning Association

Jay Dawes

EDITOR

HUMAN KINETICS

Library of Congress Cataloging-in-Publication Data

Names: Dawes, Jay. | National Strength & Conditioning Association (U.S.)
Title: Developing agility and quickness / National Strength and Conditioning
  Association, Jay Dawes, editor.
Description: Second Edition. | Champaign, Illinois : Human Kinetics, [2019] |
  Series: Sport performance series | Includes bibliographical references and
  index.
Identifiers: LCCN 2018035096 (print) | LCCN 2018053323 (ebook) | ISBN
  9781492586913 (epub) | ISBN 9781492569527 (PDF) | ISBN 9781492569510
  (print)
Subjects: LCSH: Sports sciences. | Sports--Physiological aspects. | Motor
  ability. | Motor learning.
Classification: LCC GV558 (ebook) | LCC GV558 .D45 2018 (print) | DDC
  613.71--dc23
LC record available at https://lccn.loc.gov/2018035096

ISBN: 978-1-4925-6951-0 (print)

The web addresses cited in this text were current as of October 2018, unless otherwise noted.

Senior Acquisitions Editor: Roger W. Earle; **Managing Editors:** Julie Marx Goodreau, Anna Lan Seaman, and Dominique J. Moore; **Copyeditor:** Rodelinde Albrecht; **Proofreader:** Lisa Himes, **Indexer:** May Hasso; **Permissions Manager:** Martha Gullo; **Senior Graphic Designer:** Nancy Rasmus; **Cover Designer:** Keri Evans; **Cover Design Associate:** Susan Rothermel Allen; **Photograph (cover):** Joe Robbins/Getty Images; **Photographs (interior):** © Human Kinetics, unless otherwise noted. Photos in chapter 3 on pages 51, 52, 55, 56, 58, 60, 61, 62, 63, and 65 courtesy of Jay Dawes; **Photo Asset Manager:** Laura Fitch; **Photo Production Coordinator:** Amy M. Rose; **Photo Production Manager:** Jason Allen; **Senior Art Manager:** Kelly Hendren; **Illustrations:** © Human Kinetics, unless otherwise noted; **Printer:** Sheridan Books

We thank Urbana High School in Urbana, Illinois, and the Mettler Center in Champaign, Illinois, for assistance in providing the locations for the photo shoot for this book.

Human Kinetics books are available at special discounts for bulk purchase. Special editions or book excerpts can also be created to specification. For details, contact the Special Sales Manager at Human Kinetics.

Printed in the United States of America   10 9 8 7 6

The paper in this book is certified under a sustainable forestry program.

Human Kinetics
1607 N. Market Street
Champaign, IL 61820
USA

United States and International
Website: **US.HumanKinetics.com**
Email: info@hkusa.com
Phone: 1-800-747-4457

Canada
Website: **Canada.HumanKinetics.com**
Email: info@hkcanada.com

E7354

DEVELOPING AGILITY AND QUICKNESS

SECOND EDITION

Contents

Introduction

Speed is an essential element in most sports. Speed is typically defined as the amount of time it takes to move between two points, but in sports these two points are often not in a straight line. For this reason, the ability to change direction quickly is often the difference between success and failure in many athletic endeavors. Therefore, many coaches and athletes are interested in finding effective ways to improve agility and quickness. The purpose of this book is to assist sports coaches, athletes, and strength and conditioning professionals in accomplishing this goal.

Agility and quickness are complex sporting skills that include both physical and cognitive components. According to Young, James, and Montgomery (1), the physical components of agility include those aimed at improving change of direction (COD) speed (i.e., technique, straight line speed, leg muscle qualities, and anthropometric variables), whereas the quickness-related factors are a function of perceptual and decision-making skills (i.e., visual scanning patterns, anticipation, pattern recognition, and knowledge of the situation). An example is a kick or punt returner in American football waiting patiently to receive a ball, who, upon catching it, must immediately decide which way to maneuver through the defense to gain yardage. Or imagine a point guard who dribbles down the lane and must determine whether to continue dribbling to make forward progression, pass the ball, or shoot. These are prime examples of how athletes must move and think fast to achieve success on the field or court. Thus, to maximize performance, athletic training programs must address both the physical and the cognitive components of agility and quickness. Only then will athletes be able to truly bridge the gap between practice and competition.

This second edition of *Developing Agility and Quickness* provides coaches and athletes with a resource to better understand the intricacies of developing a safe and effective training program to optimize performance. Using the latest research and advice from experienced coaches, the book provides the reader with a unique blend of science and practical application that can be immediately used to enhance athletic performance.

Chapter 1 discusses factors that influence COD speed, proper technique, body position, and the physical attributes needed for athletes to achieve high-level performance. This chapter also provides recommendations for other types of complementary training modalities that can be used to augment COD speed.

Chapter 2 explores perceptual and decision-making skills (i.e., quickness factors), such as information processing, knowledge of situations, anticipation, and arousal and anxiety levels. Athletes with high-level agility performance are better at recognizing and capitalizing on task- and game-relevant cues that give them a competitive advantage over their opponents. In many cases, these skills separate elite performers from everyone else.

Chapters 3 and 4 are new to this edition. Chapter 3 focuses on the importance of using the dynamic warm-up not only to prepare the athlete for more vigorous activity but also to develop specific skills necessary to improve movement efficiency. Chapter 4 discusses the need for the sequential development of skills based on sex- and age-related factors. These are important considerations when attempting to develop agility and quickness programs for specific populations and are the foundation for future athletic success.

Chapter 5 focuses on testing procedures and protocols to help evaluate an athlete's current strengths and weaknesses, and serve as a baseline for measuring progress over time. Once an athlete's strengths and weaknesses are identified, the coach can select drills to help the athlete continue to make improvements.

Chapters 6 and 7 present a wide variety of drills to improve agility and quickness. Many of these drills develop general motor programs and improve fundamental movement skills for future athletic success. These chapters also include suggestions and specific training drills that incorporate cognitive decision-making tasks into athletes' training programs once the athlete has mastered fundamental techniques. These unplanned, or open, drills require athletes to process information from the environment and to respond quickly with accuracy and precision. The drills included in these chapters provide a solid base of information to assist in the development of athlete-specific and sport-specific training programs.

Chapter 8 explores the basic foundations of designing agility and quickness programs by using a scientific approach to training. In chapter 9, the foundational concepts discussed in chapter 8 are put into context for specific sports. In this chapter, some of the world's leading experts and professionals from a variety of sports share their personal philosophies on agility and quickness training and their favorite drills for improving sport performance at a variety of skill levels.

This book serves as a basic guide and resource for the safe and effective development of comprehensive training programs for agility and quickness. It is loaded with valuable training tips and information that the experts in this book have taken a lifetime to develop. The NSCA hopes that readers will gain an appreciation for and a better understanding of what it takes to improve agility and quickness. Excellence does not occur by accident! It takes deliberate and focused effort. This book is an absolute must-have resource for coaches and athletes who are serious about taking performance to the next level.

Key to Diagrams

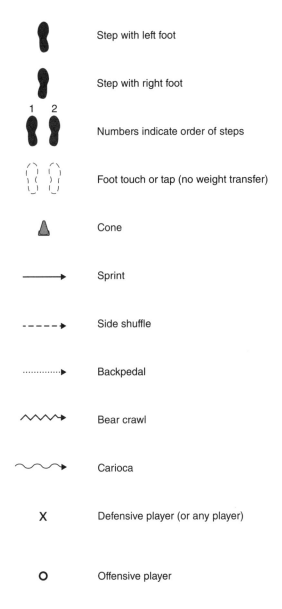

Step with left foot

Step with right foot

Numbers indicate order of steps

Foot touch or tap (no weight transfer)

Cone

Sprint

Side shuffle

Backpedal

Bear crawl

Carioca

X   Defensive player (or any player)

O   Offensive player

1 yard = 0.9 meter	40 yards = 36.6 meters
2 yards = 1.8 meters	50 yards = 45.7 meters
3 yards = 2.7 meters	3 feet = 0.9 meter
5 yards = 4.6 meters	0.3 meters = 1 foot
10 yards = 9.1 meters	1.5 meters = 1.6 yards
15 yards = 13.7 meters	3 meters = 3.3 yards
20 yards = 18.3 meters	5 meters = 5.5 yards
30 yards = 27.4 meters	10 meters = 10.9 yards

CHAPTER 1

Developing Change of Direction Speed

David N. Suprak

Most team sports, such as basketball, American football, and soccer, are characterized by rapid acceleration, deceleration, and changes of direction over relatively short distances. Further, court sports such as tennis require multidirectional first-step quickness and changes of direction within a 3 to 4 meter (9.8-13.1 feet) span (64, 117). Agility is a critical component of success in these activities as well as in many others. *Agility* has recently been defined as a rapid, whole-body change of direction or speed in response to a stimulus, and can be broken down into subcomponents made up of both physical qualities and cognitive abilities (96). One component of agility, therefore, is the ability to change direction rapidly and accurately. This chapter examines the physical qualities of speed, strength, power, anthropometrics, and technique as they relate to the development of change of direction (COD) speed.

SPEED

Athletes who can move faster than their opponents have an advantage. For example, a faster athlete may be able to get to a ball quicker than a competitor or may be able to outrun a pursuer. For this reason, athletes in most sports highly value speed. Speed is often measured by using linear (straight-line) sprinting over a distance between 40 and 100 yards (36.6-91.4 m). However, based on research and observation, it is evident that in many sports athletes are rarely required to sprint more than 20 to 30 yards (18.3-27.4 m) in a straight line before they must make some type of directional change (3, 8, 14, 89). Therefore, unless an athlete is a 100-meter sprinter, focusing

The author would like to acknowledge the significant contribution of Mark Roozen to this chapter.

the majority of time and attention on straight-ahead speed may not result in optimum performance in a given sport (33). On the other hand, since most sports require acceleration from a static state or when transitioning between movements, straight-line speed is still a valuable asset that athletes should focus on when testing and training for sports. In the following sections, specific aspects of both linear and lateral speed will be highlighted, as they relate to the development of optimum COD performance.

Sprinting is a highly technical skill, and appropriate training can improve running speed, even at the elite level. The combination of *stride frequency* (the number of strides per unit of time) and *stride length* (the distance covered in a single stride) primarily determine linear speed. In fact, *running velocity* (in meters per second) can be calculated by multiplying stride length (meters per stride) by stride frequency (strides per second) (80). So, athletes can improve linear speed by increasing stride frequency while maintaining stride length, increasing stride length while maintaining stride rate, or doing a combination of both (increasing stride frequency as well as stride length).

Many sports, with the exception of track-and-field sprinting, involve short sprints (<30 yards [27.4 m]) and rapid changes of direction or transitional movements (i.e., shuffling, chop step, etc.), followed by rapid accelerations. For this reason, a significant amount of speed training should be spent on

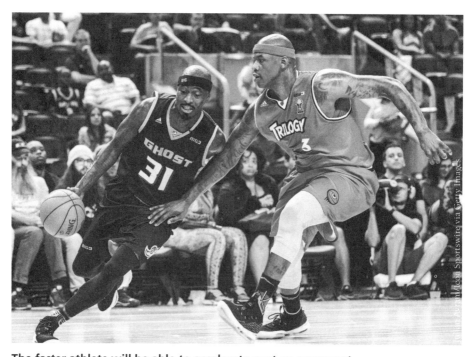

The faster athlete will be able to accelerate past an opponent.

improving acceleration, since athletes will not commonly reach maximum speed in competition (3, 8, 14, 33, 89). *Acceleration* is the rate of change in velocity, and this phase of sprinting is critical for changing directions rapidly in order to create or to close space between an athlete and the competition.

Optimal technique for linear sprinting in the acceleration phase involves four factors that maximize stride length and frequency, with the major contributor to increasing speed in this phase being stride length (67, 79).

1. The body should have a pronounced forward lean, with a torso angle of approximately 40 to 45 degrees, which results in a lower *center of mass* (COM) (63). The COM is a mechanical term referring to a hypothetical three-dimensional point about which the entire mass of the body is concentrated and balanced (75). For example, if one were to lay a pencil down on the tip of one finger and find the location at which the finger must be placed in order to balance the pencil, this location would approximate the pencil's COM. As long as foot contact remains just under or behind the COM, momentum in the forward direction should increase and braking forces should be minimized (31). Maintaining a rigid torso through bracing of the core musculature is also essential for the appropriate transfer of forces from the ground to the lower extremity and to the upper extremity, and vice versa, during the sprint.

2. When pushing off the ground during the propulsion phase, the foot touches the ground in a cocked position, with the ankle flexed upward at less than 90 degrees (dorsiflexion). Once the foot makes contact with the ground, the athlete forcefully extends the hip, knee, and ankle (termed *triple extension*) (see figure 1.1) (21).

3. During the recovery phase (when the free leg foot is not in contact with the ground), the ankle of the free leg

Figure 1.1 Proper technique for straight-ahead sprinting.

should be dorsiflexed while the knee and the hip are bent or flexed. This allows the foot to pass directly under the buttocks and permits a more rapid turnover at the hip.

4. The athlete should make certain to initiate arm swing at the shoulder with the elbow flexed at approximately 90 degrees. Emphasis should be placed on swinging the arm forcefully backward and allowing the body's stored elastic energy and stretch reflex to provide much of the forward propulsion of the arm (21).

The strength and power parameters discussed earlier in regard to COD in general apply also when considering linear speed. In the propulsion phase, the power output and the rate of force development of the hip extensors and quadriceps are important contributors to both stride length and frequency (45). In the recovery phase, the hip flexors (112) and the hamstrings (121) are the major contributors to stride frequency. The strength and power of the hip flexors is an important factor in moving the hip quickly from an extended hip position to a flexed position in preparation for the subsequent foot contact. The hamstrings have an important role as a multi-joint muscle group. Because the hamstrings cross both the hip and the knee, they are responsible for eccentrically decelerating the lower leg during the recovery phase in preparation for ground contact, while immediately transitioning to aid in hip extension for the propulsion phase of sprinting (121). This means that strengthening programs should focus on the hamstrings, both concentrically and eccentrically.

Although linear speed is an important determinant of success in many sports, athletes will not always have the luxury of moving only via a forward sprint. Athletes participating in soccer, basketball, and tennis, for example, will often have to move quickly in a lateral or a backward direction. Lateral movement, involving a shuffling motion, and backward movement, involving a backpedaling motion, are characterized by mechanics that are very different from those of linear sprinting technique. In backward movement, for example, the hamstrings will be less active and the quadriceps more active, when compared to linear sprinting (37). Lateral movement involves projection of the body in the frontal plane of motion, and therefore involves greater hip abductor demand than is observed in linear sprinting (6).For this reason, the techniques involved in quick lateral and backward movements should be practiced so that athletes can move rapidly, in any direction, while maintaining a balanced posture. Also, improving the mechanics, strength, and power of the involved musculature will result in faster movement in the lateral and backward directions.

The technical aspects of both lateral and backward movements include maintaining the COM in a low position within the *base of support* (BOS). In backward sprinting, the arm movement will be similar to that in forward sprinting, but the propulsion will be achieved through powerful quadriceps and, to a lesser degree, hip flexor action (108). In lateral movement, foot placement should remain lateral to the COM, so that propulsive forces are directed toward the direction of movement.

It is important to consider that these alternative movement patterns are often combined with decelerations and direction changes as well as with transitions to linear sprinting. Therefore, these movement patterns should be mastered by first practicing them in isolation and then incorporating them into the specific movement patterns involved in a given sport. Specific drills that can be used to improve footwork and backward and lateral movement speed will be covered in subsequent chapters of this book.

STRENGTH

Strength, or muscular strength, can be defined as the maximal force or torque produced by a muscle or a muscle group (12). Force is derived from the following equation,

$$\text{Force} = \text{Mass} \times \text{Acceleration}$$

where force represents the external force applied to an object, mass is the mass of the object, and acceleration is the change in velocity over time of that object due to the force. Therefore, force can be increased by increasing the mass of the object being moved while maintaining acceleration, increasing the acceleration of a given object's mass, or a combination of both increasing the object's mass and acceleration concurrently. Strength is an important contributor to COD expression and to athletic success in general. When considering the role of strength in agility development, consider that in acceleration, deceleration, and direction changes, the force that the athlete develops is aimed at moving and controlling his or her own body mass.

Therefore, relative strength (as compared to body mass) becomes particularly important. Many aspects of strength are important to consider when designing a program for agility development, including concentric strength, eccentric strength, and stabilization. These aspects of strength will be discussed in the subsequent sections.

Concentric Strength

Concentric strength refers to the muscular force exerted while the muscle is shortening. Concentric muscle actions can also be characterized by the performance of positive work, in which the force exerted against external resistance results in joint movement in the same direction as the force (9).

An example of concentric muscle action is the push-off during a running, jumping, or cutting motion, involving the powerful extension of the hip, knee, and ankle (triple extension; refer to figure 1.1 on page 3). Theoretically, the more force the foot exerts against the ground during running, the greater the acceleration of the body mass, leading to better performance. Likewise, the greater the force developed by the hip flexors during the recovery phase of running, the greater the forward angular acceleration of the hip. Greater hip flexor strength helps improve rate of force developed from these muscles and may allow the athlete to be positioned more quickly for the subsequent foot-strike. This results in greater stride frequency during straight-line sprinting and directional changes (30).

The scientific literature demonstrates a strong relationship between muscular strength and explosive movements, such as vertical and horizontal jumping (4, 114, 120), sprinting over distances from 5 to 40 yards (4.6-36.6 m) (20, 73, 88, 114, 120), and COD (114) movements. The relationship between concentric strength and explosive movements is even more pronounced when relative strength is considered, which factors in the athlete's size and weight. However, the relationship between concentric strength and explosive movements becomes less apparent when considering elite level athletes (24, 46, 98), suggesting a threshold in strength above which further improvements in explosive movement performance are more closely related to the rate of force development, which will be discussed in further detail later in this chapter. Maximum concentric strength is especially important in the acceleration phase of sprinting (120). Since acceleration is an integral factor in optimal COD technique, the role of concentric strength of the involved musculature is critical for performance in sports where COD is key.

Eccentric Strength

An important contributor to movements involving directional changes is the ability to decelerate the body mass quickly and under control, then rapidly accelerate again in the new direction. This ability can have positive effects not only on task performance but also on injury prevention, as most musculotendinous injuries in soccer occur during joint deceleration (102). The principal contributor to this deceleration is the eccentric strength of the involved musculature. *Eccentric strength* refers to the force exerted by a muscle as it lengthens. Eccentric muscle actions can be characterized by the performance of negative work, in which the force exerted against external resistance results in joint movement in the direction opposite to that of the force. A simple example is lowering a weight back to the starting position during a biceps curl.

An athlete with high eccentric strength is able to brake more rapidly and can therefore quickly and effectively decelerate the body while maintaining dynamic balance in preparation for a directional change (103). Conversely, inadequate eccentric strength can result in slow and inefficient deceleration and reduced ability to change direction quickly (18). In fact, eccentric strength has been shown to be a primary determinant of COD performance (18, 55, 81, 104). The relationship between eccentric strength and the ability to decelerate is exemplified by the movements in a stretch-shortening cycle. In order to minimize contact time with the ground during a stretch-shortening cycle (and during agility-type tasks), adequate eccentric strength is crucial for decelerating the body mass quickly so it can be accelerated in a new direction (56).

The ability to decelerate efficiently is important both for performance and for injury prevention. It is during eccentric muscle action that the greatest amount of force is generated (72), and this high force must be transmitted through the musculotendinous unit. One of the main contributors to proper deceleration is eccentric strength of the involved musculature. Since recent research indicates that eccentric strength is significantly correlated with COD speed (104) if these musculotendinous structures are not strong enough to withstand force during movement, poor biomechanics can lead to improper body position, increasing the chance of injury (49). On the other hand, training the eccentric component of muscle strength, through such modalities as resistance and plyometric training, can help to enhance the ability to decelerate the body mass, resulting in improved COD and athletic performance (93, 104, 119).

Stabilization Strength

The strength to support and stabilize the trunk and the joints of the lower body is an important factor that contributes to the effective application of force during COD movements (66). For example, during hip extension in the push-off of sprinting, the gluteus maximus (GM) is the *agonist* (i.e., contracting muscle). However, the GM is also responsible for producing hip external rotation, and excessive hip external rotation could result in inefficient joint alignment, thereby reducing the athlete's force production capabilities. A strong adductor magnus muscle may help better control this motion, which may improve the position of the hip joint and help to direct the force output of the GM toward forward propulsion of the body (116). Another example is the medial hamstrings and the lateral gastrocnemius muscles, which aid in controlling undesirable rotations in the frontal and transverse planes at the knee joint during various cutting maneuvers (51), thereby enhancing the performance of these movements and reducing the risk for injury (60, 61).

The strength and timing of the stabilizing contributions of these and other muscles can be enhanced by bilateral and unilateral resistance training using multi-joint movements (i.e., back squat; forward, backward, and diagonal lunges), as well as plyometric movements (19, 48, 78).

Another aspect of muscular contraction that is closely related to stability during movement is intermuscular coordination, which relates to the timing of activation of the various muscles across a joint. Intermuscular coordination is an important contributor to running gait. For example, if the hamstrings are not relaxed when the thigh is brought forward in the recovery phase of the stride, then hip flexion will be reduced, resulting in a shorter stride length. The importance of intermuscular coordination is especially clear in movements involving direction changes, where joint stability is of greater concern for the athlete. This concept is illustrated by the observation that more experienced soccer players display less co-contraction of the hamstrings and the quadriceps and more coordinated muscle activation patterns during a cutting maneuver than their less experienced counterparts (101). For these reasons, it would seem to be a prudent strategy to incorporate training focused on developing acceleration, deceleration, and change of direction change technique to improve intermuscular coordination (118) and, in turn, COD performance.

Experienced soccer players display intermuscular coordination that allows for stability in speed and changes of direction.

POWER

Power, defined as the rate of doing work (43), is an extremely important factor related to speed and agility, and may be one of the most important determinants of athletic success (106). Power can be calculated as follows:

$$\text{Power} = \text{Work} \div \text{Time}$$

In this equation, *time* refers to the period in which the work was performed. Work can be calculated with this equation:

$$\text{Work} = \text{Force} \times \text{Distance}$$

Because of the relation of work, force, and power, power can also be calculated as follows:

$$\text{Power} = \text{Force} \times \text{Velocity}$$

In this equation, *velocity* is the speed of movement in a specific direction.

The force–velocity relationship of muscle action shows that, as the movement velocity increases in a concentric muscle action, the muscle force output decreases. It should be noted that athletes cannot effectively train for power by only moving the body, or the resistance, slowly during training. As the previous equation suggests, power output can be improved by increasing force output, the velocity of movement, or both. Training methods for improving movement velocity differ significantly from those used for increasing force output, so a training program for COD development should incorporate both (23). In general terms, to maximize muscular power, athletes should first aim to improve the amount of force that a muscle is capable of producing (muscular strength) prior to performing power training. This is because an adequate amount of strength is required to control body positions when moving at high speeds. Therefore, it appears muscular strength provides a good foundation for improving power and movement economy.

Rate of Force Development

Rate of force development (RFD) is a characteristic of muscle-force output that is important for optimal functioning and closely relates to the discussion of power. This term is defined as the change in the level of force divided by the change in time to complete a task (58). To illustrate the importance of this concept, consider that maximal isometric force generation takes approximately 0.6-0.8 seconds to achieve (122). However, athletes do not achieve maximum force during high-speed activities. In sprinting, for example, the foot is only contacting the ground for about 0.1 seconds (76) for elite level sprinters. Therefore, the time constraints inherent in explosive activities, such as sprinting, jumping, throwing, acceleration, and changes of direction, dictate that force be developed quickly so that movement can occur rapidly. In these instances, the RFD becomes more important than the capability for maximum force (51).

Several authors have demonstrated the important contribution of RFD to high performance in various explosive movements, including vertical jump, sprinting, COD, and weightlifting movements (10, 85, 105). Part of the process of developing agility includes improving the RFD of the involved musculature so that explosive movements can be achieved at high forces, and athletes can impart greater forces into the ground during foot contact. The rate of muscle activation is thought to be the primary factor influencing RFD (59); however, other contributing factors may include patterns of motor unit recruitment (2), preactivation (1), fiber type composition (17), and muscle hypertrophy (115). Performing explosive exercises, such as plyometrics and Olympic lifts (push jerk, snatch), can improve RFD (41).

Stretch-Shortening Cycle

The force–velocity relationship of muscle action dictates that force output decreases as the muscle-shortening velocity increases (69). This phenomenon is obviously a disadvantage for rapid movements, such as jumping, throwing, and changing directions. However, rapid eccentric muscle actions are capable of generating high muscular forces (69). The *stretch-shortening cycle* (SSC) allows athletes to increase their force generation capabilities by performing a rapid eccentric (elongating) muscle action immediately prior to a concentric (shortening) muscle contraction. This rapid prestretching of the muscle just prior to contraction of the same muscle allows for a more rapid expression of force than when performing the concentric action alone (83).

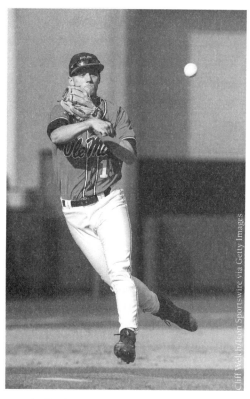

Baseball players use a high rate of force development to create a powerful throw quickly.

Three phases compose the stretch-shortening cycle: eccentric, amortization, and concentric (figure 1.2). In the *eccentric (stretching) phase*, the agonist muscles undergo a lengthening action as the athlete initiates the movement in the direction opposite to that of the intended movement. This phase is extremely important to the effectiveness of the stretch-shortening cycle, because this is where the muscle is taking advantage of the force–velocity relationship to build high forces prior to the initiation of concentric action, through both the storage of elastic energy in the tendons and fascia, and the monosynaptic stretch reflex (26). The literature suggests that both a small magnitude (small range of motion) and a high velocity of the stretching movement are important for maximizing its contribution to concentric force augmentation (47, 65).

The *amortization phase* comprises the time between the end of the eccentric phase and the beginning of the concentric phase of movement. The ability to transition quickly from the eccentric to the concentric phase of the SSC is often termed *reactive strength*, and is defined as the length of the amortization phase (42). This phase may be the most critical in the SSC, because much of the force generated during the eccentric phase can dissipate quickly.

The *concentric phase* of the SSC represents the time during which force application results in motion in the intended direction. In this phase, the previous eccentric action created increased force and power output of the agonist musculotendinous units. However, the extent to which this increased

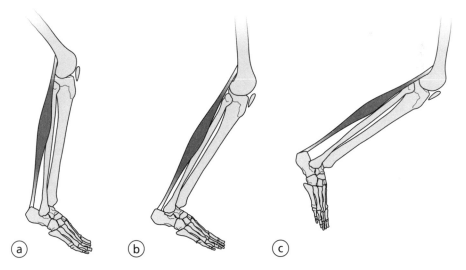

(a) (b) (c)

Figure 1.2 The stretch-shortening cycle. The period from the foot touching down to the end of the downward movement is the *(a)* eccentric phase. The transition from the eccentric phase to the concentric phase when no movement occurs is the *(b)* amortization phase. The start of the push-off from the foot leaving the surface is the *(c)* concentric phase.

force benefits the athlete is predicated on minimizing the duration of the amortization phase.

The ability of the SSC to contribute to force production is attributed to two main mechanisms, one of a neurophysiological nature and the other of a mechanical nature (26). In a neurophysiological context, improved muscular efficiency is related to the stretch reflex and the involved activity of the muscle spindles. When a muscle rapidly stretches (e.g., the rectus femoris and gastrocnemius at initial contact in a cutting maneuver), the corresponding muscle spindles, which lie parallel to the force-producing muscle fibers, also stretch. This results in a monosynaptic reflex, in which the sensory endings of the muscle spindles send a signal to the spinal cord about the change in muscle length. The spinal cord, in response, sends an excitatory signal to the corresponding muscle. These events result in the mechanical mechanism, which is a reflexive concentric action of the previously stretched muscle. This reflex may also be a protective mechanism against excessive stretching of the musculotendinous unit.

At this point, the importance of the length of the amortization phase becomes evident. The stretch reflex occurs less than 50 milliseconds after a rapid stretch (11, 13). The amortization phase should, therefore, be kept as short as possible in order to take advantage of the potential force increase that results from coupling the stretch reflex with active, concentric muscle action.

Improved muscular efficiency also results from the storage of potential (elastic) energy in the musculotendinous unit. This involves the stretching of the series elastic component (tendon) and, to a lesser extent, parallel elastic components (intramuscular fascia) of the musculotendinous unit. Elastic energy is

Recoiling muscle action increases force and power output, which allows athletes to jump with force and power.

stored within these components when the muscle is stretched. This energy is released shortly after it is stored, either in the form of the tissue recoiling to return to its original length, or as heat. In sprinting, jumping, and cutting maneuvers, the stored energy is used in subsequent force production during the propulsion phase.

Once again, the length of the amortization phase has important implications here. The elastic energy stored in the series and parallel elastic components during the lengthening action lasts only a short time before it dissipates as heat. However, if the amortization phase is kept to a minimum, the recoiling action of the series and parallel elastic components couple with the active concentric muscle action, resulting in increased force and power output. If athletes rely exclusively on muscular contraction without prestretching, they will need much more energy to do the same tasks, and they would not be able to achieve the same level of force and power output.

The SSC can have profound influences on the power output of an explosive movement while also improving movement efficiency. In order to maximize the force output of the concentric contraction in an SSC, the eccentric action should be quick (low magnitude and high velocity) and the amortization phase should be as short as possible (27, 110). These characteristics of the SSC can be improved by training, but may be independent of strength levels in trained athletes (5). Therefore, specific training of the SSC, also referred to as plyometrics, should be incorporated into a training program designed to maximize speed and COD in athletes.

ANTHROPOMETRIC VARIABLES

Anthropometric variables, such as height, weight, body fat, and length and circumference of the limbs and trunk, may play a major role in athletic success. These variables tend to predict positional and sport aptitude, as well. For example, rugby forwards tend to be taller and heavier compared to backs (25, 84), and arm span appears to be one of the best predictors of performance in adolescent 100-m swimmers (62). If two athletes are of equal body weight, the leaner athlete may be able to produce greater force than the athlete with more body fat, because a greater amount of lean muscle mass can contribute to greater force production. Furthermore, excess fat may create a larger physiological burden when the athlete attempts to change directions (27, 28). One study found that boys with a higher percent of body fat had poorer performances than their slimmer counterparts in the 40-yard (36.6 m) dash and in COD tests (7). In a study by Dawes and colleagues (28), it was found that as the sum of skinfolds increased, performance on an occupationally specific agility course decreased. Thus, by simply changing one anthropometric variable, body composition, an athlete may improve power-to-weight ratio, which may then provide a greater opportunity to improve speed and COD performance (23). These factors should be considered in the program design process for those desiring to optimize COD speed.

TECHNIQUE

Success in many sports depends on an athlete's ability to rapidly and correctly initiate and stop movement in multiple directions while maintaining proper body control and joint position. Athletes can change directions more effectively by ensuring that their body is in the best possible position to produce, reduce, transfer, and stabilize both internal and external forces. If any segment of the body is out of position, they will not be able to achieve optimal COD performance. If the body mass is under control during movement (dynamic stability), however, then the forces exerted on the ground during deceleration, changing direction, or acceleration can be directed toward increasing the velocity of movement, and less toward regaining control of the body. Thus, optimal technique is essential for maximizing COD performance and quickness, and will manifest in correct body posture, foot placement, and the BOS.

Agility performance comprises a series of discrete tasks strung together to form what is called a *serial task*. The athlete must first be able to effectively execute individual movement patterns, and then combine the various movement patterns discussed in this section in the proper sequence and at the proper time while accelerating, decelerating, and transitioning in multiple directions. Therefore, athletes should first master individual movement patterns by practicing each of the skills in a controlled environment. Next, they may combine tasks and incorporate them into the specific movement patterns involved in a given sport. They can then use specific drills to improve footwork and speed in backward and lateral movements.

To produce the movement needed to change directions, athletes should begin in a proper position. The *universal athletic position* (figure 1.3) is an effective beginning stance for a variety of movement patterns. Here, athletes slightly flex the knees and hips, slightly lean the torso forward, flatten the back, and position the head straight with eyes looking forward (22). Other common positions include a *staggered stance* (figure 1.4), such as the one used by defensive backs in football and a *three-point stance* (figure 1.5) used by defensive linemen. Athletes can incorporate these stances to add greater sport specificity to a variety of multidirectional drills.

The body posture assumed during activity will, in part, determine the positioning of the COM of the body in space. Two important concepts should be understood regarding the COM and its relation to agility expression. First, the farther from an object's COM a force acts, the more likely that force is to

Figure 1.3 The universal athletic position from the *(a)* front and *(b)* side views.

Figure 1.4 The staggered stance.

Figure 1.5 The three-point stance.

cause rotation of the body (this can also be seen using the pencil example). In *anatomical position* (standing erect with arms at the side and palms facing forward), the COM in the human body is located approximately at the level of, and a few centimeters posterior to, the umbilicus (navel). If a force is imparted on the human body above the level of the COM while standing straight up, the body will likely rotate about the feet, and if the force is great enough, it will cause the body to tip over and fall. This occurrence is related to the distance between the point of force application and the ground. The situation is similar during rapid changes of direction. If the body (the COM) is moving rapidly one way, and a person attempts to reverse the direction of movement, the reaction force exerted by the ground on the foot is more likely to cause unwanted rotation of the body if the COM is farther from the foot (if the person is standing taller). This phenomenon illustrates the importance of a lower running style for improved COD performance. Indeed, when comparing the running styles of elite track sprinters and rugby players, Sayers (95) suggested that sprinting with a high COM requires postural adjustments (lowering the COM and shortening stride lengths) to decelerate before changing direction. Therefore, a running style incorporating a slightly lower COM may be advantageous to rapid direction changes.

The second concept to be considered in relation to the COM and agility concerns the BOS. In two-foot standing, the BOS is roughly equal to the area between the two feet (50). To maintain balance, the traditional view expressed in the literature has been that the COM must remain within the confines of the BOS (99). In situations where only one foot is in contact with the ground (running, cutting, etc.), however, this view does not seem to be viable, since dynamic stability can apparently still be maintained. Even if the COM is outside the BOS, stability can still be achieved as long as the velocity of the COM is in the direction of the BOS (50). For example, in a cutting maneuver to the right, the athlete's left foot is contacting the ground to the left of the body. The area under the left foot becomes the BOS, since the right foot is not touching the ground. If this position were to be attempted in a static standing condition, the body would fall over to the right side because the COM would be far outside the BOS. However, because the momentum of the body in a cutting maneuver is moving in the direction of the planting foot (the BOS), dynamic stability can be maintained and changes of direction can be made more effectively. In fact, optimal foot placement, and therefore BOS positioning, defines direction in which the COM can be accelerated (87), since directional changes require the reorientation of the body, together with the ground reaction force, to move the COM in the desired direction (77). It therefore follows that the higher the velocity of movement (and, thus, the higher the velocity of the COM), the farther the plant foot can and should be placed from the COM in order to produce a change in direction while maintaining dynamic stability. Therefore, acceleration is optimized by contacting the ground behind the COM in relation to the direction of progression, resulting in pronounced force imparted by the foot to the ground in the direction opposite to the desired movement, and ground reaction force in the desired direction (52). This positioning of the contact foot behind the COM also results in high angular momentum in the direction of progression (34). During deceleration, the foot should contact the ground in front of the COM, and to move to the side, the foot contact should be on the side of the COM opposite the desired movement direction. In all of these movement situations, a lower COM helps to direct more of the force toward movement of the body in the desired direction, and less toward unnecessary rotation of the body. Various foot speed, ladder, and cone drills can be incorporated into the training program aimed at improving the ability to maintain dynamic stability at high speeds via correct alignment of the COM and the BOS at various velocities. These drills will be covered in subsequent chapters.

The same principles of position and body mechanics that are emphasized during power movements, such as doing explosive movements or linear speed work, are also critical when producing explosive directional changes. Thus, the propulsive forces generated through triple extension are vital for optimal COD performance. When backpedaling, athletes can achieve propulsion with the powerful action of the quadriceps and the hip flexors (figure 1.6). The arm movement is similar to that used in forward sprinting.

In many cases, as athletes attempt to change direction, they pump their arms less, allowing the hands to cross the midline of the body, or they fail

Figure 1.6 Proper body position for backpedaling from the *(a)* front and *(b)* side views.

to swing the arms from the shoulders. Unfortunately, all of these extraneous movements may reduce their ability to produce quick directional changes. In order to produce force in any direction, athletes should use a proper arm swing that originates from the shoulder. Arms flexed at approximately 90 degrees will help produce greater force and more explosive movements.

The ability to reduce speed quickly and under control is also essential to produce rapid and accurate changes in direction. Figure 1.7 shows the proper position for deceleration of a forward movement. Figure 1.8 shows the proper position for both deceleration and acceleration of forward and lateral movements. These are the optimal positions for effectively producing and reducing speed (32, 35). Notice during the forward movements (figure 1.7) that the majority of the athlete's weight is on the ball of the foot. During

Figure 1.7 After the *(a)* last normal stride, the athlete *(b, c, d)* decelerates by taking abbreviated steps until she comes to a *(e)* full stop.

Figure 1.8 *(a, b, c)* The athlete decelerates by taking abbreviated steps and *(d)* turns laterally while lowering his COM *(e, f)*. While making a lateral COD, the athlete keeps the COM low and points the lower leg in the new direction *(g, h)*. The athlete then accelerates in the new direction.

lateral movements, it is also on the medial aspect of the inside foot and on the lateral aspect of the outside foot (figure 1.8). To prepare for any directional change, the angles of the ankle and knee should be about or less than 90 degrees, and the hips and the COM should be in a low position. The foot of the outside leg should remain outside the COM and the lower leg should point roughly in the direction of the desired movement.

The transfer of forces relies on the ability to control the COM and the BOS. Athletes with high COD speed can quickly and effectively position their bodies in an optimal manner to control their COM. If the COM moves too far away from the BOS, given its momentum, the athlete may lose balance or even fall. The ability to control the COM with respect to the BOS allows athletes to transfer force and power more efficiently and to perform at higher levels.

Athletes can improve their ability to change directions with balance, body control, and minimal loss of speed by widening their BOS and lowering their COM. Figure 1.9 shows the correct position and an example of an incorrect body position during the breakdown of a lateral movement. In figure 1.9*a*, the athlete's weight is distributed evenly on the inside of the foot, and the knee is aligned over the ankle. In figure 1.9*b*, the majority of the athlete's weight is on the outside of the foot, and the ankle and knee are in a compromised position over the outside. Furthermore, notice in figure 1.9*a* how the athlete's shin is angled toward the direction of the desired movement (this is often termed a *positive shin angle*). Compare this to figure 1.9*b*, in which the athlete's shin is angled in the direction opposite to the desired movement. Not only is this angle inappropriate for generating the power necessary for explosive changes of direction but it also places the joints in a vulnerable position for injury.

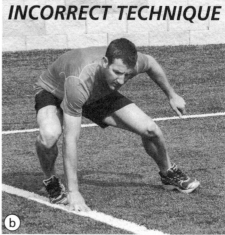

Figure 1.9 *(a)* The correct position for changing direction in lateral movement. *(b)* An incorrect body position is less effective and more likely to cause injury.

When changing direction, some sort of rotation generally must occur to transition from one movement pattern to the next (17). For example, when transitioning from a forward sprint in one direction to one in the opposite direction, many athletes begin by turning the head, immediately followed by the shoulders and the trunk. This creates a shift in the body's COM that allows the athlete to turn the pelvis and hips in the intended direction of movement (17). Others initiate the rotation at the hip joint of the free leg, as shown in figure 1.10. The aim here is for the foot of the free leg to strike

Figure 1.10 Transition movement with an open-leg knee drive. This COD skill teaches the athlete to plant and step as part of the COD motion. The athlete *(a)* begins to decelerate and *(b)* plants the outside leg, maintaining proper body position to load the muscles for the COD. The athlete *(c)* steps with the opposite leg, driving off the leg to propel in the new direction, and *(d)* sprints away.

the ground on the next step, pointing in the intended direction for the next movement (figure 1.11).

Regardless of the technique used, coaches should emphasize several specific cues to make certain the athlete is in the proper position to transition to the next movement with as little wasted motion as possible. Athletes should focus on driving the knee of the lead leg up forcefully and pivoting the hips in the new direction. Correct body position produces lower extremity joint angles that are favorable for producing optimal torque. This helps produce maximal speed of movement by encouraging rapid joint rotation in the desired direction. In order to assist in fully turning their hips and generating maximal

Figure 1.11 Transition movement with an opposite-leg knee drive. This COD skill teaches the athlete to push off as part of the COD motion. The athlete (a) lowers the COM and loads the outside leg while opening the hips and (b) lifting the inside leg to change direction. The athlete (c) pushes off with the outside leg, turns hips, and gets ready to plant the inside foot with a positive shin angle to move in the opposite direction. The athlete (d) sprints away.

power, athletes should imagine that they have a camera at their navel. They should point the lens of the camera to take a picture of the direction they wish to go. Another cue for proper arm mechanics is to drive the lead elbow back in the direction of the planting foot to rotate the upper body and assist with core rotation. This action also helps athletes get into proper running form more efficiently.

COMPLEMENTARY TRAINING

Aside from technique, there are several forms of complementary training that can be used to enhance agility performance. The following section will highlight several of these options; for a more comprehensive overview of these topics, the reader is directed to the following resources provided by the National Strength and Conditioning Association:

- ▶ *Exercise Technique Manual for Resistance Training*
- ▶ *Strength Training*
- ▶ *Developing Power*

Resistance Training

Resistance training is commonly used to increase strength, power, and muscle mass. The literature demonstrates the clear contribution that muscular strength makes to enhanced performance in explosive movements, such as jumping, sprinting, and changing directions. In general, faster athletes are able to reach higher running speeds by striking the ground with greater force over shorter durations (i.e., higher ground reaction forces and RFD) compared to slower runners (70). Therefore, increasing the maximal force-producing capabilities of the involved musculature would appear beneficial (18, 22, 29, 118). For example, increasing back squat strength has been shown to improve peak power output, 5-m, 10-m, and 20-m sprint performances, and vertical jump height following eight weeks of training in professional rugby league and soccer players (20, 23, 29).

Although there are many specific aspects of maximizing muscle force output, the basic guidelines can be summed up in terms of load used, target repetitions per set, number of sets completed, and rest intervals used between sets. A simple guideline for developing strength is to employ heavy loads (≥85% of 1RM), for six or fewer repetitions per set for 2 to 5 sets, separated by rest intervals of at least 2 minutes (97). This basic guideline can be adjusted as the athlete progresses through a training cycle, in order to bring about sustained adaptations. For example, the program can start with three sets of five repetitions with 85% 1RM, separated by two minutes, and progress to five sets of two repetitions at 93% 1RM, separated by 3 to 4 minutes. Of course, this type of training should only be undertaken when the individual has developed a sound fitness foundation and has developed proper technique in the exercises involved.

Movement specificity is an important consideration when developing a resistance training program aimed at optimizing COD performance, especially as the training status and strength levels of athletes increase. A systematic review of the literature revealed that resistance training that does not involve a countermovement has limited transfer to rapid force development in unloaded dynamic movements that involve the SSC, especially for well-trained individuals (111). In addition, limited transferability of the strength gains seen in bilateral movements was observed for unilateral movements in well-trained individuals (111). Therefore, in order to maximize task-specific gains, it would be prudent to progress from less movement specificity in the early stages of resistance training to more movement specificity as the athlete gains strength and training experience.

It is critical to progressively build the capacity to decelerate, change direction, and accelerate, and part of this process should incorporate resistance training. A periodized program emphasizing technique and work capacity early, then maximum muscle strength, then power output and RFD should help to optimize results (107).

Hip Strength

In a cutting maneuver associated with changing direction, the hip abducts and extends (rotates to the side and backward), the knee extends (straightens), and the ankle plantar flexes (toes move away from the lower leg). Hip abduction and extension is performed primarily by the gluteus maximus muscle, located on the back of the hip joint. The quadriceps muscle group performs knee extension. Finally, ankle plantar flexion is performed primarily by the gastrocnemius muscle, located on the back of the lower leg (68). With this in mind, strengthening programs should focus attention on these muscles in order to enhance propulsion in sprinting and cutting. Additionally, stabilizing musculature is important to consider, as these muscles help to ensure that force generation is properly directed, and that body control is maintained throughout the movement. At the ankle, for example, the peroneus longus (rotates the ankle to the outside) and tibialis anterior (pulls the foot up toward the lower leg) muscles stabilize the ankle during cutting maneuvers, enabling the powerful gastrocnemius to plantar flex the ankle powerfully for the COD (82). Therefore, these muscle groups may warrant special attention in the resistance training program.

Eccentric Strength

It is also important to optimize eccentric hamstring strength, because it has an important role in maintaining neuromuscular control during ground contact of both linear and COD tasks (55), helps maintain hip extensor torque, assists with dynamic trunk stabilization, and controls knee function (40). In addition, a quadriceps-dominant strategy during a cutting maneuver can predispose individuals to noncontact knee injuries (44). Therefore, the function of the hamstrings is critical to optimal COD performance, and should be trained in both concentric and eccentric muscle actions (40).

Power

As important as increased strength is to optimal COD speed development, power output and RFD improvements of the involved musculature are just as important. Several methods can be used to target power improvements. Athletes can use the same movements used for strength development (i.e., back squat, deadlift), but employ lower loads so that the movement speed is faster (27). Second, the many variations of Olympic lifts (clean, jerk, snatch, hang clean, etc.) can be used in order to incorporate the kinetic chains of both the upper and lower body. In either case, the emphasis should be placed on speed of movement, so rest intervals between sets should be between 2 and 5 minutes to minimize fatigue (97). The recommended load to use varies in the literature, but it is beneficial to select a load that elicits the highest power output. For Olympic lifts variations, a load of approximately 70-80% 1RM is recommended (38, 57). For lower body exercises, use 45-70% 1RM (53, 94, 100).

Plyometric Training

Plyometric training is a type of training that deliberately incorporates the SSC into each repetition to enhance force and power output of the concentric action during execution. Examples include vertical or horizontal jumps (either from the ground or rebounding from a drop off a box or platform), throws or passes, which use a prestretch of the involved musculature immediately prior to executing the desired movement. This type of training has been in practice since at least the 1960s, when Yuri Verkhoshansky observed that people could significantly improve their jumping and sprinting abilities using progressive jumping exercises (113). Subsequently, other authors have studied these mechanisms more in depth, and reported that plyometric training can result in increased peak force, average power and velocity of movement, heightened muscle activation, improved muscle spindle sensitivity and joint proprioception, and improved storage of elastic energy and efficiency of the stretch reflex (26, 39).

The improvements reported in performance after plyometric training have been attributed mainly to neural adaptations, since this type of training often results in enhanced neuromuscular performance without increases in muscle size (92). The specificity of these adaptations to the training type is further illustrated in that greater improvements in speed, COD, and explosiveness measures are seen when plyometric training is done in addition to resistance training, compared to resistance training alone (36). Even short-term training can be beneficial, as Ramachandran and Pradhan reported improved vertical jump and agility performance following just two weeks of plyometric training in professional basketball players (91). Therefore, short plyometric training cycles may help to enhance performance.

The literature suggests that a variety of exercise types should be employed when implementing plyometric training to optimize COD performance. This is because COD tasks require optimal control of the COM and the BOS, as previously discussed, and because they involve multiple movement modes in multiple planes of motion. For example, Thomas, French, and Hayes found that both countermovement jump and depth jump training can improve both vertical jump and agility performance (109). Further, McCormick and colleagues suggested that athletes should incorporate plyometric exercises in all planes of motion to optimize improvements in power and COD speed (74). Coaches and athletes, therefore, should consider incorporating a variety of plyometric exercises in various planes of motion in order to achieve the greatest improvements in power and COD speed.

Flexibility, Mobility Training, and Warm-Ups

Another important factor contributing to COD performance is achieving optimal flexibility of the muscles and mobility of the joints. *Flexibility* can be defined as the ability to move an individual joint through a full range of motion and is often measured in a nonweight-bearing position (54). Flexibility can be an important contributor to movement capability. For example, if the hamstrings are excessively tight, and this tightness reduces the flexibility in the hip joint, hip flexion may be hindered during the recovery phase of sprinting, and speed and agility may suffer. Tight hip flexors may restrict hip extension, reducing the power output during the triple extension during propulsion. However, this example illustrates how a lack of flexibility at the hip joint is manifested as diminished mobility. *Mobility* is a more functional term, defined as an individual's ability (or inability) to achieve an intended position or posture, and is more related to relevant movement patterns (16). While sufficient flexibility contributes to mobility, mobility also entails stability and coordination in multiple joints functioning together, and in multiple planes of movement (16). In a COD maneuver, the hip must be mobile enough to both externally rotate and extend, and the ankle must exhibit full range of plantar flexion motion, while the knee remains stable while extending. The lumbar spine must remain stable to transmit forces, while the thoracic spine and the scapula (shoulder blade) display mobility to allow the arms to aggressively rotate through the shoulder to move the body in the intended new direction. Therefore, to perform a single whole-body movement, the various joints must coordinate roles to contribute to optimal function.

Increasing flexibility at the joints that contribute to COD speed (specifically, ankle, hip, thoracic spine, and shoulder) can be accomplished via a combination of targeted static and dynamic stretching and *proprioceptive neuromuscular facilitation* (PNF). One caveat to undertaking a program of increasing flexibility is that excessive range of motion at a joint can predispose an individual to acute injury (15). In addition, recent findings indicate that, to an extent, greater levels of lower-body stiffness are associated with improved performance in tasks that involve rapid stretch-shortening cycles (90). Therefore, there appears to be an optimal range of flexibility that can contribute effectively to performance while limiting injury risk. While *static stretching* is characterized by taking the joint to the end range of motion and holding the position for several seconds (usually 15-30 seconds), PNF training involves multiple methods designed to take advantage of neuromuscular mechanisms to reflexively allow for enhanced elongation of the musculotendinous unit while stretching. It entails taking the joint to the end range, then contracting the muscle to be stretched, either isometrically or concentrically, then bringing the joint to a new, often further, endpoint and holding it (71). Both of these methods are effective at increasing joint range of motion following chronic implementation (71). However, they are also both joint-specific, and result in decreased force- and power-related performance if conducted prior to movement execution (i.e., at the beginning of a training session). Dynamic warm-ups are, therefore, recommended prior to performance of high-force or high-power movements, such as sprinting, jumping, or COD movements. *Dynamic warm-ups* involve progressive movement patterns that often exaggerate the ranges of motion that will be used in the subsequent session and challenge the involved musculature and connective tissue in functional patterns (86). If static stretching, PNF, or both are incorporated into a training program for increased flexibility to contribute to optimal mobility, these techniques should be used at the end of training sessions and competitions. Specific dynamic warm-up activities will be addressed in greater detail in later chapters.

CONCLUSION

COD speed is a critical component of performance for those involved in many team sports, and a component that can be improved if trained properly. Targeted training that focuses on correcting and optimizing technique; maximizing strength, power, and RFD of involved musculature; and enhancing mobility, and employs strategies to avoid common injuries can bring about optimal adaptations leading to desired performance improvements. The following chapters will present methods of application of the principles discussed here and focused training strategies to achieve optimal enhancement of COD speed.

CHAPTER 2

Factors Determining Quickness

Tania Spiteri
Jeremy Sheppard

The ability to identify relevant cues and execute the correct corresponding movements with minimal delay contributes to an athlete's success in competition. If an athlete misreads or mistimes these cues, it can literally cost a goal, a game, or even a championship. Numerous perceptual and decision-making factors influence a player's reactive ability, or quickness, which also affects agility.

DECISION-MAKING SKILLS

Decision-making is the ability to accurately and rapidly identify task-relevant cues within the sporting environment, process the incoming information, and select the most appropriate response. Often referred to as *reading the play*, successful decision-making requires superior perceptual–cognitive ability and physical capacity to produce a coordinated movement output in response to external stimuli. During competition when the athlete has decided which specific movement to make, based on information collected by sensory mechanisms from external stimuli, this movement is then compared to prior stored knowledge and feedback mechanisms (proprioceptive and peripheral), before being interpreted by the motor cortex (20, 35). The brain then sends a message through the spinal cord to the working muscles, producing the desired movement output (35). This response represents the collective interaction between the nervous system and intrinsic muscle properties to modulate movement output in response to input regarding the surrounding environment.

The authors would like to acknowledge the significant contribution of Jay Dawes to this chapter.

FACTORS INFLUENCING DECISION-MAKING ABILITY

Many factors can influence decision-making ability. Broadly, the task, environment, and organismic constraints influence the ability of an athlete to make rapid and accurate decisions during competition (figure 2.1).

Task Constraints

Task constraints vary between different sports, however refer to the number of players on the court, player size, speed of movement execution, object manipulation, and presentation of the stimulus. During competition, movements are typically executed rapidly, reducing the time available for athletes to identify and respond to relevant stimuli within the environment, resulting in a slower decision-making time. Further, a majority of team sports require athletes to control an object (e.g., a ball, bat, or racquet) when making and executing

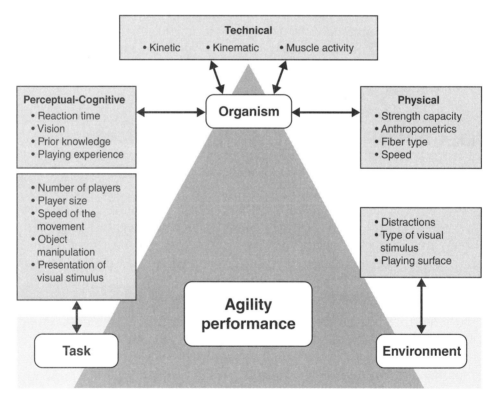

Figure 2.1 Organismic, task, and environmental constraints affecting decision-making ability.

Reprinted by permission from T. Spiteri, F. McIntyre, C. Specos, and S. Myszka, "Cognitive Training for Agility: The Integration Between Perception and Action," *Strength and Conditioning Journal* 40, no. 1 (2017): 39-46.

decisions. Research has shown that this increases the cognitive demand of the task and slows decision-making time in novices, but despite this, elite athletes have the ability to produce a faster performance (29).

Environmental Constraints

Environmental constraints describes the athletic environment in which the task occurs; specifically, the type of stimuli that athletes are required to respond to and the external distractions present that can negatively influence decision-making ability. Research in this area has revealed that a faster decision-making time is directly dependent upon prior knowledge and experience specific to the sporting context in addition to the specificity of the stimulus to the athlete's sporting environment (2). External distractions such as the number of athletes and the atmosphere of the crowd can either increase or decrease athletes' arousal and anxiety, impacting their ability to make rapid and successful decisions (34).

Organismic Constraints

Organismic constraints describe the physical, technical, and perceptual–cognitive qualities of an athlete and how these affect movement output (25). *Physical qualities* refer to the anthropometrics, general motor abilities, and strength and power capacity that can affect an athlete's ability to successfully execute the desired movement, while *technical qualities* describe an athlete's ability to sequence the required muscle actions, coordinate force application, and adopt an appropriate body position to execute a fast performance (26). *Perceptual–cognitive qualities* describe the ability of an athlete to control gaze to identify relevant cues from the environment requiring effective visual scanning, anticipation, and decision-making to formulate a rapid and accurate response, which is directly dependent upon the athlete's playing experience and prior knowledge of the game (13, 20).

In creating training programs to develop agility and quickness, coaches should first identify a perceptual–cognitive skill to be trained, then manipulate a task and/or environment constraint to develop that particular perceptual–cognitive quality. When the different task and environmental constraints of each individual sport are identified, training conditions can be manipulated to better reflect the competitive environment and develop an athlete's decision-making ability.

INFORMATION-PROCESSING CAPACITY

Information processing refers to the speed with which athletes are able to process incoming information from their environment and respond accordingly

(19, 20). Before athletes move, they must first identify the need to respond to a situation, which is achieved by identifying and collecting environmental cues from a variety of sensory mechanisms, including the auditory, visual, and somatosensory systems (20). For example, a running back waits for the quarterback to provide the auditory command to signal the start of a play. As he prepares to grab the handoff from the quarterback, he collects visual information about the position of the defense in an attempt to find a gap to run through. As would-be tacklers try to grab him, his somatosensory system gives his central nervous system feedback about the manual pressure the opponents are applying to his pads and his body. Given this information, the player may be able to spin away from the attack.

This scenario illustrates that the complex interactions between the athlete, the task at hand, and the environment impact the ability to make rapid and accurate decisions during competition. The human model for information processing describes the interaction between an athlete's perceptual ability to identify and interpret relevant stimuli and cognitive ability to program and execute an appropriate response based upon retrial of information from stored memory (figure 2.2). Thus, the outcome and accuracy of the response depends on how specific the stored information is to the given situation (4, 20). Several variables affect the speed at which information processing occurs,

Running backs respond to a variety of environmental cues, allowing them to elude opponents.

including stimulus clarity, intensity, type, specificity, and level of experience (19).

Stimulus clarity refers to the extent to which the stimulus is well defined and clear (e.g., in focus versus out of focus), while

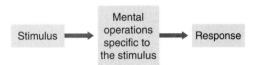

Figure 2.2 Information processing model.
Adapted from R.H. Cox, *Sport Psychology: Concepts and Applications*, 7th ed. (New York: McGraw-Hill, 2012), 133.

stimulus intensity describes the magnitude of the stimulus (e.g., loudness, brightness, and so on). The greater the clarity or intensity of an environmental stimulus, the faster the athlete will be able to identify the stimulus within the environment and process the relevant information (19). *Stimulus type* describes the type of stimulus presented and can also influence the speed at which a stimulus is initially identified. The time required to respond to a visual stimulus (approximately 180-200 milliseconds) is greater than the time required to respond to an auditory stimulus (approximately 140-160 milliseconds), while kinesthetic reaction time is the fastest (averaging 120-140 milliseconds) (20, 30).

Stimulus specificity describes the level of similarity of the given stimulus to the actual competitive environment (19, 20). As mentioned, reacting to a stimulus requires processing based on retrieval of information from memory. If there is a greater similarity between a stimulus used in training to those presented during competition, information-processing speed should improve. Studies investigating differences between experts and nonexperts have identified the need for a specific training stimulus in order to detect differences in perceptual–cognitive expertise enabling athletes to utilize sport-specific decision-making to replicate game-specific conditions (2, 5, 13). Research has shown that while a generic stimulus, such as a light, may train an athlete to recognize and react by training basic information processing, it is not a valid measure to develop perceptual–cognitive ability or for gauging athletic performance (6). Using a more specific stimulus, such as another person to move and respond to, allows athletes with anticipatory expertise to identify relevant kinematic cues from their opposition earlier in stimulus presentation and respond faster (1, 2, 11, 33).

Finally, the athlete's level of experience has a profound effect on overall quickness. For example, athletes who are able to read or expect the next play based on their opponents' formation have a greater anticipatory advantage than those unable to identify these task-relevant cues. The ability to read the opposing player's actions is largely based on repetition and competitive experience over time (12, 22, 35).

Coaches should consider this information when developing drills to train agility and quickness; implementing a generic stimulus (e.g., light, whistle, or voice commands) creates a controlled reactive environment, exposing athletes to employ a basic goal-directed search strategy to improve reactive ability. Replicating the competitive environment in training is a critical factor to develop decision-making ability and increase the potential to transfer from training to competition. Creating *temporal* (timing of stimulus presentation) and *spatial* (direction of the stimulus) variability within the training environment exposes athletes to the unpredictable nature of competition, enabling them to practice scanning the environment for relevant cues. Finally, the specificity of the stimulus used should be directly related to gamelike situations that the athlete might experience. For example, a sprinter should respond to a sound stimulus, since the same type of cue is used to initiate track events. In contrast, a sport-specific stimulus for a defensive lineman in football would involve movement, since football players look for visual stimuli in competition.

FACTORS INFLUENCING REACTION TIME

The ability to process information in a relatively short period allows athletes a tactical advantage when a rapid motor response is needed. *Reaction time*, described as the time between stimulus presentation and the onset of motor response (20), is often used as a measure of information-processing speed and decision-making ability. Many factors can influence reaction time, including the rate and speed of movement execution, the number of stimulus-response alternatives, the length of time between the presentation of multiple stimuli, and the location of the stimulus within the visual field (20).

The number of stimuli in the environment and the total number of possible actions largely determine the athlete's ability to select an appropriate response (19, 20). Typically, reactions are classified as either *simple* or *choice* (19). *Simple reaction time* refers to the presentation of a stimulus that has only one correct response, such as a gun being fired to signal the start of a sprinting race. *Choice reactions* require an athlete to select an appropriate response to one of several unanticipated stimuli (20). According to Hick's law, the amount of time required to prepare a response to a stimulus depends on the possible number of responses present (19). As the number of stimuli in the environment increases, the athlete has a greater number of alternative responses to select from in order to perform the correct motor task, increasing the amount of time required to execute a particular movement (19). Choice-reaction time is important for sports that require athletes to respond to the movements of other players and to select appropriate responses based on these movements. For example, as defenders in lacrosse follow their opponent downfield, they must watch their opponent's body position, the offensive patterns of the opposition, and the location of their own teammates in order

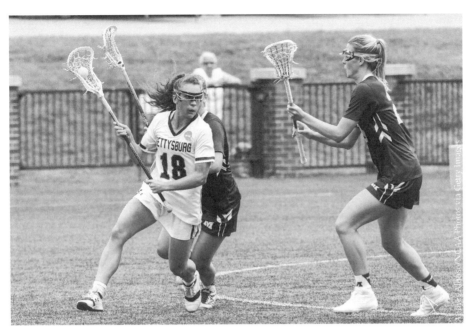

Sports such as lacrosse create a chaotic environment in which players must react to multiple stimuli.

to take the most appropriate action and to best defend against the offensive attack.

When an athlete is responding to two closely spaced stimuli, a delay in processing speed is often observed; this is called the *psychological refractory period*. This delay in response represents the limiting factor in processing speed: the response to the second stimulus is delayed because the athlete is still processing (and responding to) the first stimulus (10). An example of this is a fake performed in many sports to deceive the opposition. In this type of play, an athlete indicates the initial stages of one movement and then quickly performs another movement to its completion. Performing a fake initially gives the opposition incorrect cues so that they cannot respond correctly or quickly enough to effectively defend the second, or actual, movement. Another example is if a pitcher appears to be about to deliver the baseball to the plate but instead attempts a pickoff, this may cause the base runner a momentary delay, resulting in being picked off at that base. When an athlete is responding to two closely spaced stimuli during an agility task, differences in decision-making time have been observed in faster and slower athletes when responding to the first stimulus; however no difference was evident in response time between groups when responding to the second stimulus (27). Despite faster athletes being able to produce a faster overall performance, which is likely due to their organismic contrasts (physical and technical ability), a delay in response time is still observed in athletes responding to two closely spaced stimuli.

In sport, responding in the same direction as an opponent or pass where the stimulus and the response occur on the same side produces compatible mapping. Conversely, moving in the opposite direction will result in incompatible mapping because the stimulus and response occur on opposite sides. The term *stimulus-response compatibility* describes the spatial correlation between the stimulus and the appropriate response (8), with research concluding that reaction time is faster following a compatible rather than an incompatible stimulus (15). One study has investigated differences in response times during defensive (compatible) and offensive (incompatible) agility tasks, finding differences in both decision-making time and movement output between the two tasks, with a faster performance observed when athletes were instructed to change direction and follow their opponent (defensive agility) (27). Since both defensive and offensive movements are required throughout a game, it is important to measure an athlete's response times under both compatible and incompatible stimulus-response conditions in order to make agility training programs more specific for an athlete's individual needs.

From a training perspective, many experts believe simple reaction time is much harder to alter through training because it is primarily related to genetics and to the speed of the central nervous system. However, training and experience may significantly improve choice-reaction time (20). For this reason, athletes should incorporate some form of sport-specific reactive-agility training into their overall strength and conditioning programs to improve their ability to respond quickly to multiple stimuli in a chaotic sport environment. Early studies involving anticipation and reaction time were based on generic stimuli and generic athletic responses (9), failing to accurately assess sport-specific decision-making and anticipation. Previous studies have utilized projected images and three-dimensional human stimuli (other opponents) for athletes to respond to, allowing individuals with anticipatory expertise to recognize specific kinematic cues earlier in stimulus presentation and to respond faster; this proved to be a better discriminator between levels of expertise compared to other generic stimuli (5, 6, 23). These findings indicate that sport-specific protocols that utilize perceptual skills (such as pattern recognition and anticipation) may be best for establishing the appropriate context, or link, to skills in a particular sport (1).

ANTICIPATION

When athletes can accurately predict an event and organize their movements in advance, they can initiate an appropriate response faster than if they had waited to react to a stimulus. With experience, they gain greater knowledge

Patrick Gorski/Icon Sportswire via Getty Images

Through anticipatory cues, an experienced hockey player can gain a competitive advantage over opponents.

of how long it takes to coordinate their own movements (known as *effector anticipation*) with certain environmental regularities and opponent tendencies in a given situation (*perceptual anticipation*). In addition, if athletes can predict the location of an object within their environment (*spatial anticipation*) and identify when it will occur (*temporal anticipation*), they will be able to form an appropriate response before the stimulus is presented. Athletes who anticipate accurately can gain a competitive advantage over their opposition. Anticipation is possible in nearly all sports. For example, by watching how an opponent pivots or moves the stick, a hockey player can get an idea of the direction an opponent is going or what movement the opponent is trying to execute.

Anticipation appears to be a trainable factor that affects decision-making ability, because athletes improve and refine their search strategies and pattern recognition and gain more knowledge though more playing experience (1, 13, 16, 18, 22). The primary goal in training anticipation should be to improve decision-making ability and response accuracy, before enhancing response speed, before training the ability to locate and identify correct cues from the environment, and before focusing on speed of identification.

KNOWLEDGE OF SITUATIONS

The knowledge of specific sporting situations can help athletes react more quickly to environmental cues. Prior situational knowledge of an opponent's strengths and weaknesses, court or field position, and event probability information can assist athletes when they are searching for relevant cues to enable a faster response. For example, the trajectory or spin of a ball, the direction and speed of an opponent, or the opposition's position are all possible patterns that an experienced athlete may use to gain advantage over those with less experience. In many sports, the better athletes are at recognizing and interpreting these patterns, the greater their potential for reacting quickly and accurately to the given stimulus (19, 20). An increased awareness of the surrounding environment has been found to increase the visual representation of sport-specific cues, subsequently leading to an increase in motor activation of the muscles involved in skill execution (24, 35). The increase in corticospinal motor-evoked potentials enables elite athletes to prepare the body sooner for the upcoming response compared to novice athletes (35), resulting in a shorter response programming phase of the human information-processing model (see figure 2.2). In a sport like American football, specific cues may alert the defense whether a passing or a running play is about to occur. Defenders who are able to interpret these cues quickly are more likely to be in the correct position sooner to make a necessary play.

This ability to recognize specific patterns is a skill that athletes can develop through experience and learning. Both the amount and the type of practice are important. As players' knowledge of a particular situation increases and they become more familiar with the optimal movement response in relation to the stimulus displayed, their reaction time, or quickness, will improve. For this reason, during the initial stages of learning, athletes should perform closed, pre-programmed agility drills for technique mastery. Performing a shuttle run drill, for example, will allow athletes to become familiar with the most suitable body position

Knowledge of sport situations allows an experienced player to read a ball for a successful return.

to adopt when decelerating and reaccelerating, because such a drill teaches and enforces correct movement patterns to be drawn upon during reactive game scenarios. However, as athletes perfect technique and gain greater experience in their respective sport(s), open, unplanned quickness drills with appropriate cues may better improve their sport performance, because the training will be more specific.

AROUSAL LEVEL

Arousal, or an athlete's overall level of central nervous system excitement and activation, plays a significant role in the ability to perform both quickly and accurately. The inverted *U* hypothesis further explains the relationship between arousal and performance (20, 34). Figure 2.3 shows the inverted *U* hypothesis, which states that arousal facilitates performance to a certain point. If the arousal level is too low or too high, the athlete fails to produce high-level performance (14, 34). The zone of optimal functioning is the level of arousal for the best integration of both the mental and physical processes associated with maximal performance (14, 34). It is typified by several factors, including improved automaticity and the increased ability to identify task-relevant cues and to ignore environmental cues that are irrelevant to performance (20).

If athletes' arousal levels are too low, they may focus too much on irrelevant environmental cues. Since their environmental focus may be too broad, these perceptual distractions may not allow them to pick up on relevant environmental stimuli. Perceptual narrowing, or tunnel vision, may also occur as arousal levels continue to rise. This may hinder an athlete's ability to identify task-relevant cues, thus increasing reaction time.

Ideally, athletes can identify the optimal level of arousal required to switch focus from broad to narrow. For example, when tennis players serve a ball, they initially have a broad focus as they scan the court to determine where they would like to hit the ball. They would

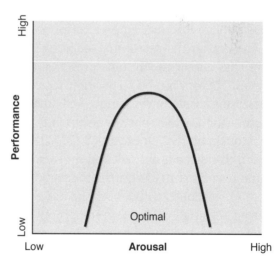

Figure 2.3 Inverted *U* principle.
Reprinted by permission from B.D. Hatfield and G.A. Walford, "Understanding Anxiety: Implications for Sport Performance," *National Strength & Conditioning Association Journal* 9, no. 2 (1987): 58-65.

then switch to a narrow focus during the serve. Once the serve is complete, they switch back to a broader focus to track their opponent and to anticipate where the opponent will return the ball.

For this reason, during practice athletes may benefit from using open-skilled tasks that replicate competitive game situations that may be perceived as stressful. Changing the speed of movement execution or placing a time constraint on a task, for example, may increase an athlete's arousal level, not only changing their perception of the task but also increasing the perceptual–cognitive demand required to execute the correct responses. Drills that force players to perform in a competitive situation enhance their confidence and skill in adapting and executing movement under various situations. This game-like environment also allows players to adapt their skills and better control their arousal levels under the pressure of competition.

INFLUENCE OF PERCEPTUAL–COGNITIVE FUNCTION ON MOVEMENT OUTPUT

Agility is a context-specific movement requiring athletes to sequence necessary muscle actions, adopt an appropriate body position, and systematically coordinate force and impulse in order to produce a fast performance that matches the most appropriate movement solution in response to a given situation (12, 25). As a result, movement produced in competition may not reflect optimal technique; rather it reflects the ability of an athlete to successfully control and coordinate movement in response to various task and environmental constraints to produce a faster performance.

The greater the perceptual–cognitive skill athletes have to identify relevant cues earlier in stimulus presentation the more they are able to adopt a more appropriate body position to execute movements at a faster pace. Possessing a faster processing speed during agility tasks can result in muscle preactivation, which has been shown to protect against injury and increase subsequent movement execution (27, 32). Increasing preparatory muscle activation through a faster reaction time can increase rate of force development and muscular stiffness during the early phase of movement, enabling more force to be applied throughout the movement (27). Greater force production during both the braking and the propulsive phase of agility movements has been observed when athletes produce a faster decision-making time, resulting in a faster agility performance (26). Further, a faster initial reaction to the stimulus allows athletes to enter a lower, more advantageous body position to better direct force throughout the movement (32). In contrast, a subsequent delay in processing speed, resulting in a longer decision-making time, has been associated with decreased neuromuscular control as a result of insufficient time for the central nervous system to implement appropriate postural adjustment strategies, compromising performance outcomes (27).

Coaches should consider this information when developing agility and quickness training programs. Implementing random practice conditions where the individual skills or movements are executed in a random order requires athletes to continuously modify their biomechanics to develop a coordinated and adaptive movement. Varying the speed and distance available to execute drills manipulates the constraints of the task, thus altering the physical and technical requirements of the drill. The overall goal of training should not be movement perfection; rather it should be to provide athletes with the opportunity to develop an adaptable movement solution to a wide variety of movement problems. This allows athletes to produce the optimal movement output when responding to various stimuli in competition.

VISION TRAINING

The visual system is perhaps the most dominant sensory system (20), to which a majority of information is sourced to guide and direct movement output. Currently, research into visual training programs used are shown to be generalized programs aiming to improve basic visual functions (such as acuity, eye tracking, and depth perception) and subsequently sports performance by using repetitive eye exercises in response to generic stimuli (21). Studies have found that these generic programs show improvements in choice-reaction time and peripheral vision speed, but they fail to show improvements in task-specific decision-making ability (21).

Task-specific perceptual–cognitive research shows distinct differences between experts and nonexperts in visual search strategies (7, 11, 13), suggesting that experts use a search strategy involving fewer fixations of a longer duration, have the ability to anticipate cues in advance, and can recognize and recall familiar patterns of play, enabling them to make rapid and accurate sport-specific decisions. Specifically, elite athletes have been found to fixate centrally to identify cues from the proximal body (e.g., trunk and hips) and use their peripheral vision to monitor surrounding areas of play, enabling them to be more effective in tactical situations to successfully evade their opponents and produce a faster performance (2, 16, 17). In contrast, novice athletes appear to be dependent upon obvious kinematic cues sourced from distal body segments (e.g., arms, legs, and feet), placing them at a disadvantage during competition, because they have to wait until their opponent completes a movement in order to execute the appropriate response.

From a training perspective, it is important for coaches to develop drills and expose athletes to practice scenarios that require search strategies similar to competition conditions. This will allow athletes to develop their ability to detect appropriate cues within their environment and learn to adapt and alter their movement output in response. As perceptual expertise is developed from prior knowledge and exposure to situations, developing drills in training that allow athletes to identify and respond to sport-specific stimuli under varying task and environmental conditions will hopefully allow them to transfer these skills over to competition, resulting in improved decision-making.

MENTAL SKILL TRAINING

The ability of an athlete to control mental and emotional elements assists task performance by improving concentration, confidence, and psychological well-being during competition (3). Sports psychologists typically use mental practice in conjunction with physical practice as a training tool to alleviate the risk of overtraining and to assist athletes who are away from practice facilities or who have restrictions in movement because of an injury, to visualize and rehearse their performance.

Mental rehearsal describes the process of practicing the procedural elements (steps) of a skill used to increase skill efficiency (31). For example, focusing on extending the shoulder, elbow, and wrist prior to releasing the ball during a basketball free throw allows athletes to visually practice the key components of the movement in a controlled environment. Mentally rehearsing the procedural elements of an agility task in a coordinated smooth and accurate manner can have a positive outcome on an athlete's physical execution of the movement (20), potentially assisting with improving motor performance of the skill.

Mental imagery and visualization describes the process of an athlete visualizing themselves performing the whole movement. This type of practice has been shown to activate the muscles that would be used if physical execution of the movement occurred and has been shown to have a positive priming effect on the body prior to competition (20, 28, 31). For athletes practicing mental imagery, both *procedural knowledge* (knowing how to execute the movement) and *declarative knowledge* (what they currently know about the movement) are critical, because imagining the skill and actually performing it needs to be as closely executed as possible for the effective transfer of learning.

There are many guidelines to enhance the imagery process, specifically concerning the environment in which to practice, the perspective in which to imagine movements, and incorporating the correct emotional context to the skill or movement being visualized (8, 24). Athletes should be encouraged to perform mental imagery in a quiet, relaxing place with no external distractions so they can focus their attention when visualizing the skill. Once relaxed, the athlete should aim to recall as much sensory information from visual, temporal, acoustic (hearing), olfactory (smell), and kinaesthetic (body) awareness of the skill as possible. This creates a more realistic simulation to be visualized. The athlete should then attempt to view the movement either through a first-person or a third-person perspective. Athletes "seeing" themselves perform the movement through their own eyes (first person) or through the eyes of another person observing them (third person) dynamically changes the perspective of the image created. The type of perspective that works best appears to be dependent upon the type of skill, with research suggesting that first-person perspective works best for individuals who perform open skills (e.g., agility) (20). Finally, specific focus on the emotional content associated with the skill should be retrieved, replicating the desired arousal and attentional processes involved before visualizing the skill.

Implementing these practice conditions could assist the athlete with improved decision-making during skill execution by providing a clearer description of the desired movement output in the response programming phase of the information processing model. This may result in a faster movement output by assisting athletes to focus their attention on task-relevant cues leading to improved performance in competition.

CONCLUSION

Athletes' ability to achieve optimal agility and quickness depends largely on their perceptual and decision-making skills. In order to fully develop these capabilities, athletes must continue to gain experience identifying task-relevant cues in their respective sports by training in gamelike conditions and by using sport-specific training cues and methods aimed at improving perceptual–cognitive abilities and decision-making skills.

Warm-Up Methods and Techniques for Agility Training

Logan Lentz Kell
Doug Lentz

It is an essential and standard practice for athletes to warm up before they practice or compete. The purpose of a well-designed warm-up is to enhance performance and decrease the likelihood of injuries (4, 12, 16, 17). The warm-up also provides an ideal time to learn and rehearse movement skills such as jumping, landing, accelerating, decelerating, and the other various modes of locomotion. The opportunity for mental preparation that this segment of the training session provides is equally important because it sets the tone for the work to follow. An appropriate warm-up reaps several physiological benefits that can positively affect an athlete's performance. The warm-up should increase blood flow to active muscles (21), raise core body temperature (21), enhance metabolic reactions (10), and disrupt temporary connective tissue bonds (8, 13). These effects can aid the athlete by yielding improvements in rate-of-force development (3, 13), improvements in reaction time (3, 13), improved oxygen delivery to the lungs and working muscles (21), and improvements in acute measures of muscle strength and power (6, 10, 12, 13). In addition, the increased production of synovial fluid located between the joints will acutely enhance the dynamic flexibility, or mobility, of the joints (5, 21). Another benefit is that the warm-up helps facilitate the breakdown of glycogen, which is the source of energy most often used for exercise; this translates to more energy available for the athlete (11, 14).

The mental aspect of the warm-up often does not receive the attention it deserves. The warm-up provides the perfect opportunity for athletes to shut off concerns from the outside world and concentrate on the activities that are about to commence. Effective warm-up sessions direct focus and active participation by both coaches and athletes; even responsible athletes can benefit from performing movements under the diligent eyes of the coach. This means that the coach must actively engage in cueing and teaching these movements to help athletes create the appropriate intent with each movement. For example, a coach instructing athletes on proper plyometric mechanics during a practice session might cue the athletes during a warm-up to pretend they are landing on hot coals; this image could help prepare them for quick landings and explosive takeoffs. Reinforcing proper cues during the warm-up offers a less stressful platform for learning.

Proper posture and body positioning are critical in all physical activities for optimizing performance and reducing injury risk and for maintaining body balance and the proper arrangement of supporting structures. Research supports the contention that correct posture is a prerequisite of a healthy lifestyle (15, 20) but today's athletes live in a world that does not necessarily promote good posture. Excessive use of phones and computers, carrying heavy school or work bags, and poor posture while studying or watching television are just a few examples of habits that prohibit the maintenance of correct posture. The warm-up offers a good opportunity to educate and then reinforce proper posture and body positioning. Here are some simple ways to address this issue.

- ▶ Keep the head up at all times and always look straight ahead.
- ▶ When landing and decelerating, hinge at the hips and do not round the back to dampen the force with the hips and knees.
- ▶ Maintain proper foot alignment and spacing when jumping and landing; for example, takeoffs from a two-footed jumping position should have the feet at hip width or slightly wider; conversely, when landing, land with both feet closer to shoulder-width distance apart.
- ▶ Distribute weight appropriately for different movements; for example, when starting mechanics from a stationary staggered stance, most of the weight should be placed on the lead leg to optimize horizontal force into the ground.
- ▶ Maintain proper shin angles, especially during the initial driving strides while accelerating. The intent should be to drive the leg back behind the body and fully extend at the hip, knee, and ankle. A significant part of this technique is to begin with a positive shin angle that is a forward tilting of the lower leg bones. A negative shin angle during initial acceleration indicates that the foot is too far in front of the body, which would create excessive braking forces during footstrike.

Because there are many important components to a typical practice or competition, it can be very challenging to coach such technical aspects after the warm-up is over, so the warm-up itself offers an excellent opportunity to refine body positioning and posture as it relates to athletic performance.

There are certain challenges and considerations that coaches must address with respect to the warm-up. For example, while it would be ideal to allow 10 to 20 minutes for the warm-up period, time constraints may reduce that period significantly in real life. Coaches often only have only 5 or 10 minutes of quality work to prepare the athletes for the ensuing practice, so they must consider several factors when determining the length of the warm-up. For example, if the agility session for the day is going to be of higher intensity, the coach may want to allow a slightly longer warm-up period to make sure that the athletes are adequately prepared for the session. It has been well established that a subnormal body temperature has an adverse effect on neuromuscular performance (22, 23). In colder weather, it would therefore be prudent to minimize the time between warm-up and the agility session so that athletes will not cool down before the session begins. Conversely, research also reveals that heat stress reduces a person's ability to achieve maximal metabolic rates during exercise and that, during exercise-induced heat stress, competing metabolic and thermoregulatory demands for blood flow make it difficult to maintain an adequate cardiac output (1, 24). Therefore, in warmer, more humid weather, the duration and intensity of the warm-up should be shortened to minimize the risk of fatigue and heat-related illness. Another potential obstacle during warm-ups may be space limitations. If this is an issue, it is advisable to have back-up exercises and movements that can be performed easily and safely in a small area.

Proper warm-ups should be taught in a systematic fashion. The following guidelines should be adhered to during all warm-ups.

- ▶ Begin with simple movements such as marching. Once the athletes demonstrate a level of proficiency with the marches, progress to skipping; as these simple movements become less difficult, progress the athlete to more complex movements and variations.

- ▶ Make sure that the movements are performed slowly enough to achieve an acceptable level of performance before attempting to go to full speed.

- ▶ Rehearse bilateral work before incorporating unilateral skills, especially with takeoffs and landings. Training ladders may be useful to help improve rhythm, timing, and coordination. The literature supports closed skill movements in various directions over prearranged distances to build correct movement patterns in novice athletes (12, 18). After a high level of technical proficiency is attained, these tools may no longer be as beneficial from a skill development standpoint. However, they can certainly be included as part of a dynamic warm-up because they will prepare the body physiologically (e.g., increased heart rate, breathing rate, perspiration rate, etc.).

▶ Perform unloaded or bodyweight movements with proper movement patterns before considering adding some form of external resistance (e.g., resistance tubing). Training sessions should be performed no later than 15 minutes after termination of the warm-up (2). It has been demonstrated that the positive effects of warm-up begin to dissipate after 15 minutes (9); ideally, therefore, the athletes should be ready to practice as soon as the warm-up ends.

▶ Be sure to keep the warm-up appropriate to the fitness levels of the participants. The warm-up should prepare the individuals for training and/or competition without being so stressful as to cause fatigue.

COMPONENTS OF A WARM-UP

Most athletes will arrive at a practice session after sitting in a car for varying lengths of time. Being sedentary for an extended period can produce many unwanted physiological effects for athletes who are about to move. For example, heart rate and blood flow slow down; additionally, a seated position over time can tighten the hip flexors. It has been observed that female athletes with hip flexor muscle tightness exhibit less gluteus maximus activation and lower gluteus maximus and biceps femoris coactivation (19). Individuals with hip flexor muscle tightness appear to use different (unwanted) neuromuscular strategies to control lower extremity motion (19). For this reason, the first thing a coach should do in warm-up is the get the athletes moving by performing some form of general, light cardiovascular activity such as calisthenics, which consist of a variety of gross motor movements performed in a rhythmic or cyclical manner (e.g., jumping jacks or mountain climbers). One of the great things about calisthenics is that, because they are performed with body weight only, they can be performed in a limited space, without additional equipment, and the number of movements performed is almost limitless. Start with slower, lower-intensity efforts such as marching in place, arm swings, alternating toe touches, and jumping jacks. As the exercises increase in number, intensity and speed of movement should also increase.

The next phase of the warm-up should focus on enhancing joint mobility and activating the neuromuscular system to prepare it to perform efficient muscular contractions (7). Before an agility practice session, particular attention should be given to the joints and musculature of the lower extremities. This does not imply that the upper extremities are neglected, only that a greater portion of the warm-up will be focused on the lower body, since this body region will be stressed more heavily during the training session. Performing movements that are more specific to the sport being trained is an essential element for improving the transfer of training effect (8). For example, when training volleyball athletes, jumps, landings, and short change-of-direction drills make perfect sense based on the size of the playing area and the demands of a match. Therefore, coaches should include drills and movements in the warm-up that are specific not only to the sport being trained but also to the positions of the athletes who are playing that sport.

DYNAMIC WARM-UP DRILLS

This section describes numerous drills that can be included in a sport-specific dynamic warm-up. In general, when selecting drills, the coach should focus on progressing drills from those that are simpler to those that are more complex. In designing the dynamic warm-up, the coach should also select drills that can be safely and easily performed given space and time constraints. Table 3.1 provides a list of the warm-up drills (in order from simpler to more complex) included in this chapter.

Table 3.1 Dynamic Warm-Up Drills

Drill name	Page number
Stationary arm warm-up	50
Standing ankle circles	51
Standing hip external rotation/circumduction	51
Standing hip internal rotation/circumduction	52
Walking high knee pull	52
Leg swings front to back	53
Leg swings side to side	54
Lateral lunge squat and walk	55
Front and back lunge	55
Multidirectional reaching lunge	56
Straight leg toy soldier march	57
Lunge walk with a twist	57
Standing/traveling quad stretch	58
Stationary and traveling inchworm	59
Elbow to instep walk	60
Forward, backward, and lateral march	60
Front, back, and lateral skip	61
Power skip	61

(continued)

Table 3.1 Dynamic Warm-Up Drills *(continued)*

Drill name	Page number
Linear acceleration to deceleration	62
Shuffle to deceleration	62
Backward run to deceleration	63
Tuck jump	63
Horizontal jump and stick	64
Hop and stick	65
Butt kick	66

Stationary Arm Warm-Up

The athlete sits with legs out in front, heels touching the ground, knees slightly bent, arms at the side, and elbows bent at a 90-degree angle. (The exercise may also be performed in a standing position.) The athlete begins by moving one arm forward and the other backward so that one hand is at eye level and the opposite hand is near the back hip pocket. Then, the athlete moves the front arm to the back and the back arm to the front, starting at about half speed, then increasing speed when proper technique and form is achieved. At any point, if the athlete breaks technique or form, the coach should stop the warm-up. The athlete builds up speed for 12 to 15 seconds or until form is broken. The athlete may repeat as desired with proper breaks between sets for full recovery. This dynamic warm-up can also serve as a technique drill for learning or reinforcing proper arm mechanics during running.

(a) **Sitting version.**

(b) **Standing version.**

Standing Ankle Circles

The athlete stands tall near a wall with one or both arms fully extended for support. The athlete stands on one leg, flexes the knee of the other leg, and rotates the ankle of the free leg for 10 repetitions in a clockwise direction. The athlete should perform this action slowly through a full range of motion. The athlete then performs this same drill counterclockwise and, when finished, repeats the drill with the other foot.

Standing Hip External Rotation/Circumduction

The athlete stands tall near a wall with one or both arms fully extended for support. The athlete stands on one leg, flexes the hip and knee of the other leg, and rotates the entire free leg externally through as full a range of motion as possible for 10 repetitions in a slow, controlled fashion and, when finished repeats the drill with the other leg.

Standing Hip Internal Rotation/Circumduction

The athlete stands tall near a wall with one or both arms fully extended for support. The athlete stands on one leg, flexes the hip and knee of the other leg, and rotates the entire free leg internally through as full a range of motion as possible for 10 repetitions in a slow, controlled fashion and, when finished repeats the drill with the other leg.

Walking High Knee Pull

The athlete begins by flexing one hip and lifting the knee on that side as high as possible. Then, the athlete grabs the leg just below the knee with both hands and pulls the knee toward the chest, keeping the chest up. The athlete returns the raised leg to the ground and repeats the action with the other leg. The exercise is continued by alternating legs with each step as the athlete walks forward for 10 yards (9.1 m). The athlete should also focus on dorsiflexing the ankles on each repetition. This drill can also be performed in place if space is limited.

Leg Swings Front to Back

The athlete stands next to a stable surface, fully extends the arm closest to that surface, and places the hand against it for support. The athlete then swings the leg closest to the surface forward and backward as quickly as possible. During the leg swing, the athlete slightly flexes the knee of the support leg and rises on the ball of foot, keeping the swing leg ankle in a dorsiflexed position and not allowing the hips to rotate throughout the movement. The athlete swings the leg as high as possible while still maintaining control of the movement. The athlete should perform 10 to 15 repetitions, and then turn to face the other direction and repeat with the other leg.

Forward swing.   Backward swing.

Leg Swings Side to Side

The athlete faces a stable surface, fully extending both arms to shoulder height, and places both palms against the surface for support. The athlete lifts one leg and swings it from side to side across the body as quickly as possible. During the leg swing, the athlete slightly flexes the knee of the support leg and rises on the ball of the foot. The athlete should keep the swing leg ankle in a dorsiflexed position and not allow the hips to rotate throughout the movement. The athlete swings the leg as high as possible while still maintaining control of the movement. The athlete should perform 10 to 15 repetitions on each leg.

Swing across.   **Swing out to the side.**

Lateral Lunge Squat and Walk

The athlete extends the arms directly in front of the chest at approximately shoulder height. The athlete takes an elongated step to the side. Once the foot touches the ground, the athlete flexes the knee of the lead leg and lowers the body until the top of the thigh is approximately parallel to the ground. The arms remain extended throughout the duration of this drill to assist with balance. The knee of the lead leg should not move forward past the toes. The trailing leg should remain extended but should not be locked. Those with limited flexibility might perform the movement with slight flexion in the knee.

For lateral lunge squat, the athlete returns to the starting position by extending the flexed leg, flexes the other knee into the lunged position, and performs 8 to 12 lunge squats by alternating sides. For the lateral lunge walk, the athlete brings the foot of the extended leg back and places it next to the other foot, momentarily pausing in the standing position, and then takes another elongated step in the same direction. The athlete continues for 10 yards (9.1 m) and then reverses the movements to lateral lunge walk 10 yards (9.1 m) back to the original starting position.

Front and Back Lunge

The athlete starts with the feet in a parallel position and begins the movement by taking an elongated step forward (front lunge) or backward (back lunge) with a lead foot, maintaining an erect torso throughout the entire movement. When the lead foot touches the ground, the athlete points it straight ahead, or slightly inverts it, and flexes the trailing knee slightly. To begin the downward movement, the athlete flexes the lead hip and knee and lowers the trailing knee until it is 1 to 2 inches (2-5 cm) above the ground, keeping the lead knee directly over the lead foot through-

out the entire movement. The athlete's weight is evenly distributed between the lead foot and the ball of the trailing foot. The athlete begins the upward movement by pushing off the ground with the lead foot, then brings it back to the starting position in one fluid motion without allowing any extra steps. The athlete alternates lead foot and repeats the movement, and performs 8 to 12 repetitions per side.

Multidirectional Reaching Lunge

The athlete takes a step forward with one leg and begins the downward movement by hinging at the hips while keeping the back in a neutral position (a). During the hinge, the athlete slightly flexes both the lead knee and the trailing knee and reaches toward the lead foot with both arms. After reaching as far as possible with the hands, the athlete returns to the starting position. Next, using the same leg, the athlete takes a step laterally, hinges at the hips, flexes at the knee, and reaches toward the lead foot (b). After returning to the starting position, and still using the same leg, the athlete takes a step forward at a 45-degree angle (c). Again, the athlete hinges at the hips, flexes at the knee, and reaches toward the lead foot. Upon completion of the reach, the athlete returns to the starting position. The athlete alternates lead legs and begins the three-part sequence to the other side.

Straight Leg Toy Soldier March

While walking forward, the athlete swings one leg forward as high as possible, keeping it straight. The athlete reaches the contralateral arm out in front at about shoulder height and uses it as an anatomical target for the swinging foot. The athlete rotates the ipsilateral arm back behind the body to counteract the movement and to help control balance. The athlete continues walking forward, swinging and extending the opposite leg and arm. The athlete performs the drill for 10 yards (9.1 m), alternating arms and legs with each step.

Lunge Walk with a Twist

The athlete extends the arms directly in front of the chest at approximately shoulder height and takes an elongated step forward. Once the foot contacts the ground, the athlete flexes the hip and knee of the lead leg until the top of the thigh is approximately parallel to the ground. The athlete then rotates the hips and shoulders as far as possible toward the lead leg. If possible, the athlete should keep the arms extended. If necessary, the athlete can slightly flex the elbows for better balance and control. The athlete should not move the knee of the lead leg forward past

the toes on that side nor allow the knee of the trailing leg to contact the ground. The athlete rotates the hips and shoulders back to neutral, returns to the starting position by stepping forward with the trailing leg, and then repeats the exercise, leading with the opposite leg. The athlete performs this drill for 10 yards (9.1 m), alternating the lead leg with each step.

Standing/Traveling Quad Stretch

The athlete begins by flexing one knee and raising that heel toward the buttocks and then grabbing hold of that ankle with the ipsilateral hand while maintaining an upright position. The athlete's chest is up and the torso is erect, and there is no flexion at the hips. The athlete extends the contralateral arm straight above the head and holds this position for 2 to 3 seconds. The other foot remains flat on the ground throughout the movement. After the hold, the athlete releases the ankle and extends the knee back to the starting position while also lowering the arm back to the side. Upon completion of the movement, the athlete alternates legs and repeats the movement. The exercise can be completed in place for 8 to 12 repetitions per leg or while traveling over a 10-yard (9.1 m) distance, taking a step after each hold.

Stationary and Traveling Inchworm

The athlete starts in a standing position and begins the movement by hinging at the hips and reaching toward the toes. The athlete places the hands on the ground while keeping the hips elevated and the legs extended. The heels should be flat on the ground when the hands reach the ground. If flexibility does not allow, slight knee flexion may be necessary. At this point, the athlete slowly walks the hands out until the athlete reaches a plank position. Upon reaching the plank position, the athlete pauses momentarily and then slowly walks the hands back toward the feet. Throughout the movement, the athlete keeps the legs extended, without knee flexion, and the heels as flat as possible on the ground. Once the athlete reaches the starting position, he or she immediately walks the hands back out for the next repetition.

When completing the traveling inchworm, the athlete should not return to the starting position by walking the hands back toward the toes, but instead inch the feet toward the hands before walking the hands back out. The athlete can complete the drill in place for 8 to 12 repetitions per leg or while traveling over a 10-yard (9.1 m) distance.

Elbow to Instep Walk

The athlete begins by taking an elongated forward step with one leg and then flexing the ipsilateral elbow and bringing the hand to chin level. The athlete begins the downward movement by flexing the lead hip and knee and allowing the trailing knee to lower to a point just above the ground. The athlete then attempts to touch the ipsilateral elbow to the instep of the lead leg while maintaining balance. The contralateral hand should remain in contact with the ground during this action to maintain balance. After making elbow contact with the instep, the athlete pushes through the lead foot, lifting the torso up and the trailing leg forward until back in the starting position. The athlete alternates lead legs and repeats the movement. The exercise can be completed in place for 8 to 12 repetitions per leg or while traveling over a 10-yard (9.1 m) distance.

Forward, Backward, and Lateral March

The athlete begins by lifting the left leg with the hip flexed at 90 to 120 degrees while at the same time lifting the right arm with the elbow flexed at 90 degrees. As the left leg is raised, the athlete dorsiflexes the left ankle, moving it close to the buttocks. As the right arm and the left leg come back down, the athlete lifts the opposing limbs with the same motion. When the athlete strikes the ground with the ball of the foot (not the heel), the footstrike occurs just slightly in front of the takeoff position as the athlete travels forward (for the forward march), slightly in back of the takeoff position as the athlete travels backward (for the backward march), or slightly lateral of the takeoff position as the athlete travels laterally (for the lateral march). It is important for the athlete to maintain an erect torso throughout the movement. The exercise can be completed in place for 8 to 12 repetitions per leg or while traveling over a 10-yard (9.1 m) distance.

Front, Back, and Lateral Skip

The guidelines for the three skip variations are the same as for the three march variations except that the athlete pushes off the ground for more upward extension as the legs are alternated. The athlete begins by lifting the right leg with the hip flexed at 90 to 120 degrees while at the same time lifting the left arm with the elbow flexed at 90 degrees. As the right leg is raised, the athlete dorsiflexes the right ankle, moving it toward the buttocks. As the left arm and the right leg come back down, the athlete lifts the opposing limbs with the same motion. The athlete forcefully pushes off the ground as soon as the foot makes contact to minimize ground contact time as much as possible. It is important for the athlete to maintain an erect torso throughout the movement. The exercise can be completed in place for 8 to 12 repetitions per leg or while traveling over a 10-yard (9.1 m) distance.

Power Skip

Before performing power skips, the athlete must demonstrate the ability to skip. To power skip, the athlete drives the free knee upward as aggressively as possible and simultaneously uses an aggressive arm action to create an exaggerated skip with more vertical displacement. The athlete should try to skip as high and as far as possible on each jump or stride, and perform 8 to 12 repetitions per leg or over a 20-yard (18.3 m) distance.

Linear Acceleration to Deceleration

The athlete begins in a forward jog. As the athlete anticipates the need to decelerate, he or she does so by flexing at the hips to lower the center of mass. Simultaneously, the athlete's strides should decrease in length. Unlike accelerations, which should be on the balls of the feet, decelerations should use a heel-to-toe foot action. The athlete should attempt to keep the weight balanced and not too far forward.

Shuffle to Deceleration

The athlete begins by shuffling laterally (with feet pointing forward), and as he or she approaches a predetermined stopping point, the athlete should brake with the weight on the outside of the inside foot and on the inside of the outside foot. The athlete's hips should be flexed and the body should lean away from the direction of the shuffle (see photo; the athlete was decelerating from moving to his right).

Backward Run to Deceleration

The athlete begins by backpedaling, and as he or she approaches a predetermined stopping point, the athlete should brake. The athlete's hips should be flexed with the shoulders leaning away from the direction of the backpedal.

Tuck Jump

The athlete stands with feet shoulder-width apart and the body in an upright position, not flexing at the waist. The athlete jumps up, bringing the knees up to the chest and then grasps, or attempts to grasp, the knees with the hands before the feet return to the ground. The athlete should land in a standing position. After performing the tuck jump successfully, the athlete should attempt to repeat the jump immediately and perform 6 to 10 repetitions of the drill.

Horizontal Jump and Stick

The athlete starts in a one-quarter to one-half squat position with the feet hip- to shoulder-width apart. The athlete uses a big arm swing and countermovement (a quick flexing of the hips and knees), then jumps forward as far as possible. The athlete should land on flat feet, with the predominance of the weight on the balls of the feet. The athlete should strive for stable, balanced landings, and perform 6 to 10 repetitions of the drill.

Hop and Stick

The athlete stands on one slightly to moderately flexed leg and then uses a counter-movement and a big arm swing forward to hop forward and land on the same leg. The emphasis is on a stable landing with minimal knee valgus. The athlete performs 6 to 10 repetitions of the drill per leg.

Butt Kick

Beginning in a jog, the athlete attempts to lift the heel of the lower leg up to bounce off the underside of the buttocks (see photo). As the hip and the knee flex, the knee comes forward and up (not seen in photo). The athlete performs the drill over a distance of 10 to 20 yards (9.1-18.3 m).

CHAPTER 4

Age and Sex Considerations

Jennifer Fields
Margaret T. Jones

Children are not miniature adults, so age and sex considerations should be addressed when designing and implementing speed and agility programs. In particular, youth undergo two critical periods before and after peak height velocity, in which they are more sensitive to training adaptations. Targeting these windows of opportunity may enhance performance responses (21). In addition, puberty marks a time when sex-related divergences take place. Thus, coaches should be aware of how these differences may affect both injury risk and performance.

AGE

Chronological age, which refers to a single time point after the date of birth, is frequently used to characterize young athletes. But because children do not grow at a constant rate, there are considerable interindividual differences in physical development at any given chronological age. For example, there will be substantial variations in height and body weight in a group of 14-year-old children as a result of differences in the age of onset and the progress of puberty (19) (figure 4.1). Therefore, it may be better to classify children based upon their *biological age*, or their stage of pubertal development. This age classification addresses the interaction between growth, maturation, and training (2).

Techniques available to the strength and conditioning practitioner for the purpose of assessing biological age include longitudinal growth curve analysis, percentages and predictions of final adult height, and, most commonly, the prediction of age from peak height velocity (21, 22). *Peak height velocity*

(PHV) refers to the maximum velocity of growth in stature and has been used to characterize developments in performance relative to a child's growth spurt (22). PHV can be calculated using the following anthropometric measurements: sex, date of birth, standing height, sitting height, and weight (17, 26). By objectively measuring the rates of change in height, children may be better trained according to biological status rather than chronological age (2). The average age of PHV is 12 years in girls, and 14 years in boys (2); however, these are best regarded as an approximation.

Figure 4.1 Differences in size between athletes of the same age.

Windows of Opportunity

There are two major *windows of opportunity*, or critical periods of accelerated adaptation, in which the development of speed and agility are critical in a child's life (2, 21) (table 4.1). While these skills are trainable throughout childhood, the windows of opportunity are considered a prime time for children to be exposed to proper movement mechanics. This first window of accelerated adaption occurs prior to PHV between the ages of 6 to 8 years in girls and 7 to 9 years in boys (2). This period is characterized by an increase in rate of sprint speed and explosive strength improvement (44). Therefore, this critical period is where speed responses will be maximized (2). For accelerated improvement of their motor abilities, prepubescent children may benefit most from training that requires high levels of neural activation, such as plyometrics and sprint training (21, 44). While improvement in speed has been observed prior to PHV (24, 44) declines in performance have been demonstrated during and following PHV (24). Speed and agility, therefore, should be of primary emphasis prior to PHV throughout this first window of opportunity.

Table 4.1 Windows of Opportunity

Stage	Boys (age)	Girls (age)	Activities	Goal
1	7-9 yrs	6-8 yrs	• Form drills • Speed drills • Agility drills • Plyometric drills	• Motor skill development • Improve neural activation • Increase in rate of sprint speed • Increase explosive strength
2	14 yrs	12.5 yrs	• Strength development • Power development • Speed drills • Agility drills	• Increase strength • Increase power and explosive strength • Maximize sprint and agility performance

The second window of opportunity occurs approximately 12 to 18 months following PHV and often coincides with *peak weight velocity* (PWV) (5, 6). The PWV is associated with a rapid growth in body mass and usually occurs during the PHV in boys (~14 years) and about 6 months after PHV in girls (~12.5 years) (36). During this time, adolescents undergo periods of rapid gains in muscle mass ensuing from increased circulating androgen concentrations (44). Increases in muscle mass, resulting from larger muscle fibers, allow for a greater force-production capacity, leading to increased strength (30). Muscular strength has been closely associated with running speed (13, 14), change of direction speed (29, 39), and plyometric ability (27), such that 70% of the variability in motor skills may be attributed to differences in muscular strength (40). Since strength is the foundation of subsequent power and speed, increases in strength during this stage will assist youth in further advancements in their speed and agility performance. The increases in androgen concentration and lean muscle will increase muscle force and rate of force development, further enhancing change of direction (COD) agility. Therefore, the second window is another critical time to emphasize speed and agility training in youth programs.

Agility can be divided into two predominant categories: *COD speed* (technique, straight sprinting speed, lower limb strength) and *cognitive function* (perceptual and decision-making processes) (37, 49). Since COD speed involves lower limb strength and straight running speed, agility training should be incorporated in prepubertal years with an emphasis on coordination and movement patterns. During this time, children undergo rapid developments in brain maturation and neural plasticity (35); therefore, developing motor control and basic COD techniques are critical. Once youth reach adolescent years, they should progress to more sport-specific agility movements.

Several perceptual variables may influence agility, such as visual scanning, knowledge of situation, pattern recognition, and anticipatory qualities (37). Research suggests that cognitive capacities increase during late childhood (girls: 8-9 years; boys: 10-11 years) and adolescence (girls: ~12 years; boys: ~14 years) (8, 10, 33), and so repeated exposure to speed and agility drills throughout this time may result in faster response times (1). However, during a growth spurt, increased limb length can result in decrements in motor control performance, a concept commonly referred to as *adolescent awkwardness* (21). During this stage of development, many of the skills learned previously will need to be reemphasized (21). Therefore, agility should be introduced early in the prepubertal years and continuously progressed and reinforced as the child ages through adolescence. Monitoring growth rates may help coaches identify adolescent awkwardness and adjust the content of training sessions accordingly.

Practical Application

Most importantly, coaches need to ensure that content is age appropriate. For example, a group of middle school football players should not be performing the same speed and agility training tactics as professional athletes from the National Football League. Effective age-appropriate program design and implementation will contribute to athlete success in both speed and agility development. During the first window of opportunity, special attention should be paid to body awareness and body control with proper movement mechanics. Once motor skills are successfully performed, speed will develop. Therefore, a strong focus on form is crucial during the prepubescent years. Since speed has been shown to decrease during and following PHV, it is recommended that coaches incorporate speed and agility training during earlier prepubescent stages (girls: 6-8 years; boys: 7-9 years). The addition of these skills earlier in youth development may reduce speed disparities associated with the onset of PHV.

Following PHV, the second window of opportunity is characterized by increases in strength due to surges in androgens, specifically testosterone, growth hormone, and insulin-like growth factor. Strength is closely associated with speed, change of direction, and plyometric ability; therefore, the second period is critical for further improvements in speed and agility and drills that address the aforementioned should be included into the training program design.

It is important for coaches to be aware of adolescent awkwardness. Routinely monitoring stature and body weight of athletes in order to identify growth spurts may help practitioners to recognize this phase. During adolescent awkwardness, limb lengths increase but muscles have yet to reach full size or strength (32), which contributes to reductions in motor skill performance. Therefore, coaches may choose to spend more effort reviewing optimal movement patterns for athletes at this time. Spending more time on form and technical skill will allow the athlete to retrain the control needed to attain subsequent high levels of speed and agility. Practitioners will likely need to modify existing motor patterns with reduced loads (18).

Additionally, risk of injury may be heightened during PHV (11). For example, before PHV there is a decrease in bone mineral density, leading to increased risk of bone fractures (11). Further, changes in limb length and mass resulting from growth place disproportionately increased stress on muscle-tendon junctions, bone-tendon junctions, ligaments, and growth cartilage (11). Such imbalances, coupled with the loading demands of sport, may make the affected youth prone to musculoskeletal and overuse injuries (11). Increases in body mass and height of center of mass without corresponding adaptations in strength and power can lead to excessive loading on the musculoskeletal system during dynamic and reactive actions (16, 28). Females, specifically, have an increased risk of knee injury due to their increasing body size without the appropriate increases in hip and knee strength to support their skeleton (28). Females experience a widening of the hips, thus increasing the Q angle of the knee (38). Larger Q angles are associated with increased pressure on the lower extremities (38); therefore, coaches should be sure to select biologically age-appropriate drills and encourage proper recovery.

With youth training, it is recommended that emphasis be placed upon exercise programs that promote physical development, reduce injury, and enhance fitness behaviors across the age spectrum. *Long-term athlete development* (LTAD) refers to the habitual development of athleticism over time to improve health and fitness, enhance physical performance, and reduce the relative risk of injury (18). A list of the pillars of successful LTAD is provided in table 4.2. This model emphasizes age-appropriate exercises since children's anatomy and physiology differ from those of adolescents in muscle structure (15, 31), size (12), activation patterns (12), and function (13). Structured training that focuses on age-appropriate drills and movement patterns will provide superior results and reduce the risk of overtraining. Coaches should also educate youth about how their drills will translate into improved performance in their sport. This understanding will help motivate children and build a lifelong future of healthy and enjoyable engagement in sport and physical activity (18).

Table 4.2 Ten Pillars of Successful Long-Term Athletic Development

Number	Description
1	Long-term athletic development pathways should accommodate the highly individualized and nonlinear nature of the growth and development of youth.
2	Youth of all ages, abilities, and aspirations should engage in long-term athletic development programs that promote both physical fitness and psychosocial well-being.
3	All youth should be encouraged to enhance physical fitness from early childhood, with a primary focus on motor skill and muscular strength development.
4	Long-term athletic development pathways should encourage an early sampling approach for youth that promotes and enhances a broad range of motor skills.
5	The health and well-being of the child should always be the central tenet of long-term athletic development programs.
6	Youth should participate in physical conditioning that helps reduce the risk of injury to ensure their ongoing participation in long-term athletic development programs.
7	Long-term athletic development programs should provide all youth with a range of training modes to enhance both health- and skill-related components of fitness.
8	Practitioners should use the relevant monitoring and assessment tools as part of a long-term athletic development strategy.
9	Practitioners working with youth should systematically progress and individualize training programs for successful long-term athletic development.
10	Qualified professionals and sound pedagogical approaches are fundamental to the success of long-term athletic development programs.

Reprinted by permission from R.S. Lloyd, J.B. Cronin, A.D. Faigenbaum, G.G. Haff, R. Howard, W.J. Kraemer, and J.L. Oliver, "National Strength and Conditioning Association Position Statement on Long-Term Athletic Development," *Journal of Strength and Conditioning Research* 30, no. 6 (2016): 1491-1509.

SEX DIFFERENCES

It is important for coaches to gain an understanding of sex-related differences associated with speed and agility training. During the prepubertal years, boys and girls follow similar rates of growth and maturation. Therefore, strength, speed, power, and coordination are comparable (5), and prepubertal boys and girls can follow similar speed and agility programs.

Body Composition

With the onset of puberty, hormonal changes lead to sex-related divergences in body size and body composition. In girls, increases in estrogen production lead to increased fat deposition; conversely, in boys, increases in testosterone production result in increased bone formation, muscle synthesis, and lipolysis (43). Whereas preadolescent boys and girls display testosterone levels between 20 and 60 ng/100ml, males experience a tenfold increase, with levels reaching up to 600 ng/100ml following puberty (19). Boys develop fat-free mass at a rapid rate while the gain in girls begins to plateau at approximately age 12. On average, adult males will have 20 kg (44.1 lb) greater fat-free mass compared to adult females (43). Since males experience a dramatic growth in fat-free mass and muscle size, their body fat percentage often decreases during and following puberty. Conversely, rising estrogen rates leads to increased fat mass, resulting in girls having an average of 5 to 6 kg (11-13.2 lb) greater fat mass than boys (22). In summary, women generally have higher body fat, less muscle, and lower total body weight than men following sexual maturation (19, 43).

In addition, force-production capabilities differ significantly during and after puberty. The surge in anabolic hormones experienced by males increases muscle cross-sectional area, which results in greater force production, strength, and power output (34). Typically, females have from 41 to 45% smaller cross-sectional area of upper body muscles and a 25 to 30% smaller cross-sectional area of lower body muscles (25). Between 10 and 16 years of age, pubertal boys have shown upper- and lower-body strength increases by 3.9 and 2.5 times, respectively (7). Girls generally exhibit little change in strength and coordination throughout puberty (5); rather, strength and power output reach a plateau around the age of 16 years (34). The absence of such adaptations in girls reduces force-production capabilities during sport (15). Pubertal boys have shown a 7.3% increase in vertical jump height whereas no increases were observed in girls of the same ages (15). Compared to boys, postpubertal girls reduced their vertical jump takeoff phase in comparison to their prepubertal assessments (15). From the ages of 13 to 16, significant differences were observed between boys and girls in the squat jump, counter-movement jump, rebound jump, and average power, with males consistently outperforming females (41).

Strength and power are highly correlated with speed and change of direction because athletes must be able to accelerate their bodies while applying maximal forces to the ground (9, 46). Sprint performance is commonly examined in three phases: acceleration phase (0-10 m), transition phase (10-36 m), and maximal running speed (36-100 m). The acceleration phase requires powerful extensions of all leg joints, particularly from the gluteus maximus and the knee extensors (9). In the maximal running phase, there is an increased involvement of the hamstrings, gluteus maximus, and adductor magnus muscles that play an important role in forward propulsion. Due to the increases in strength and power following puberty, males experience a corresponding improvement in sprint performance, whereas females have reached a plateau (9).

Risk of Injury

During puberty, female athletes undergo sex-specific physiological processes that may affect performance: increased fat mass, differential rates of development of neuromuscular strength, altered center of mass, widening of the hips, increased Q angle (38), commencement of menstrual cycle, increased joint laxity, increased knee valgus angle; and increased reliance on quadriceps-dominant landing strategies, all of which have been associated with an increased risk of a noncontact anterior cruciate ligament (ACL) injury. Prior to puberty, no differences in ACL injury rates are seen between boys and girls; in fact, ACL sprains are not commonly found in prepubescent children (47). However, immediately following PHV, girls are at significantly higher risk of developing an ACL injury (42).

Female athletes have a risk of ACL injury that is two to six times the risk male athletes playing at similar competitive levels in the same sports (28). In particular, female athletes from soccer and basketball are at greatest risk for injury. A five-year study examined 461 men's and 278 women's soccer teams and determined the rate of ACL injury in females was more than double that of males (0.31 vs. 0.13) (44). The same study examined 531 men's and 576 women's basketball teams, and results indicated the ACL injury rate in women was more than four times that of men (0.29 vs. 0.07). The high rate of noncontact ACL injury observed in basketball can be attributed to planting and cutting (29%), straight-knee landing (28%), and knee hyperextension (26%) (1). Female basketballers experience a greater number of injuries compared to males because of the sex-specific physiological processes that occur during puberty.

Unlike boys, girls do not experience significant neuromuscular adaptations during puberty, despite an increase in body growth. Puberty marks a stage where neuromuscular imbalances emerge in girls, causing increased lower-extremity joint loads during sports (15). Specifically, females experience an imbalance in ligament control of the joints; an overreliance of quadriceps strength compared to hamstrings, resulting in an imbalance in strength, recruitment, and coordination; and an imbalance in strength and coordination patterns between the right and left lower extremities (28). Compared with male athletes, female athletes are more susceptible to these imbalances, which are considered to be important contributors to an increased risk of ACL injury (20).

Practical Application

As explained, sprint performance and change of direction abilities tend to decline following PHV in both girls and boys (17). Because girls reach PHV earlier than boys (girls: 12 years; boys: 14 years), a training emphasis on sprinting and agility is recommended at a younger age for girls than for boys (24). Earlier incorporation of drills designed to enhance speed and change of direction will attenuate performance decrements associated with the onset of puberty (20).

During puberty, sex differences emerge in body composition, force production, and strength and power output. Consequently, it is the strength and conditioning practitioner's responsibility to reduce these disparities commonly observed in female athletes and to prioritize strength training in program design (1).

Resistance training should be incorporated prior to, and following, the adolescent growth spurt, around the age of 14 in males and 12 in females (21). The incorporation of resistance exercise, specifically for female athletes, may help reduce increases in fat mass and body fat experienced during puberty (38). In addition, resistance training may lead to improvements in force, strength and power production, which can translate to overall sport performance (4). Particular attention should be placed on lower extremity strengthening (e.g., gluteus maximus, quadriceps, hamstrings, abductors, and adductors) to enhance speed and change of direction (9). For sprint athletes who achieve maximal running speeds over 36 to 100 m (40), it may be beneficial to incorporate speed-strength training, a method utilizing maximal forces at high velocities (e.g., jump squat) (9).

Because pubertal females are at heightened risk for injury, particular attention must be paid to girls during the maturation stage of development. Increases in joint laxity are associated with increased incidence of musculoskeletal injury (48), and coaches should be cognizant of proper form during speed and agility drills. Resistance training should emphasize the strengthening of gluteal and hamstring muscles (e.g., walking lunges, wall sits, reverse and forward lunges, glute hamstring raises, stiff-legged deadlifts) and plyometrics with proper landing mechanics (e.g., lateral hops, forward hops, single-legged hops, vertical jumps, depth jumps) (14, 23). Appropriate incorporation of these exercise techniques may result in an 88% decrease in ACL injury (23). With proper coaching and exercise prescription, resistance training can offset increased risks of noncontact injury.

CONCLUSION

Emphasizing speed, agility, and plyometrics within the first window of opportunity will improve neural activation, sprint speed, and explosive strength. The second window of opportunity, following PHV and PWV, should include activities to increase strength and power development while maximizing sprint performance. Coaches must be cognizant of the sex-related differences in body composition and neuromuscular adaptations that occur with the onset of puberty. Awareness of injury risk and prevention will allow practitioners to design and implement age- and sex-appropriate exercise programs to optimize effectiveness and decrease injury risk.

CHAPTER 5

Testing, Assessment, and Monitoring of Agility and Quickness

Robert Lockie

It is important for coaches to understand the components of agility before selecting an appropriate testing program for their athletes. Sheppard and Young (74) have described agility as being composed of two broad factors: change of direction (COD) speed and perceptual and decision-making factors. *Change of direction speed* is the physical component of agility, which incorporates technique, the ability to accelerate and decelerate, strength, and power. For a task to be truly defined as agility, it needs to involve some form of perception and decision-making, which includes visual scanning, knowledge about the current situation (e.g., recognizing formations on offense and defense in football), pattern recognition, and anticipation. *Agility* requires a reactive element; some form of external stimulus (e.g., an opponent) drives the need for the athlete to change direction. *Quickness* has been defined as a multiplanar skill that incorporates a combination of acceleration, reactive ability, and explosiveness (58), which in essence is the ability to read and react to a situation (87).

Nimphius, Callaghan, Bezodis, and Lockie (59) stated that the act of changing direction can take place in both planned and reactive situations. Accordingly, coaches must know what they are actually assessing when they select a test. If all the actions are preplanned, then the test will provide a metric of COD speed. If there is an external stimulus involved, then this will more likely test agility and quickness. However, before describing the specific

The author would like to acknowledge the significant contribution of Jason Jones to this chapter.

process for selecting a specific test, it is first important to understand why to test athletes. There are several reasons the use of testing can be beneficial for the coach and athlete:

▶ *Predicting athletic potential.* Field testing can be used to predict the potential for an athlete to be successful at a particular sport (55). In order to do this, the test should be as specific to the sport as possible with regard to specific movement patterns, muscle group recruitment, and test duration to increase the validity and accuracy of the test's predictability. For example, the pro-agility shuttle and three-cone test used in the National Football League (NFL) combine to assess collegiate football players prior to the NFL draft (28, 69, 76).

▶ *Identification of strengths and weaknesses.* Appropriate testing can be used to determine those physical, physiological, and biomechanical qualities that could be targeted for improvement in athletes (55). Specific to COD speed and agility, coaches may select tests to identify whether an athlete has the requisite technique or decision-making abilities specific to their sport (74). Furthermore, certain tests could also be used to determine recovery from injury progress during rehabilitation. For example, the 505 agility test could identify differences in performance (33) and movement patterns (59) that may be indicative of lower-limb injury.

▶ *Evaluation of progress.* One of the foundations of testing athletes is to determine the change in performance as a result of a training block (55). If the athlete progresses and improves, this informs the coach that the program was effective. If the athlete does not, the coach can then modify the program where appropriate to be more effective.

▶ *Comparison to normative data.* Coaches can also use the results of test data from athletes to make comparisons to athletes within a specific team or compare to normative data from a comparable population or elite-level athletes (43, 56). This can provide a greater context for the measurement of COD speed or agility for an athlete. Normative and descriptive data for many tests included in this chapter can be found in resources provided by the National Strength and Conditioning Association, such as *Essentials of Strength Training and Conditioning* and *NSCA's Guide to Tests and Assessments*.

▶ *Goal setting.* The results of test data can also be used by the coach to set goals for the athlete and provide motivation (23, 54). Lockie, Risso, Giuliano, Orjalo, and Jalilvand (43) have noted that practitioners should be aware of the effects that superior or inferior performance on a test could have on the athlete. Test performance could influence an athlete's motivation, anxiety, or other psychological factors (81, 86).

Just as NFL teams use testing to evaluate players, coach and athletes at all levels can use testing to predict and improve performance.

Thus, the coach must effectively communicate what the results of a test mean and how they will be used to adjust the training program going forward. For example, a lower than expected test score could be used to motivate an athlete to improve.

TEST SELECTION AND ADMINISTRATION

In order to monitor the development of COD speed, agility, and quickness in athletes, it is essential that coaches select appropriate tests that are specific to the activities of an athlete's sport. A number of factors must be considered when selecting an appropriate test of agility and quickness. This involves considering the specific demands of the test, such as the type of direction changes required, duration, and whether a stimulus is included. Two reviews have provided detailed information as to the strengths and limitations of numerous COD and agility tests (59, 67). This chapter will provide information about a number of issues the coach must consider when testing COD speed, agility, and quickness.

VALIDITY, RELIABILITY, AND ACCURACY

Validity relates to whether a test measures what it is supposed to measure, which is essential for appropriate athlete data collection (23). *Reliability* refers to the repeatability or consistency of a test (55). This means that if a test is administered on two occasions during which performance should not have changed, the same (or very close to the same) result is attained. A test can be valid but not reliable, and vice versa. For example, the vertical jump is a valid and reliable test of lower-body power (64, 72). It does not, however, provide a valid metric for COD ability. *Accuracy* relates to how closely a test measures what the actual performance was (84). The adopted test procedures can influence accuracy; for example, automated timing procedures tend to produce more accurate results than handheld timing methods (22, 51). Thus, it is important for a coach to select a test and procedures that are valid, reliable, accurate, and specific to COD speed, agility, and quickness. As will be discussed, there are several factors that can influence the validity, reliability, and accuracy of data from COD speed, agility, and quickness tests. These range from the procedures adopted during testing to the design of the actual test itself.

TESTING PROCEDURES

According to the National Strength and Conditioning Association, COD speed, agility, and quickness tests should be completed at the start of a testing session or else day-before fatigue from other tests or daily activities can negatively influence performance (55). McGuigan (55) stated that this is required because of the high skill component that is typically required in these types of tests. Coaches should attempt to conduct any testing at the same time of day across multiple sessions because *circadian rhythms* (i.e., an individual's internal biological processes) can influence athletic performance (1). Weather can also influence test performance, although conducting COD speed, agility, and quickness testing indoors can reduce the influence of factors such as heat, wind, and rain, while also providing a consistent testing surface (55). If testing must be conducted outdoors, ideally the weather should be temperate. Faster linear sprint performances have occurred in temperatures above 77 degrees F (25 degrees C) (17), although warmer conditions can result in a faster rate of fatigue across multiple trials (15). Therefore, coaches should always make a record of the temperature and conditions of testing sessions conducted outdoors.

The surface used for COD speed, agility, and quickness testing can affect test performance. For example, Gains, Swedenhjelm, Mayhew, Bird, and Houser (14) detailed that collegiate football players performed the pro-agility shuttle 3% faster on field turf when compared to grass. Coaches may also consider contextual specificity when deciding on locations for testing. A soccer coach may prefer to use field turf or grass for testing, rather than a hardwood floor, because that is what the athletes play on. However, the coach may not always be allowed to select the surface used for testing, and may be limited by the available locations. Where possible, nonslip surfaces should be used, and footwear should be adopted as appropriate to this surface. Depending on the surface area used for testing (e.g., grass vs. field turf vs. indoor court), athletes should use footwear (e.g., cleats for football and soccer players, basketball shoes for basketball players) and clothing (e.g., appropriate training attire) specific to their competition equipment.

The coach should also conduct testing within the confines of the number of staff available to administer tests. This is essential when attempting to assess a large group of athletes. Coaches may have athletes rotate in a specific order to ensure sufficient recovery between trials (44). Specific instructions should be provided to staff regarding how to administer tests, and the instructions, feedback, and encouragement should be provided to athletes. This is essential to ensure consistency with procedures among a group of athletes. Test results may be provided to the athlete in order to provide motivation for subsequent trials (55), but this is up to the discretion of the coach and again should be consistent across athletes and testing sessions. The coach should also conduct an appropriate warm-up and cool-down on the testing day and repeat these in all testing sessions in the future for consistency.

TESTING EQUIPMENT

Ideally, a coach should have access to equipment such as timing gate systems that allow for the recording of more accurate data. Handheld stopwatch timing has been adopted in the literature with tests such as the pro-agility shuttle (8, 52), and experienced timers can record reliable and consistent data (22). However, stopwatches (or timing applications available on cell phones and tablets) are limited by an individual's reaction time and thus tend to feature larger measurement errors compared to other electronic timing methods (19). If a coach does not have access to electronic timing devices, then to limit measurement error, explicit instructions regarding stopwatch operation, body position relative to the start and finish of the test, and the start and stop protocols should be provided (22). In addition, if times are being recorded via a handheld device, the coach may also need to supply data sheets, clipboards, and pens to record the data. To allow for a faster reaction time, Mayhew, Houser, Briney, Williams, Piper and Brechue (51) have recommended that the index finger rather than the thumb be used to initiate timing procedures.

Nonetheless, electronic timing devices such as timing gates should ideally be used for testing. A timing gate consists of a light source or transmitter and an optical pickup or reflector (5). The transmitter and reflector are positioned opposite each other, forming a gate that can be run through, and the light beam from the transmitter hits the reflector and is bounced back to the transmitter where it is detected. The time is recorded via a tablet or handheld personal computer (PC) synchronized with the gates, which also means the coach may not need to use pen and paper to record data. A number of different timing gate systems are available to the coach. Some examples include Brower Timing Systems (Knoxville, USA), which use a single beam between the gates (20); Swift Speedlight (Swift Performance, Lismore, Australia), which is a modulated dual-beam system with light beams positioned at two heights (5); and the SmartSpeed system (Fusion Sport, Sumner Park, Australia), which is a single-beam system that uses error detection and postprocessing of the signal data (78). Each system has strengths and limitations, so coaches should have knowledge of them and how they affect the athletes' test results to determine which system is most beneficial given their known strengths and limitations.

The coach should also consider the required start procedures for a test when using timing gates. The Fusion Sport SmartSpeed system can allow the use of an in-beam start, where the athlete starts between the gate (thus within the beam), and their movement from the beam will initiate timing. This approach has been used for the pro-agility shuttle, typically started from a three-point stance (40, 44). Otherwise, depending on the structure of the test, athletes may start a certain distance behind the timing gate to initiate timing procedures (e.g., T-test, three-cone test, and Illinois agility test). Distances of 0.3 meters (11.8 in.) (47, 48) and 0.5 meters (19.7 in.) (37, 40) behind the timing gate have been used previously. Other tests, such as the 505 agility test, involve a flying start through the timing gate. Nevertheless, the major concern when assessing the same population of athletes over extended periods of time is that the coach uses the same start procedures consistently across test sessions.

TEST DESIGN

Coaches should consider the actual distance traveled within a COD speed or agility test and how this relates to the sport of the athletes. Nimphius, Callaghan, Bezodis, and Lockie (59) noted that one of the main limitations with many COD speed and agility tests is the influence linear sprinting can have on test performance. This essentially means that although athletes may have weaknesses executing direction changes, if they have greater linear speed, this may hide these shortcomings in tests that feature longer distance sprint efforts. Nimphius, Callaghan, Bezodis, and Lockie (59) used the pro-agility shuttle as an example; this test features a total of 20 yards (18.3 m) of linear sprinting and only two 180-degree direction changes. Previous research has suggested that entry velocity into a direction change and exit velocity from a direction change are the best measures of COD ability (71). However, this is very difficult to measure in the field. This has led to an alternate metric of COD speed called the *COD deficit* (36, 60, 61). The COD deficit is calculated by analyzing the difference between a COD test with one direction change and a linear sprint over an equivalent distance (59). This determines the impact that the direction change has on an athlete's movement speed. For example, when adopting a test such as the 505, if a coach also measures 10-meter (10.9 yd) sprint performance, the COD deficit can be calculated by the following formula (60):

$$\text{COD deficit} = 505 \text{ agility test time} - 10\text{-meter sprint time}$$

A greater COD deficit, which indicates lesser COD ability, demonstrates that an athlete slows down more prior to a cut or does not accelerate as effectively after a cut. Inclusion of the COD deficit allows the coach to have two measures of COD ability: the total test time and the COD deficit. Nevertheless, coaches should select tests that involve sprint distances appropriate to the sport of their athlete.

If a COD speed or agility test is completed over a longer duration, the limiting factor may not be COD ability. Instead, metabolic limitations may greatly affect the performance of a test (83). Maximal efforts exceeding 6 seconds will involve a transition from the phosphagen energy system to fast glycolysis being the dominant energy system (21). As a result, performance decrement could be the result of fatigue due to the depletion of creatine phosphate within the muscles, as opposed to lesser COD ability. This can be an issue with the Illinois agility test, which, depending on the population, can have a duration of 14 to 18 seconds (25, 46, 83). The 60-yard (54.9 m) shuttle (duration of 11-14 sec) (37, 38, 53) and the Arrowhead test (duration of 8-9 sec) (3, 37, 42) may also have this limitation. Coaches should be aware that if they use tests such as these, they may not be exclusively analyzing COD speed. Rather, these tests may assess the ability to complete longer distance sprint efforts that incorporate direction changes (37).

Coaches should also consider the angle of direction changes performed within a test, because the movements required and the ability to effect the direction change are dependent on this (59). Accordingly, the coach should select a test that involves direction changes that relate to the athlete's sport. For example, the pro-agility shuttle features a three-point stance and lateral movements that are specific to the sport of football (28, 69, 76). The 505 agility test, which features an up-and-back 180-degree direction change is similar to the cuts completed in basketball (77) or running between the wickets in cricket (32).

Tests that isolate COD performance from each leg, such as the 505 agility test, could also be used to identify bilateral deficits between legs (6, 32, 33, 47, 48, 62, 63). Although no research has clearly established limits for between-leg differences in COD actions, a 10% disparity in strength and power tests have been noted as an indicator of leg dysfunction (79, 80). Nonetheless, Lockie, Callaghan and Jeffriess (33) noted that even a 2% difference in 505 agility test times between legs was meaningful in recreational male and female athletes that had a history of ankle sprains, in that those athletes that had experienced an ankle sprain were slower on the affected limb. This type of information could be useful in detailing whether an athlete changes direction from one leg more effectively than from the other (59), or whether they have appropriately recovered from a lower-limb injury (18, 33).

NUMBER OF TRIALS

COD speed, agility, and quickness testing will often feature a number of trials to ensure either consistent or the best performance by an athlete, which may not be achieved if only one trial is performed. For example, three trials have been recommended for linear sprint testing in order to achieve a reliable best time (57). However, the number of trials may be limited by the time available for testing, particularly if a large number of athletes need to be assessed. For example, American football combine testing typically features two trials of tests such as the pro-agility shuttle and the three-cone test (24, 40). Cronin and Templeton (5) intimated that due to the reliability of a good timing lights system, coaches may only need to record one or two trials to gather reliable information. Coaches should have athletes complete at least two or three trials of their selected COD speed, agility, or quickness tests, although two trials may be sufficient if time is limited. However, in determining the optimal number of trials the coach should also decide whether the fastest performance, or the average of the trials, is needed.

EXTERNAL STIMULUS

As stated, for a test to be considered an assessment of agility or quickness, there must be some type of external stimulus in which the athlete is required to react. COD speed tests do not feature any form of stimulus, because all movements and direction changes required in the tests are explained to the athlete and preplanned prior to performance. Paul, Gabbett, and Nassis (67) have provided a detailed review of the current strengths and limitations of agility in the literature. Certain challenges for conducting agility and quickness tests must be considered by the coach. The first is the structure of the test. The most common format used for assessing reactive agility is a Y-shaped test, where the athlete moves either left or right to complete a 45-degree cut and sprint in response to a stimulus that is positioned in front of the athlete. However, this structure may not always be appropriate (67) since not all sports feature situations that require a relatively simple decision during match-play to cut either left or right. Nonetheless, a Y-shaped agility test (16, 26, 39, 65) or a reactive agility test, which requires a left or right cut in response to a stimulus (10, 13, 75), tend to be the models most easy to reproduce in the field.

The stimuli used in reactive agility tests can be illuminated arrows, flashing lights, video projections, and humans (67). Several timing gate systems are designed to allow for a flashing light to create the stimulus. A Y-shaped test using lights as the stimuli has differentiated between academy and club rugby union players (16), and semiprofessional and amateur basketball players (39). Lockie, Jeffriess, McGann, Callaghan, and Schultz (39) suggested that this could be related to superior visual scanning capacities in higher-level athletes. However, light stimuli are generally not specific to sport, and do not allow for the use of perceptual cues that elite athletes actually use in their sport (59, 67). As a result, other agility and quickness tests have incorporated video projections or a human stimulus (67). Further, Paul, Gabbett, and Nassis (67) noted that while video projections can allow for uniformity with the stimulus, they are generally not practical to use outside of a laboratory.

The use of a human performing a movement the athlete has to react to is arguably the most sport-specific form of agility testing. However, this is dependent on the actions performed by the human stimulus; their movements, and how the athlete is supposed to react to those movements, should be made as specific to the sport as possible (67). Despite the potential variability that could occur when relying on a person to initiate a response from an athlete, previous research has shown that the use of human stimuli can result in valid and reliable data (13, 75). However, Paul, Gabbett, and Nassis (67) noted that athletes should be familiarized to an agility test with a human stimulus before actual data collection is conducted. They also recommended that a stringent approach be taken with instructions for both the person acting as the stimulus, and the required response options for the athlete.

COD SPEED, AGILITY, AND QUICKNESS TESTS

This section is divided into three subsections: shorter distance COD speed tests, longer distance COD speed tests, and reactive agility and quickness tests. For each test, the coach will need to use either a stopwatch or electronic timing gates to record performance and will need a measuring tape to measure the required distances. If timing gates are to be used, the diagrams of the tests display where these should be positioned. The number of cones required for each test is noted, in addition to the test procedures.

With regard to the start position, a two-point stance generally refers to a standing start position where the feet are positioned in a comfortable staggered stance (figure 1.4 on page 15). The weight is predominantly on the front leg, which is flexed at the hip and knee to load the leg, and the opposing arm to the front leg is positioned in front of the body. The back leg is positioned by slight extension at the hip, and the knee is also flexed. A three-point stance refers to a start where the front and back legs, and opposing arm to the front leg, are in contact with the ground, in a position similar to a track start (see figure 1.5 on page 15). The hand of the opposing arm to the front leg is positioned level with the starting line. The front leg is positioned approximately 16 to 20 inches (about 40-50 cm) behind the front hand, and the rear leg is positioned behind the front leg. When the athlete raises the hips from the three-point stance, the front knee should have an angle of approximately 90 degrees, while the rear knee should be at an angle of approximately 120 degrees.

Table 5.1 provides a list of the speed, agility, and quickness tests included in this chapter.

Table 5.1 Speed, Agility, and Quickness Tests

Test name	Page number
SHORTER DISTANCE COD SPEED TESTS	
Pro-agility shuttle	87
505 agility test	88
Adapted 505 agility test	89
COD deficit	90
Three-cone test	91
Modified T-test	92
LONGER DISTANCE COD SPEED TESTS	
Illinois agility test	93
60-yard shuttle test	94
Arrowhead test	95
T-test	96
REACTIVE AGILITY AND QUICKNESS TESTS	
Y-shaped agility test	97
Reactive agility test	98

Shorter Distance COD Speed Tests

PRO-AGILITY SHUTTLE

The purpose of the pro-agility shuttle is to assess the ability to accelerate, decelerate, and move laterally to the left and right, in addition to completing 180-degree cuts from each leg. This test is a staple for American football (28, 40, 44, 69, 76) but has also been used to assess soccer players (37, 38, 42, 50, 52, 68).

Test Layout

Three pairs of cones should be positioned 5 yards (4.6 m) apart to form a straight line that covers a total distance of 10 yards (9.1 m). The starting line is in the middle of the 10-yard (9.1 m) distance. The cones should be positioned such that they represent three lines: left, center (the start and finish line), and right.

Procedures

Football athletes should use a three-point stance with the feet parallel to start the test. For athletes from other sports, an athletic position with the feet parallel should be used. Once ready, the athlete turns to the right and runs 5 yards (4.6 m) to touch the line with the right hand. The athlete then turns and sprints 10 yards (9.1 m) to the opposing line and touches it with the left hand. Finally, the athlete turns and finishes by sprinting back to and through the start and finish line. Failure to touch the line each time results in termination of the test. Timing begins as soon as the athlete moves out of the start position and stops when the athlete passes through the finish line. The coach should allow the athlete to complete at least two trials, one with movement initiation to the right, one with movement initiation to the left.

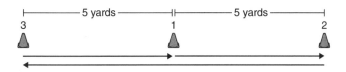

505 AGILITY TEST

The 505 agility test can assess the ability to accelerate and decelerate while navigating a challenging 180-degree direction change and can be used to determine COD ability for each leg (31, 33). This test has been administered for a range of athletes from sports such as rugby league (6, 13), rugby union (29), soccer (35, 41, 49), football (36), netball (9), basketball (77), softball (62, 63), and cricket (32, 60).

Test Layout

The 505 agility test is conducted over a 15-meter (16.4 yd) distance. Two cones should be placed at the starting line, timing line (10 meters [10.9 yd] away from the starting line; the timer or timing gate should be positioned here), and turning line (5 meters [5.5 yd] away from the timing line). Where possible, the lines should be indicated on the ground.

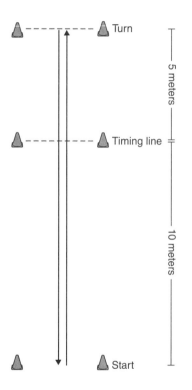

Procedures

The athlete should use either a two- or a three-point stance to start the test. Once ready, the athlete sprints past the timing line to the turning line. The athlete should then place either the left or right foot on the turning line, and sprint back through the timing line. Time is recorded from when the athlete initially passes through the timing line and is stopped when the athlete passes the line following the 180-degree direction change. The coach should allow the athlete to complete at least two trials; one where the right foot is placed on the turning line, and one where the left foot is placed on the turning line. The data can be averaged between the two legs, or the coach may analyze performances from both legs individually.

ADAPTED 505 AGILITY TEST

Lockie, Jalilivand, Orjalo, Giuliano, Moreno, and Wright (36) adapted the 505 agility test (commonly abbreviated to A505) to make it potentially more specific to football players by basing the distances on yards rather than meters. This may make the test easier to set up on football fields because the distances are already indicated on the ground. Lockie, Jalilivand, Orjalo, Giuliano, Moreno, and Wright (36) documented that the A505 agility test correlated with the times recorded for the traditional 505 agility test and was able to discriminate between position groups (i.e., the backs were faster than the linemen).

Test Layout

The structure of the A505 agility test is the same as that of the 505 agility test. However, the A505 agility test is conducted over a 15-yard (13.7 m) distance. The distance between the starting line and the timing line is 10 yards (9.1 m), and the distance between the timing line and the turning line is 5 yards (4.6 m).

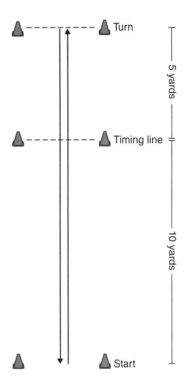

Procedures

The procedures for the A505 agility test are the same as that for the 505 agility test. As with the 505 agility test, athletes should complete at least two trials for the A505 agility test, one turning off the right leg, and one turning off the left leg. Again, as with the 505 agility test, the coach can average data between the two legs, or analyze performances from each leg individually.

COD DEFICIT

The COD deficit is an alternate metric of COD ability, and it is used to calculate the impact that a direction change has on a sprint performance relative to a linear sprint over an equivalent distance (59). This has been calculated from the first direction change in the pro-agility shuttle (61), the 505 agility test (60), and the A505 agility test (36). In order to calculate the COD deficit, the coach should record the athlete's performance in a test such as the pro-agility shuttle, the 505 agility test, or the A505 agility test. The coach should also record linear sprint time over a 10-yard (9.1 m) distance for the pro-agility shuttle and the A505 agility test, or a 10-meter (10.9 yd) distance for the 505 agility test. COD deficit can then be calculated via the following formulas:

Pro-agility shuttle COD deficit = Pro-agility 10-yard split time − 10-yard time

505 COD deficit = 505 agility test time − 10-meter time

A505 COD deficit = A505 agility test time − 10-yard time

Depending on the design of a COD speed test, and whether split times that isolate a direction change within the test can be recorded, COD deficit could also be calculated for other tests.

THREE-CONE TEST

The three-cone test assesses acceleration, deceleration, lateral movement, and maneuverability. This test is also a staple COD speed test for football players (28, 40, 44, 69, 76), and has been used to test rugby league players (12).

Test Layout

Three cones are positioned in the shape of an *L*. Cone 1 is the start cone, cone 2 sits at the 90-degree corner, while cone 3 is at the other end of the *L*. The distance between the cones is 5 yards (4.6 m). The three-cone test can be set up such that *L* bends toward left or right.

Procedures

The athlete should use either a two- or a three-point stance to start the test. Once ready, the athlete runs forward toward cone 2, bends down and touches the ground with the hand before running back to cone 1 and touching the ground with the hand (*a*). The athlete then runs back to cone 2 and around the outside of it, weaves inside cone 3, and around the outside of cones 3 and 2 before finishing at cone 1 (*b*). Timing starts from when the athlete moves until when the athlete sprints back past the starting line following the final sprint in the test. The coach should allow the athlete to complete at least two trials, one where the athlete has to turn to the right, and one where the athlete has to turn to the left.

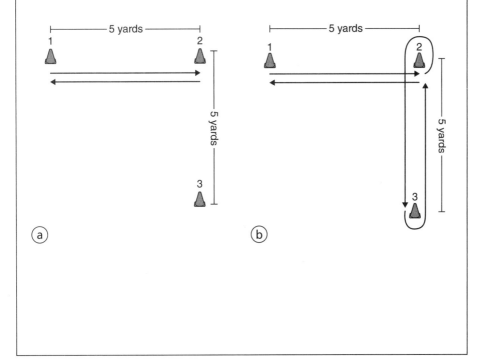

MODIFIED T-TEST

The modified T-test is a shortened version of the traditional T-test (see the longer distance COD speed tests section) that was originally designed for soccer players (70). Sassi, Dardouri, Yahmed, Gmada, Mahfoudhi, and Gharbi (70) demonstrated that the modified T-test correlated with the traditional T-test when performed by college-age men and women, over distances potentially more specific to team sports. This test has subsequently been used to assess COD speed in team sport athletes (e.g., soccer, basketball, netball, softball, rugby league, rugby union, Australian football) (47, 48), and lacrosse players (30).

Test Layout

Four cones are placed in the shape of a *T*. The start and finish line is cone 1. Cone 2 is placed 5 meters (5.5 yd) away from cone 1. Cones 3 and 4 are positioned 2.5 meters (2.7 yd) to the left and right of cone 2, respectively.

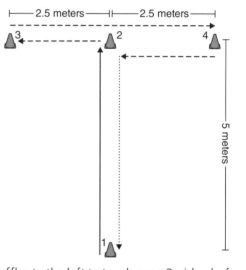

Procedures

The procedures for the modified T-test are the same as that for the traditional T-test. The athlete should use either a two- or a three-point stance to start the test. Once ready, the athlete sprints forward to touch the top of cone 2. The athlete then side-shuffles to the left to touch cone 3, side-shuffles to the right to touch cone 4, side-shuffles back to the left to touch cone 2 again, before backpedaling through the starting line to finish the test. Time is started from the initiation of movement until the athlete returns past the starting line. The hand that is on the same side as the shuffle direction (i.e., the left hand when shuffling to the left, and the right hand when shuffling to the right) is used to touch the cone. Athletes must not to cross their feet when side-shuffling, and they must touch the cone each time. Failure to do so results in termination of the trial. Athletes should complete at least two trials for the modified T-test, one where the athlete shuffles to the left first, and one where they shuffle to the right first. As for the T-test, the data can be averaged between the two directions, or the coach may analyze performances for each side separately.

Longer Distance COD Speed Tests

ILLINOIS AGILITY TEST

The Illinois agility test is a longer-effort COD test that incorporates linear sprinting, weaving and maneuverability about cones, and acceleration and deceleration to execute harder cuts. This test has previously been used to assess field hockey (27), rugby union (25), soccer (82), Australian football (46), and squash (85) players as well as police officers (2, 66).

Test Layout

The Illinois agility test requires eight cones. Four cones are used to indicate an area that is 10 meters (10.9 yd) long and 5 meters (5.5 yd) wide. In the center of the area 2.5 meters (2.7 yd) away from the 10-meter (10.9 yd) sides of the area, four cones are placed 3.3 meters (3.6 yd) apart.

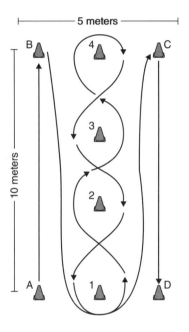

Procedures

The athlete should use either a two- or a three-point stance to start the test. Once ready, the athlete sprints from cone A to cone B and then cuts around this cone to sprint toward cone 1. The athlete then weaves in and out of cones 1 through 4 using a zigzag motion, circles cone 4, and then returns to cone 1, weaving through the center cones in the opposite direction. The athlete then sprints to cone C, cuts around this cone, and sprints to cone D to finish the test. Time is started from the initiation of movement until the athlete passes cone D. Athletes must step around or over the cones. Failure to do this results in test termination. At least two trials should be allowed for this test.

60-YARD SHUTTLE TEST

The 60-yard (54.9 m) shuttle features movement patterns similar to those of the pro-agility shuttle, except that it is performed over a longer distance. This test stresses the ability to accelerate, decelerate, and perform lateral movements under greater anaerobic strain than shorter agility tests. Accordingly, the test has been used to assess football (28, 53) and soccer (37, 38, 68) players.

Test Layout

Four pairs of cones should be positioned at 0 yards (start and finish line), 5 yards (4.6 m), 10 yards (9.1 m), and 15 yards (13.7 m) from the starting line. The cones represent lines 1, 2, and 3.

Procedures

The athlete should start from either a two- or a three-point stance with the feet parallel, and should face toward the right. Once ready, the athlete sprints to the first line (step 1) and touches the line with the left hand before sprinting back to touch the starting line with the right hand (step 2). The athlete then sprints to touch the second line with the left hand (step 3) before sprinting back to retouch the starting line with the right hand (step 4). Lastly, the athlete sprints to touch the third line with the left hand (step 5) and then sprints back through the start and finish line (step 6). Time is started from the initiation of movement until the athlete returns back past the starting line. Failure to touch the line each time results in termination of the test. The coach should allow the athlete to complete at least two trials: one where the athlete faces the right to start the test and one where they face the left. When facing toward the left to start the test, the right hand is used to touch lines 1, 2, and 3, while the left hand is used to touch the starting line. The data can be averaged between the two trials, or the coach may analyze each trial separately.

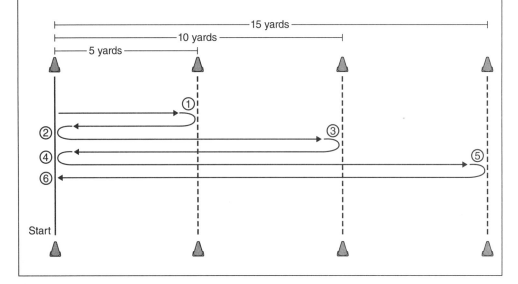

ARROWHEAD TEST

The Arrowhead test was originally designed to assess soccer players (37, 42). This test has been shown to delineate between youth and professional male soccer players, providing some measure of discriminant validity (3).

Test Layout

Six cones are required for this test. Two are used to indicate the starting line. One cone should be placed 10 meters (10.9 yd) away from the middle of the starting line, with two cones placed 5 meters (5.5 yd) to the left and right of this cone. A final cone is placed 15 meters (16.4 yd) away from the middle of the starting line (a).

Procedures

The athlete should use either a two- or a three-point stance to start the test. Once ready, the athlete sprints to the middle cone (step 1), turns to the left or right to sprint around the side cone (step 2), and sprints around the top cone (step 3) before sprinting back through the starting line (step 4) (b). Time is started from the initiation of movement until the athlete returns past the starting line. Athletes must step around and not over the cones. Failure to do this results in test termination. The coach should allow the athlete to complete at least two trials; one where the athlete turns to the left and one where they turn to the right. The data can be averaged between the two directions, or the coach may analyze each side separately.

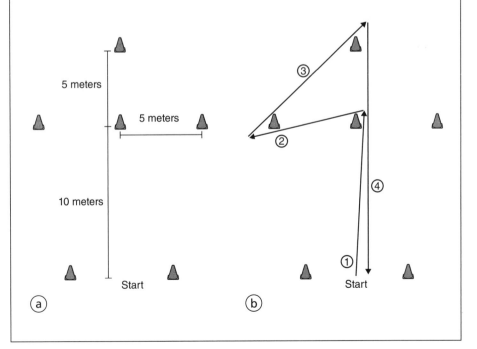

T-TEST

The T-test assesses COD speed via linear acceleration, deceleration, lateral movements via side-shuffling, and backpedaling (i.e., backward running) (73). As a result of the movement required in this test, it has been used to assess police academy cadets (4), recreational male and female athletes (45), and athletes from the sports of basketball (7, 77), volleyball (11), and soccer (52).

Test Layout

Four cones are placed in the shape of a *T*. The start and finish line is cone 1. Cone 2 is placed 10 yards (9.1 m) away from cone 1. Cones 3 and 4 are positioned 5 yards (4.6 m) to the left and right of cone 2, respectively.

Procedures

The athlete should use either a two- or a three-point stance to start the test. Once ready, the athlete sprints forward to touch the top of cone 2, side-shuffles to the left to touch cone 3, side-shuffles to the right to touch cone 4, side-shuffles back to the left to touch cone 2 again, and then backpedals through the starting line to finish the test. Time is started from the initiation of movement until the athlete returns past the starting line. The hand that is on the same side as the shuffle direction (i.e., the left hand when shuffling to the left, and the right hand when shuffling to the right) is used to touch the cone. The athlete is not to cross the feet when side-shuffling, and must touch the cone each time. Failure to do so results in termination of the trial. The coach should allow the athlete to complete at least two trials, one where the athlete shuffles to the left first, and one where they shuffle to the right first. The data can be averaged between the two directions, or the coach may analyze each side separately.

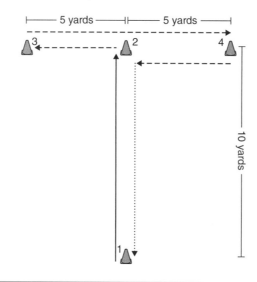

Reactive Agility and Quickness Tests

Y-SHAPED AGILITY TEST

The Y-shaped agility test is performed with timing gates that provide reactive conditions via a flashing light stimulus. Although this type of stimulus may not be sport-specific, it does allow for the assessment of how quickly an athlete can visually scan the environment (39). This type of test has been used to assess agility in basketball players (26, 34, 39), rugby union players (16), and athletes from other sports (e.g., field hockey, soccer, and racket sports) (65).

Test Layout

Four timing gates are used for this test. The start gate is positioned on the starting line, the second gate is positioned 5 meters (5.5 yd) away from the start gate, and the third and fourth gates are positioned 5 meters (5.5 yd) away at 45-degree angles from the center of the trigger gate. The coach should make sure that the timing gate system can allow control over which gate will illuminate within each trial, such that the coach knows but the athlete does not.

Procedures

The athlete should use either a two- or a three-point stance to start the test. Once ready, the athlete sprints through the start and trigger gates. He or she should be told not to try to anticipate which gate will illuminate, so that they will be better prepared to cut in either direction. Once the illuminated gate is spotted after the athlete passes through the trigger gate, the athlete should execute a COD as quickly as possible to sprint through this gate. If the athlete does anticipate which gate will illuminate, the trial is disregarded and reattempted. The coach should use enough trials to ensure an equal number of attempts to left and right.

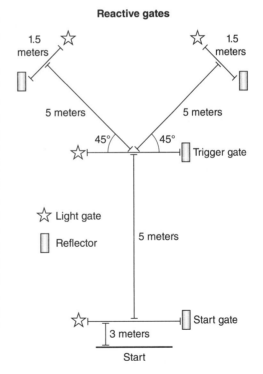

Reprinted by permission from M.D. Jeffriess, A.B. Schultz, T.S. McGann, S.J. Callaghan, and R.G. Lockie, "Effects of Preventative Ankle Taping on Planned Change-of-Direction and Reactive Agility Performance and Ankle Muscle Activity in Basketballers," *Journal of Sports Science & Medicine* 14, no. 4 (2015): 864-876.

REACTIVE AGILITY TEST

The reactive agility test is an example of a test that can incorporate a human stimulus. This type of test may allow an athlete to use specific visual cues with which to execute a direction change. This test was originally used to assess Australian football players (75) but has also been adopted for rugby league players (10, 13).

Test Layout

Two cones are used to mark a starting line (a). Timing gates are positioned 5 meters (5.5 yd) to the left and right of the center of the starting line, 2 meters (2.2 yd) forward of the starting line. Thus, the timing gates should be 10 meters (10.9 yd) apart from each other. A further timing gate is positioned opposite the starting line; this gate is used to initiate timing when the tester (i.e., a human stimulus) steps through it.

Procedures

The athlete should start with the feet parallel behind the starting line. The tester stands opposite the athlete behind the timing gate. The tester initiates movement to begin the timing of the test (b). The athlete reacts to the movement of the tester by sprinting forward and cutting left or right in response to what the tester does. The athlete should be told to recognize cues as quickly as possible and not to try to anticipate the direction the tester will step. The tester has four options to present to the athlete, all of which involve steps of approximately 0.5 meters (19.7 in.):

1. Tester steps forward with the right foot, and athlete changes direction to the left

2. Tester steps forward with the left foot, and athlete changes direction to the right

3. Tester steps forward with the right foot, then left foot, and athlete changes direction to the right

4. Tester steps forward with the left foot, then right foot, and athlete changes direction to the left

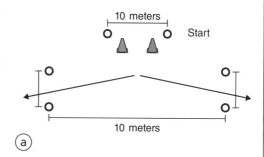

The test time is stopped when the athlete sprints through the left or right timing. Response accuracy should be emphasized; if the athlete does anticipate which direction the tester will step and completes an inaccurate response, the trial is disregarded and reattempted. The coach should use enough trials such that the athlete can respond to each of the four options.

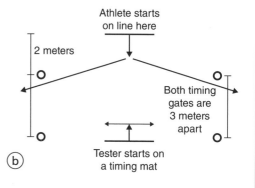

Reprinted from J.M. Sheppard, W.B. Young, T.L.A. Doyle, T.A. Sheppard, and R.U. Newton, "An Evaluation of a New Test of Reactive Agility and Its Relationship to Sprint Speed and Change of Direction Speed," *Journal of Science and Medicine in Sport* 9, no. 4 (2006): 342-349, with permission from Elsevier.

CHAPTER 6

Change of Direction Speed Drills

Mark Roozen

As discussed in other chapters throughout this book, proper footwork, body position, technique, and the ability to accelerate and decelerate are essential components of being able to change direction with skill and precision. This chapter provides numerous change of direction (COD) speed drills designed to teach the athlete the essential skills and movement mechanics required for high-level agility performance. It is critical that these movements are mastered so athletes can apply these mechanics effectively and efficiently in the context of their specific sport.

The drills in this chapter are set up into basic footwork drills and those that require the athlete to move between several different points or markers. A key to remember when performing or coaching these drills is that doing more drills is not necessarily better. Having a long list of COD speed drills is beneficial for adding variety to a training program and reducing monotony, but randomly selecting drills may not allow an athlete to master the proper movement mechanics or high levels of skill necessary for success in sport. Rather, drill selection should be based on the demands of the sport and on the level of movement mastery and skill and the developmental level of the athlete.

Included in this chapter are points for identifying the key movement mechanics for COD speed and agility drills. Also included are recommendations and suggestions on how to select and progress COD drills based on the athlete's level. Gaining a greater understanding of these foundational concepts will enhance an athlete's potential to maximize the benefits from each training session.

The author would like to acknowledge the significant contributions of Mike Nitka and David Sandler to this chapter.

It is important to plan progressions into the training program to ensure that an athlete learns proper COD speed technique for acceleration and deceleration in multiple directions. This will help prepare the athlete for the development of efficient movement skills. In the following section, the key movement mechanics needed to accelerate and decelerate efficiently are discussed.

ACCELERATION AND DECELERATION MECHANICS

Acceleration from an in-place (static) or an in-motion (rolling) start is essential in sport. A key to acceleration while running forward is the *triple extension position*, which is characterized by a coordinated and powerful extension of the ankle, knee, and hip (2). This powerful movement allows an athlete to propel the body rapidly forward by creating significant ground reaction forces (GRF). Based on Newton's third law of motion (for every action there is an equal and opposite reaction), the more GRF the athlete is able to produce in the limited amount of time the foot is in contact with the ground, the faster he or she should be able to propel the body in the intended direction. The same holds true when looking at COD or lateral-movement training.

When decelerating the body, or braking, the *triple flexion position* is used to reduce speed and prepare for the COD. This position is characterized by flexion of the ankles, knees, and hips. In this case, the greater the braking force the athlete is able to create, the quicker he or she will be able to slow down and reposition the body to prepare for the next movement required.

When coaching COD speed or agility drills, several key points should be emphasized (1, 2).

Posture

During acceleration, the athlete's center of mass should be in front of the base of support (i.e., the feet). This allows optimal body positioning for the production of GRF to increase horizontal propulsion. This lean should not be achieved by flexing at the waist; instead, the coach should be able to observe an imaginary line intersecting the ears, down through the torso, hip, knee, and ankle of the supporting leg when the athlete's knee is fully extended just before the foot loses contact with the ground. The athlete's head should be in line with the torso and the torso in line with the legs during linear acceleration movements (figure 6.1).

When decelerating, or braking, the forward lean seen during forward acceleration is not evident. This is because, in order to decrease the body's momentum, the torso must assume a more erect posture compared to the lower body and greater posterior lean during deceleration. This action of the torso moves the center of mass behind to the base of support. This allows the lower body to get into a better position to brake the horizontal propulsion created during acceleration (figure 6.2).

Arm Action

The athlete should be instructed to run with the arms flexed at approximately 90 degrees when accelerating. However, it should be noted that during the backswing the athlete's elbow will likely extend beyond 90 degrees due to the forces produced from the powerful backward swinging of the arms. This forceful backward swinging of the arms uses the stretch reflex and provides much of the power needed to propel the body. The hands should not cross the midline of the body in order to help counteract the rotational forces of the lower extremities. In general terms, the longer an athlete's stride length the larger the arm swing will be because arm speed and leg speed are dependent on one another. In other words, as arm swing increases so will stride length (and vice versa).

When decelerating, the arms will continue to move primarily in the sagittal plane (i.e., swing forward and backward), although the range of motion at the shoulder and the amplitude of the arm swing will be reduced when

Figure 6.1 Triple extension position during acceleration.

Figure 6.2 Triple flexion position during deceleration.

shorter strides are used to slow the body down or to prepare for a change of direction. When moving laterally or into the athletic position, the arms should be at the sides of the body.

Leg Action

Explosive takeoffs require extending the hip, knee, and ankle in a synchronized manner to generate GRFs. When performing acceleration drills, athletes should be instructed to keep their ankle in a dorsiflexed position and use a *punch-and-drive action* (i.e., punch the knee and drive the foot into the ground). During footstrike, the athlete's weight should be on the ball of the foot. This action will minimize braking forces and maximize propulsive force. The angle of the athlete's shins to the ground will be acute (less than 90 degrees) initially and will increase slightly with each successive stride. During acceleration, stride length will start out short; the longer the athlete accelerates, stride length will gradually increase. Ground contact time will be the greatest with the first stride and will also gradually decrease as stride length increases. Similarly, stride frequency will start out slowly because of the initial longer ground contact times required to overcome inertia, and will increase gradually with each stride.

During deceleration the opposite occurs; the athlete's weight should be more toward the heel at footstrike to reduce propulsive force and maximize braking forces. The angle of the athlete's shins to the ground will be greater than 90 degrees initially and will decrease slightly with each successive stride. Ground contact time will also gradually increase as the athlete attempts to slow down and prepare to assume a preparatory stance or transition into another movement, such as a lateral shuffle, backpedal, or cut.

DRILL SELECTION AND PROGRESSION

As noted earlier, not every drill is appropriate for all athletes or for every sport. Two key factors for drill selection are to understand

1. the different levels of movement skill and training age of the athletes and
2. the movement requirements commonly performed in the sport (e.g., traveled distance, movement patterns, amplitude and direction of movement, and required level of force).

The following are some basic considerations and recommendations for programming and progressing COD speed and agility drills.

▶ **Begin with a dynamic warm-up.** It is important to warm up appropriately before performing any type of agility or quickness training. Proper warm-up increases blood flow to the muscles, increases neurological activity, and gives the athlete time to prepare mentally for the workout. One of the most effective ways to prepare the body for physical activity is to perform dynamic warm-up activities. Furthermore, this type of movement preparation may also help reduce an athlete's risk of injury. The dynamic warm-up is covered extensively in chapter 3.

▶ **Progress from lower-intensity drills to higher-intensity drills.** The intensity of a COD speed drill can be quantified in terms of the speeds being traveled, the number of cuts or changes of direction required, and the duration of the drill. In general terms, intensity and volume are inversely related. In other words, the greater the number of cuts and the greater the amount of force an athlete is required to absorb when decelerating, the greater the amount of fatigue that will accrue. As fatigue builds, the athlete's ability to maintain proper technique decreases, which may lead to the athlete's adopting poor movement patterns in the future rather than using proper COD speed mechanics. Therefore, if the intensity of a COD speed drill is high, the athlete should perform fewer repetitions to minimize the potential for injury and overtraining.

▶ **Progress from closed drills to open drills.** *Closed COD speed drills* are those in which the movement pattern is known. There is a fixed pattern to the movements involved in performing the drill (e.g., *sprint from cone A to cone B to cone C*). All of the drills featured in this chapter are closed drills. As an athlete progresses, *open COD speed drills* (also called *quickness drills*) should be incorporated into the training program. During an open drill, athletes must react to a visual or auditory cue signaling in which direction they should sprint. Open drills are discussed in greater detail in chapter 7.

▶ **Emphasize quality rather than quantity.** The importance of proper technique cannot be overstated. Many times, coaches ask athletes to execute COD speed drills as fast as possible regardless of how the distance is traveled. Developing coordinated movement patterns with good technique provides the best foundation for long-term success. Thus, coaches should initially allow athletes to run drills at half to three-quarter speed to emphasize good body mechanics. As the athletes demonstrate proficiency, the speed of these drills should be increased until they are working at full speed. If their technique starts to break down, they should slow down!

Table 6.1 provides a list of the speed and agility drills included in this chapter.

Table 6.1 Speed and Agility Drills

Drill name	Page number
LINE DRILLS	
Forward and backward line hops	106
Lateral line hops	106
Scissors	106
Forward and backward line hops (traveling laterally)	106
Lateral line hops (traveling forward and backward)	107
Traveling scissors	107
180-degree traveling line hops	107
LADDER DRILLS	
One in the hole	110
Two in the hole	110
Lateral two in the hole	111
Skip	111
Cha-cha	111
Ickey shuffle	112
Ladder carioca	112
Crossover (in and two steps out)	113
Hopscotch	113
Ali shuffle	114
Lateral one in the hole	114
Two in, two out (traveling laterally)	114
Slaloms	115
Cherry pickers	115
180s	116
DOT DRILLS	
Forward and back	118
Diagonal jumps	118
V drill	118
M drill	118
Figure eight	118
Hopscotch	118
TWO-CONE DRILLS	
Forward run	119
Backpedal	119
Lateral shuffle	119
Two-cone carioca	120

Drill name	Page number
TWO-CONE DRILLS	
180-degree drill	120
Figure-eight shuffle	120
Figure-eight run	121
THREE-CONE DRILLS	
90-degree round	122
90-degree cut	123
L drill	124
T drill	124
FOUR-CONE DRILLS	
Square run	125
Four corners drill	125
Bear crawl and backpedal drill	126
X drill	126
Z drill	127
FIVE-CONE DRILLS	
M drill	127
Star drill	128
Star drill with bear crawl	128
Butterfly drill	128
Hourglass drill	129
Attack and retreat drill	129
DRILLS WITH SIX OR MORE CONES	
Pro-agility race	130
S drill	131
Snake drill	131

LINE DRILLS

Coaches and athletes commonly use line drills to improve footwork, speed, and coordination. Line drills are excellent for the beginner because they are relatively simple and require limited equipment. In fact, all that is needed is a boundary line on a gym floor or a sports field, or a chalk line drawn on a resilient nonslip surface. They can also be adjusted for age and ability by increasing the length of the movement down a line or, if it is a timed drill, the length of duration can be adjusted. The following are examples of line drills and their variations.

Forward and Backward Line Hops

The athlete stands parallel to the line and then hops back and forth over it with the feet together for a specified time period or number of repetitions. After the athlete lands for each hop, he or she should immediately push off again and hop to the other side of the line, without any extra hops or bounces.

Single-Leg Variation
Hopping back and forth over the line can also be performed on one leg. The athlete should complete the drill for a specified time period or number of repetitions. The drill should be performed equally on each leg to ensure balanced training.

Lateral Line Hops

The athlete stands perpendicular to the line and then hops side to side over it for a specified time period or number of repetitions.

Single-Leg Variation
Hopping side to side over the line can also be performed on one leg. The athlete should complete the drill for a specified time period or number of repetitions. This drill should be performed equally on each leg to ensure balanced training.

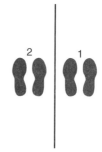

Scissors

The athlete stands parallel to the line and then steps across with the right foot, straddling the line with the left foot behind it. Next, the athlete shifts the feet rapidly, moving each foot to the opposite side of the line, and continues the drill by changing the position of the feet with a scissor-like motion.

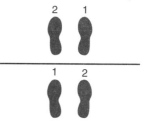

Forward and Backward Line Hops (Traveling Laterally)

The athlete stands with shoulders parallel to the line and then hops forward and backward over it with feet together. At the same time, he or she moves laterally down the line for a specified time period or a predetermined distance. The athlete should travel to both the right and left sides to ensure balanced training.

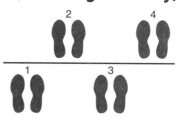

Lateral Line Hops (Traveling Forward and Backward)

The athlete stands with shoulders perpendicular to the line and then hops side to side over it with the feet together. He or she moves forward down the line, hopping from side to side, until reaching the end, and then returns to the starting position by hopping backward from side to side. This is done for a specified time period or a predetermined distance. The athlete should keep both feet together for the duration of the drill.

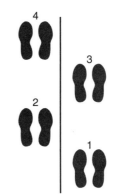

Single-Leg Variation
Hopping side to side over the line can also be performed on one leg. The athlete should complete the drill for a specified time period or number of repetitions. The drill should be performed equally on each leg to ensure balanced training.

Traveling Scissors

The athlete stands with shoulders parallel to the line and then steps across the line to straddle it with one foot in front of the line and the other behind it. He or she rapidly alternates the position of the feet, moving them forward and backward in a scissor-like motion while moving laterally down the line for a specified time period or a predetermined distance. This drill should be performed to both the right and the left side to ensure balanced training.

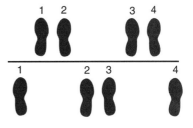

180-Degree Traveling Line Hops

The athlete stands on the line with shoulders and hips parallel to it. Next, he or she hops to the side while rotating the body 180 degrees in the air, landing on the line facing in the opposite direction. The athlete continues hopping and traveling laterally down the line for a specified time period or a predetermined distance. Both feet must land on the line for each hop.

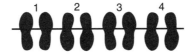

Single-Leg Variation
This drill can also be performed on one leg. As with the two-footed version, the athlete hops down the line, rotating the body 180 degrees with each hop. The foot must land on the line with each hop. The athlete performs the drill for a specified time period or a predetermined distance. This drill should be executed equally on each leg to ensure balanced training.

Using Alternative Patterns

Using alternative patterns can increase the complexity of these basic line drills and reduce the risk of boredom. The basic structure of each of the drills is unchanged, but instead of using a straight line, athletes can perform the drill around other shapes to add challenge and variety. Possible options include a zigzag line, a rectangle, an oval, a triangle, or a double line (figure 6.3).

Adding a line (figure 6.3*e*) can increase the intensity and metabolic demand of each drill. For example, in the forward and backward line hops, athletes can hop with both feet over the first line, then over the second line. Without pausing, they can immediately jump backward over the second line and then the first. Coaches should place the lines approximately 12 to 18 inches (30-46 cm) apart. If an athlete cannot maintain balance, stability, and body position, coaches should shorten the distance between the lines and then increase the distance again when the athlete is able to manage a greater workload.

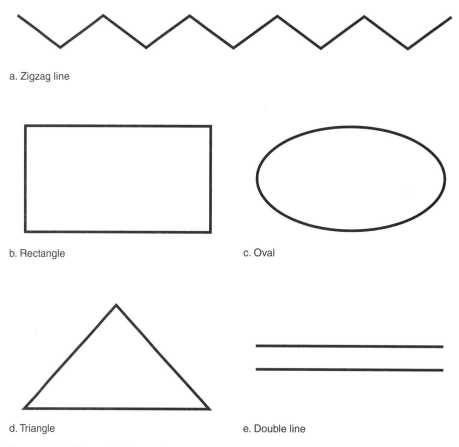

a. Zigzag line

b. Rectangle

c. Oval

d. Triangle

e. Double line

Figure 6.3   Alternative line patterns.

Adding Auditory or Visual Stimuli

Coaches can add external stimuli to any of these drills to create a reactionary component. For example, a partner or coach can call out random directional cues (e.g., "Change direction!" or "Stop!") during the line drills, and the athlete must respond quickly and effectively. Moreover, coaches can introduce visual stimuli for greater sport specificity. An example is periodically tossing a ball to an athlete during a drill. To challenge cognitive and decision-making skills, coaches can prearrange several cones and require athletes to stop what they are doing and immediately sprint to a cone when prompted by a visual or verbal cue.

LADDER DRILLS

Ladder drills can be an excellent tool for teaching beginners basic body control and awareness, developing rhythm and tempo, and learning basic body mechanics when producing and reducing force. These drills may also have value for the rehabilitation of athletes and can be used as a functional return-to-play tool after injury (3).

Most speed and agility ladders are made of plastic rungs that are attached to nylon straps to form boxes. Typically, the rungs are set approximately 12 to 18 inches (30-46 cm) apart; however, the box size can be adjusted by sliding the rungs up or down the nylon straps. Coaches may wish to alter the size of each box periodically so that an athlete is forced to adjust stride length. These adjustments in foot placement are analogous to what happens in competition.

When performing these drills, the athlete should progress from drills that are simple to those that are more complex. Initially the athlete should focus on performing each drill as quickly as possible with good body control and technique. Athletes who are unable to maintain proper form should be encouraged to execute the movement at a slower speed.

One in the Hole

The athlete stands at the end of the ladder with shoulders and hips parallel to the rungs and then steps into the first box of the ladder with one foot. Next, the athlete steps into the following box with the opposite foot and repeats the process down the ladder. The athlete repeats this drill, this time leading with the opposite foot.

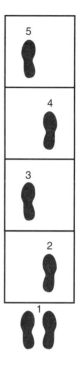

Two in the Hole

The athlete stands at the end of the ladder with the shoulders and hips parallel to the rungs. The athlete steps into the first box with one foot and then steps into the same box with the other foot. This pattern is continued through the ladder. The athlete should alternate the lead foot on subsequent trials.

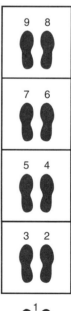

Lateral Two in the Hole

The athlete stands sideways at the end of the ladder so that the hips and shoulders are perpendicular to the rungs. With the foot closest to the ladder, the athlete steps into the first box and then steps the other foot into the same box, placing it next to the lead foot. The athlete should not cross the legs; instead, he or she continues by moving laterally down the ladder, stepping first with the lead foot and then moving the other foot into the same box. The athlete repeats this drill, leading with the opposite foot.

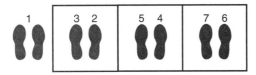

Skip

Skips can be used to increase the complexity of one in the hole, two in the hole, and lateral two in the hole ladder drills. To perform this variation, the athlete steps into each box using a skip-step, or step-hop, pattern. The skip pattern requires the athlete to take off and land with the same leg. In contrast, regular patterns require athletes to alternate legs between takeoff and landing. Before doing a skip pattern in the ladder, coaches should make sure the athlete can skip 10 to 15 yards (9.1-13.7 m).

Cha-cha

The athlete stands to the side of the first box with shoulders and hips perpendicular to one side of the ladder. With the leg closest to the ladder, the athlete steps laterally into the far half of the first box and then steps the other foot into the same box. With the first leg, the athlete then steps to the outside of the ladder (on the opposite side of the starting point) and follows with the trailing foot. The athlete takes another step to the side with the first leg and then steps diagonally into the far half of the second box, leading with what was previously the trailing foot. Now, he or she steps into the second box with the trailing leg (formerly the leading leg). The athlete continues this pattern to the end of the ladder, stepping into and out of the boxes and switching the leading leg all the way through.

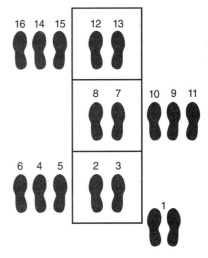

Ickey Shuffle

The athlete stands to the side of the first box with hips and shoulders perpendicular to the sides of the ladder. With the foot closest to the ladder, the athlete steps laterally into the far half of the first box and then immediately steps the other foot into the box. Next, the athlete steps outside the box on the other side with the lead foot and then steps with the other foot into the next box. This step is immediately followed by the outside foot. The athlete performs the same pattern of stepping out on the other side of the ladder, continuing this pattern down the ladder, alternating legs and sides of the ladder. To further challenge kinesthetic awareness and movement proficiency, the athlete can perform this drill moving backward.

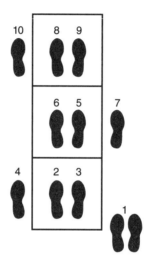

Ladder Carioca

The athlete stands at the end of the ladder with hips and shoulders perpendicular to the rungs, and with the foot farthest from the ladder steps laterally into box 1 by crossing the outside foot in front of the other leg. The athlete steps into box 2 by moving the trailing leg behind and beyond the original lead leg. Next, he or she steps into box 3 with the original leading leg, crossing it behind the foot in box 2. The athlete steps into box 4 by moving the foot from box 2 in front of the other leg and to the side, and then continues moving laterally, alternating the front and back movement of the trailing leg. The athlete then repeats the drill, leading with the opposite foot.

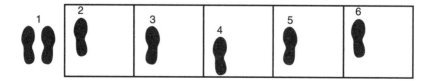

Crossover (In and Two Steps Out)

The athlete stands to the side of box 1 with the hips and shoulders perpendicular to the sides of the ladder and then crosses the outer leg in front of the other to step into the center of box 1. The athlete then moves the other leg behind the lead leg, across the ladder, and outside the first box. This movement is followed quickly by the first leg. Next, the athlete crosses the outside leg over to step into the center of box 2. This pattern is repeated down the ladder. The athlete should take two steps to the outside of each box and should do a crossover step into the center of each one.

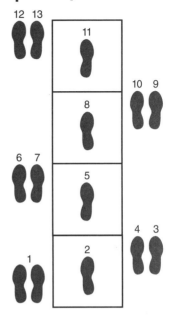

Hopscotch

The athlete stands with the feet straddling the first box of the ladder. The left foot is on the left side and the right foot is on the right side. The hips and shoulders should be parallel to the rungs. The athlete quickly hops into box 1, landing on one foot. After landing, he or she immediately hops forward, landing so that the feet straddle box 2. Then, the athlete quickly hops into box 2, landing on the other foot. The athlete continues this pattern down the ladder, hopping with both feet outside the ladder and alternating the landing foot inside the boxes.

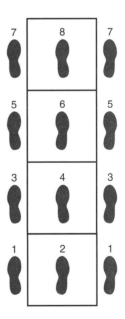

Ali Shuffle

The athlete stands to one side of box 1, which is formed by the first and second rungs of the ladder. The hips and shoulders should be perpendicular to the rungs. The athlete hops, moving the foot closest to the end of the ladder into box 1 and the other foot to the side. Using a scissor-like motion, he or she hops again, stepping the foot behind the ladder into box 2 and moving the original lead foot behind box 2. The athlete continues, switching feet and traveling laterally down the ladder. This drill should be completed in both directions (alternating the lead leg) to ensure balanced training.

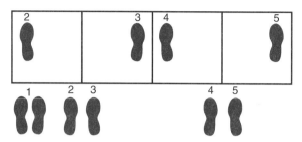

Lateral One in the Hole

The athlete stands to one side of box 1 between the first and second rungs of the ladder. The hips and shoulders should be perpendicular to the rungs. The athlete touches the foot closest to the second rung in and out of the center of box 1 and then shuffles laterally to the outside of box 2, leading with the same foot. The athlete again taps the lead foot in and out of box 2 and continues to shuffle laterally down the ladder, touching the lead foot into each box. He or she repeats this drill facing in the opposite direction, leading with the other foot and placing it in each box.

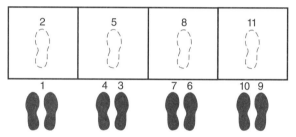

Two In, Two Out (Traveling Laterally)

The athlete stands to the side of the first box with the hips and shoulders perpendicular to the rung and steps into the center of box 1 with the foot closest to the second rung. The other foot follows immediately. As the second foot enters the box, the athlete steps the first foot back out diagonally to face box 2. The other foot follows immediately. The athlete shuffles down the ladder laterally, placing both feet in turn in each box of the ladder. This drill is repeated in the opposite direction, with the lead legs switched.

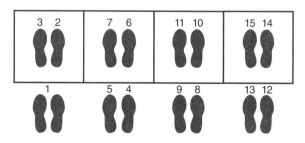

Slaloms

The athlete stands to the side of the first box with the hips and shoulders parallel to the rungs, hops with both feet into the center of box 1, and then immediately hops with both feet out of the box to the other side. Next, the athlete hops diagonally with both feet into the center of box 2 and then immediately hops out diagonally with both feet on the other side, landing at the top of the box. This zigzag pattern is continued down the ladder. This drill may also be performed laterally or backward.

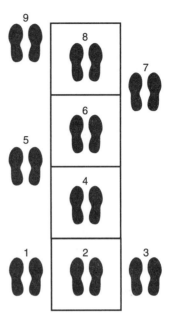

Cherry Pickers

The athlete stands at the end of the ladder with hips and shoulders parallel to the rungs and then hops forward and lands with one foot outside box 1 and the other foot in the center of it. The athlete bends forward, reaches down with the hand opposite the foot in the box, and touches the ground directly in front of the foot in the box. The athlete then hops into box 2, switching the leg position so that the outside leg goes to the center of the box and the inside leg lands outside it. He or she bends down and again touches the ground in front of the leg in the box with the opposite arm. The drill is continued down the ladder, alternating foot and hand positions. This drill can also be performed moving backward.

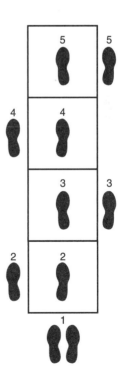

180s

The athlete stands with the feet straddling the first rung of the ladder. The hips and shoulders should be perpendicular to the rungs. The athlete jumps to the side, rotating 180 degrees, and lands straddling the next rung. This pattern is continued down the ladder.

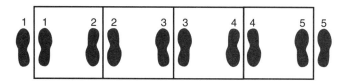

DOT DRILLS

Dot drills are commonly used by athletes to help improve foot speed, kinesthetic awareness, and reactive strength. These drills involve three phases: landing, amortization (ground contact), and takeoff. It is important to understand these three phases in order to maximize the effectiveness of these types of drills.

The *landing phase* starts as soon as the muscles start to experience an eccentric movement. This rapid eccentric stretch of the muscle activates the *stretch-shortening cycle* (SSC) (4). The SSC employs the energy-storage capabilities of the serial elastic components of the muscle tissue and stimulates the stretch reflex to facilitate a maximal increase in muscle recruitment over a minimal amount of time (4). The *amortization phase* is the time on the ground and represents the amount of time from landing to takeoff (4). If the amortization phase is too long, the energy gained through the eccentric action will dissipate as heat, and athletes lose the benefit of using stored elastic energy to help forcefully propel the body. The *takeoff phase* comprises the *concentric action* (shortening of the muscle fibers) and the use of the SSC that follows amortization (4). During this phase, the stored elastic energy within the muscles can be used to increase jump height, speed of movement, and distance traveled.

Dot drills are referred to as multiple-response drills because they involve either single- or double-leg movements repeatedly performed. These drills often include a change of direction or body orientation. Within this drill category, there are varying levels of intensity.

▶ *Beginner single-response drills* involve moving forward and backward, or side to side on both legs. Upon landing, the athlete should pause to show that good body control can be achieved and maintained prior to performing the next movement. The purpose of this pause between movements is to establish that the athlete has body control before progressing to multiresponse drills with little rest between repetitions. While these types of drills are relatively easy to perform, they set the stage for the more difficult progressions. The primary focus of these drills is to develop sport-specific kinesthetic awareness and the ability to change direction quickly under control.

▶ *Intermediate multiresponse drills* incorporate forward, backward, and side-to-side movement or rotation patterns within the same drill. The objective of these drills is to perform them as quickly as possible, while maintaining the proper body position. The primary focus is to change direction as quickly as possible under control despite the fact that the movement patterns and skill levels are more complex.

▶ *Advanced multiresponse drills* incorporate forward, backward, and side-to-side movement or rotation patterns on a single leg. These types of drills increase the intensity of the drill being performed and require the athlete to have sufficient strength and body control to execute these movements properly.

The basic dot drill setup requires arranging five cones (or dots) in an X pattern. Alternatively, these markers can be made by using chalk or applying tape to the workout surface if in a training facility, or by using field-marking paint if outdoors on grass or turf. Each dot should be approximately 4 inches (10 cm) in diameter. The dots that make up the perimeter should be placed 3 feet (0.9 m) apart and numbered as follows: the center dot is 1, the top left corner as the athlete looks at the square is 2, the right top corner is 3, the bottom left corner is 4, and the bottom right corner is 5 (figure 6.4).

The dot drills provided in this section can be used to help improve an athlete's COD skills and reactive abilities and they are programmed by number of rounds per pattern, length of time, or total training volume (i.e., reps × sets).

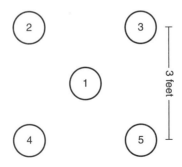

Figure 6.4 Dot drill setup.

Forward and Back

This basic foot-speed drill focuses on rapid forward and backward changes of direction. The pattern for this drill is 4, 2, 4 or 5, 3, 5.

Diagonal Jumps

The purpose of this drill is to develop rapid COD speed while moving forward, backward, and diagonally. The pattern for this drill is 2, 1, 5, 1, 2 and 3, 1, 4, 1, 3. Both patterns should be performed to ensure balanced training.

V Drill

This is a basic foot-speed drill that focuses on forward, backward, and diagonal changes of direction. The pattern for this drill is 1, 2, 1, 3.

M Drill

The purpose of this drill is to develop foot speed in forward, backward, lateral, and diagonal patterns. The pattern for this drill is 4, 2, 1, 3, 5. The athlete repeats this drill in reverse, using a 5, 3, 1, 2, 4 pattern to change the direction of movement. The athlete starts on the dot listed first in the pattern and faces the same direction throughout the duration of each drill pattern.

Figure Eight

The purpose of this drill is to improve kinesthetic awareness and COD speed. The pattern for this drill is 2, 3, 1, 4, 5, 1, 2. The athlete repeats this drill in reverse, using a 2, 1, 5, 4, 1, 3, 2 pattern to change the direction of the movement. The athlete starts at dot 2 each time.

Hopscotch

The athlete starts with one foot on dot 4 and the other on dot 5, facing dots 1, 2, and 3. The athlete jumps and lands with both feet on dot 1 and then jumps forward again and lands with split feet on dots 2 and 3. The athlete repeats this pattern, hopping backward to return to the starting position.

CONE DRILLS

Cones are typically used as landmarks to set up a variety of pre-programmed agility drills. The purpose of each of the agility drills in this section is to improve movement through a series of pre-planned direction changes. Cone drills can also be turned into semi-open drills by creating movement options and having the athlete respond to an external stimulus.

Within a drill, movement patterns can also be varied which changes up the drill and work being done. In most examples, unless indicated, all movement is a forward jog, run, or sprint with COD. To change the drill, a variety of movements can be used: backpedal, slide, shuffle, carioca, etc. In this section, several different cone drills and agility patterns are presented. It should be noted that these are merely suggestions and coaches are only limited by their own creativity when developing these types of drills. Furthermore, the tests featured in chapter 5 of this text also make excellent agility training drills. However, to avoid redundancy, they have not been featured in this section.

Two-Cone Drills

Coaches place two cones apart from one another at a set distance that works best for their sport or activity. In most situations, a distance of 5-10 yards (4.6-9.1 m) is adequate. Athletes can perform numerous drills with this setup to improve basic changes of directions. The following are just a few suggestions.

Forward Run

The athlete starts in front of cone 1. When ready, the athlete sprints forward to cone 2. Upon reaching it, the athlete comes to a complete stop in the athletic position, then immediately turns, accelerates in the opposite direction and sprints past cone 1.

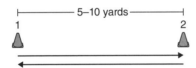

Backpedal

The athlete starts just in front of cone 1, facing away from the cones. When ready, the athlete backpedals to cone 2. Upon reaching it, the athlete immediately turns and backpedals to cone 1. The focus of this drill should be on keeping the hips low and maintaining the athletic position.

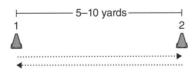

Lateral Shuffle

The athlete starts in an athletic position facing cone 1. When ready, the athlete shuffles 5 yards (4.6 m) to cone 2, keeping the hips low and the hips, shoulders, and torso parallel to the cones. Upon reaching cone 2, the athlete immediately shuffles back to cone 1. The feet should not cross during this drill.

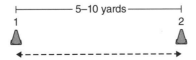

Two-Cone Carioca

The athlete starts in an athletic position facing cone 1. Keeping the hips low, she moves laterally by crossing the trailing leg in front of the other leg (*a*), stepping out with the lead leg (*b*), crossing behind with the trailing leg (*c*), stepping out with the lead leg, and so on. The athlete should keep the hips, shoulders, and torso parallel to the cones. When the athlete reaches cone 2, she should repeat the movement back to cone 1, using the opposite leg for the crossover and cross behind steps.

180-Degree Drill

The athlete starts beside cone 1, sprints to cone 2, uses short, choppy steps to go around the cone, and then accelerates back to cone 1. When rounding the cone, the athlete should stay as close to it as possible. This is done by shifting the body's center of mass toward the turning side. The athlete should repeat the drill, performing turns to both the right and the left.

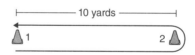

Figure-Eight Shuffle

The athlete starts facing cone 1 (and remains facing the same direction throughout the drill) and shuffles diagonally toward, above, and then clockwise around cone 2. When cone 2 is in front of the athlete, he or she shuffles diagonally toward, above, and then counterclockwise around cone 1, creating a figure-eight pattern. The athlete should repeat the drill, starting in front of cone 2 and creating a figure-eight pattern around cone 1 and then around cone 2.

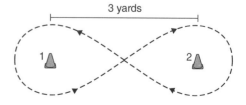

Figure-Eight Run

The athlete starts facing cone 1 and sprints toward the left of cone 2 and then clockwise around cone 2. When cone 2 is to the right, the athlete sprints toward the right of cone 1 and then counterclockwise around cone 1, creating a figure-eight pattern. The athlete should repeat the drill, starting in front of cone 2 and creating a figure-eight pattern around cone 1 and then around cone 2.

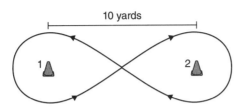

Once the athlete has mastered the technique in these basic drills, the coach can combine each of these tasks in different ways to create a wide variety of movement patterns, such as progressing from simple, *discrete movements* (one movement) to *serial tasks* (a combination of movements). The examples of movement combinations that follow are drills. The athlete can add more variety by touching each cone with the preferred hand.

▶ The athlete sprints forward to cone 2 and then backpedals to cone 1.

▶ The athlete sprints forward to cone 2 and then shuffles back to cone 1.

▶ The athlete shuffles to cone 2 and then backpedals to cone 1.

▶ The athlete shuffles to cone 2 and then sprints back to cone 1.

▶ The athlete shuffles first to cone 2, back to cone 1, and then turns 90 degrees and sprints past cone 2.

▶ The athlete backpedals to cone 2 and then sprints back to cone 1.

▶ The athlete backpedals to cone 2 and then shuffles back to cone 1.

Three-Cone Drills

Adding a third cone allows for different combinations of movements and increases the complexity of the drills. To set up for three-cone drills, coaches should place three cones in a straight line, spaced 5 yards (4.6 m) apart.

While performing three-cone drills, athletes must maintain a good athletic position. They should also use short, choppy steps to go around the cones. The 180-degree drill in the previous section provides good training for three-cone drills. Athletes can use a variety of movement combinations for three-cone drills. Additionally, all of the drills in the previous section can be modified for three cones. The following examples are just some of the possible combinations for three-cone drills.

▸ The athlete sprints forward to cone 2, turns 180 degrees, and back-pedals to cone 3.

▸ The athlete sprints forward to cone 2, turns 90 degrees, and shuffles to cone 3. He or she repeats this drill, facing the opposite direction during the shuffle.

▸ The athlete sprints forward to cone 2, performs a 360-degree turn around it, and sprints to cone 3.

▸ The athlete shuffles to cone 2, turns 90 degrees, and backpedals to cone 3.

▸ The athlete shuffles to cone 2 and then back to cone 1, then immediately turns 90 degrees and sprints past cone 3.

▸ The athlete backpedals to cone 2, turns 180 degrees, and then sprints past cone 3.

▸ The athlete backpedals to cone 2, turns 90 degrees, and then shuffles past cone 3. He or she repeats this drill, facing the opposite direction during the shuffle.

Coaches can also use drills created specifically for three cones. Some drills presented here use the basic cone setup discussed previously and others use different layouts.

90-Degree Round

This beginning movement pattern teaches body position, body control, and how to adjust to forces during movement. Three cones are set up in an *L* shape 10 yards (9.1 m) apart. The athlete starts inside of cone 1, keeping the hips, shoulders, and torso parallel to the cone. When ready, he or she turns and sprints toward cone 2. As the cone is approached, the athlete slows down slightly, moves to the outside, makes a 90-degree turn around cone 2, accelerates out of the turn, and then sprints past cone 3.

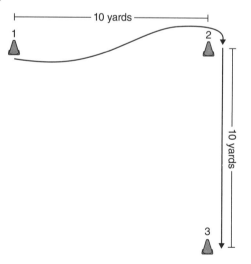

90-Degree Cut

The purpose of this drill is to develop quick transitions between high-speed agility movements. Three cones are set up in an *L* shape 10 yards (9.1 m) apart (*a*). The athlete starts outside of cone 1. When ready, he or she sprints to cone 2. As the cone is reached, the athlete drops down into a good athletic position, makes a sharp lateral cut (*b* and *c*), and sprints past cone 3. This drill should be performed in both directions for an equal number of repetitions.

L Drill

The purpose of this drill is to maintain sport-specific balance and the ability to accelerate during quick directional changes. Three cones are set up in an *L* shape 10 yards (9.1 m) apart. The athlete starts outside of cone 1 and, on a cue, sprints from cone 1 to cone 2 and drops down into an athletic position by slowing down, lowering the center of gravity, and squaring up the feet. The athlete then performs a sharp 90-degree cut and accelerates to cone 3. He or she makes a 180-degree turn around cone 3 using short, choppy steps and then accelerates back to cone 2. The athlete makes another sharp 90-degree cut and sprints back to cone 1. This drill can also be set up to be performed in the opposite direction.

T Drill

Three cones are set up in a straight line, with each cone 5 yards (4.6 m) from the next. These are cones 2, 3, and 4. A fourth cone (cone 1) is placed perpendicular to cone 3, about 10 yards (9.1 m) away. (Although this drill technically uses four cones, it fits with the three-cone drills because the first cone is used only as a starting point.) The resulting *T* pattern is commonly used to develop rapid acceleration, deceleration, and explosive COD. Starting at cone 1, the athlete sprints to cone 3, cuts left, and then sprints to cone 2. Using short, choppy steps, the athlete performs a 180-degree turn around cone 2, and then sprints to cone 4. He or she then performs a 180-degree turn around cone 4, sprints back to cone 3, cuts left, and then accelerates past the cone 1.

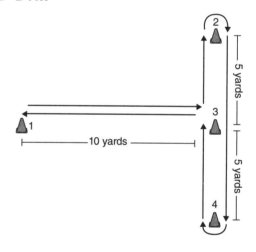

Four-Cone Drills

As athletes advance in their progressions, they should add a variety of movement patterns, including forward, backward, and lateral movements, as well as different angles, such as a 45-degree lateral drop (i.e., a backward zigzag step). Adding cones increases the complexity of the drills and requires more mobility and body control, since athletes move in multiple directions and accelerate and decelerate in different patterns. The following drills require four cones set up in a square. Each side of the square should be 10 to 15 yards (9.1-13.7 m) long.

Square Run

The athlete starts in an athletic position outside of cone 1, with the hips, shoulders, and torso perpendicular to the cone. When ready, or on a cue, he or she sprints to cone 2, returns to an athletic position, makes a 90-degree cut, and then sprints to cone 3. The athlete continues this pattern around all of the cones until reaching cone 1 again. This drill should be run both clockwise and counterclockwise. The athlete can also run backward or shuffle laterally through the cones.

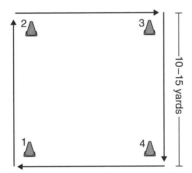

Four Corners Drill

The athlete starts in an athletic position outside of cone 1, with the hips, shoulders, and torso perpendicular to it. When ready, or on a cue, he or she sprints to cone 2, shuffles to cone 3, backpedals to cone 4, and finally shuffles back to cone 1 to finish the drill.

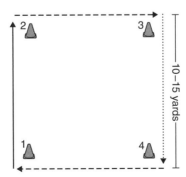

Bear Crawl and Backpedal Drill

This drill uses a pattern similar to that of the four corners drill, but a bear crawl replaces the shuffle (*a*). The athlete starts in an athletic position outside of cone 1, with the hips, shoulders, and torso perpendicular to it. When ready, or on a cue, he or she sprints to cone 2, turns to face cone 3, assumes a bear-crawl position (*b*), and crawls to cone 3. At cone 3, the athlete stands up as quickly as possible, faces away from cone 4, and then backpedals to cone 4. Here, the athlete turns to face cone 1, returns to the ground, and bear crawls back to cone 1.

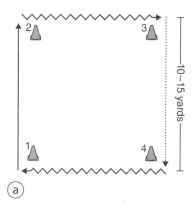

Variation

This drill can be performed using a variety of movement patterns (e.g., shuffle, sprint, or carioca). Additionally, bear crawls can be performed moving forward, laterally (while continuing to face forward), backward, or using a combination of these movements.

X Drill

The athlete starts in an athletic position outside of cone 1, with the hips, shoulders, and torso perpendicular to it. When ready, or on a cue, he or she sprints to cone 2, backpedals around it, and continues to backpedal diagonally to cone 4. At cone 4, the athlete plants, turns, and sprints around it, and then runs forward to cone 3. At cone 3, the athlete backpedals around it and continues to backpedal diagonally to cone 1 to finish the drill. The movement pattern in this drill can be varied by starting with a sprint and then performing a shuffle.

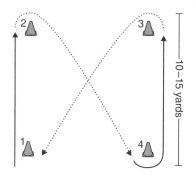

Z Drill

The athlete starts in an athletic position outside of cone 1 facing cone 2. When ready, or on a cue, he or she sprints to cone 2, makes a drop cut toward cone 3, and then sprints to cone 3. At cone 3, the athlete makes a final cut toward cone 4, and then sprints to cone 4.

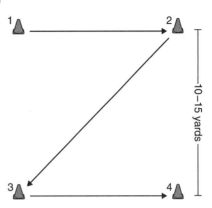

Five-Cone Drills

Five-cone drills once again add more markers, increasing the complexity of movement, the demands on body position, proper agility form, and technique. The drills in this section require four cones set up in a square with one cone in the center. The cones around the perimeter are numbered 1 through 4, and cone 5 is in the middle. The sides of the square should be 10 to 15 yards (9.1-13.7 m) long.

M Drill

The athlete starts in an athletic position outside of cone 1, with the hips, shoulders, and torso perpendicular to it. When ready, or on a cue, he or she sprints to cone 2. After reaching it, the athlete returns to an athletic position and plants the outside foot to change direction as the cone is passed. From cone 2, the athlete shuffles diagonally to cone 5, then returns to an athletic position, plants one foot, and then sprints to cone 3. After reaching it, the athlete returns to an athletic position, plants the outside foot, and then backpedals to cone 4. After passing it, the athlete plants the outside foot, and then shuffles laterally back to cone 1. This drill should be performed in both directions to ensure balanced training.

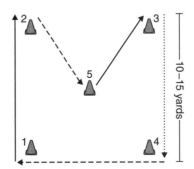

Star Drill

The athlete stands outside of cone 1, facing the center of the box (and continuing to do so throughout the drill). On a cue, the athlete sprints diagonally to cone 5, backpedals back to cone 1, and then shuffles to cone 2. At cone 2, the athlete turns and sprints diagonally to cone 5, backpedals to cone 2, and then shuffles to cone 3. Next, he or she sprints diagonally to cone 5, backpedals to cone 3, and then shuffles to cone 4. At cone 4, the athlete turns, sprints diagonally to cone 5, and then backpedals to cone 4. To finish the drill, the athlete shuffles from cone 4 to cone 1. The athlete should perform this drill in the opposite direction and change the movement pattern.

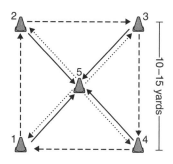

Star Drill with Bear Crawl

This variation of the star drill develops total-body agility. The athlete stands in an athletic position at cone 1 facing the center of the box. On a cue, he or she sprints diagonally to cone 5 and then bear crawls back to cone 1. The athlete then stands and shuffles to cone 2 while facing the center of the box. At cone 2, he or she turns and sprints diagonally to cone 5 and then bear crawls back to cone 2. Next, the athlete stands and shuffles to cone 3 while facing the center, sprints diagonally to cone 5, bear crawls back to cone

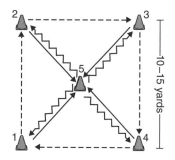

3, and returns to a standing position to shuffle to cone 4 (while facing the center of the box). Then the athlete turns and sprints diagonally to cone 5, bear crawls back to cone 4, and finishes the drill by standing again and shuffling to cone 1. The athlete should reverse the direction to change shuffle and movement patterns.

Butterfly Drill

The athlete stands in an athletic position at cone 1, facing the center of the box. On a cue, he or she sprints diagonally to cone 5 and shuffles around cone 2, leading with the left leg. The athlete sprints to cone 2 and then continues sprinting to cone 5. Next, the athlete shuffles to cone 3, again leading with the left leg, and then sprints around cone 3 and continues to cone 5. The athlete then shuffles with the left lead leg to cone 4 and sprints around it and back to cone 5. To finish the drill, the athlete shuffles back to cone 1 (start), leading with the left leg. The athlete should repeat this drill, leading with the other leg on the shuffles.

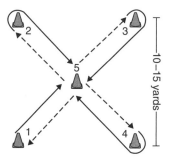

Hourglass Drill

The athlete starts in an athletic position at cone 1, facing the center of the box (*a*). On a cue, he or she cariocas (leading with the right leg) to cone 4. At cone 4, the athlete sprints diagonally to cone 5 and then turns and backpedals diagonally to cone 3. Next, he or she shuffles to cone 2, leading with the right leg and facing the center of the box and then sprints to cone 5. At cone 5, the athlete shuffles (leading with the left leg) to cone 3 (*b*), sprints back to cone 5, shuffles (leading with the left leg) to cone 4, and then sprints back to cone 5. To finish the drill, the athlete shuffles, leading with the left leg, to cone 1. To alter the pattern, the athlete may change the lead leg on the shuffles and replace the sprinting to cone 5 with backpedaling.

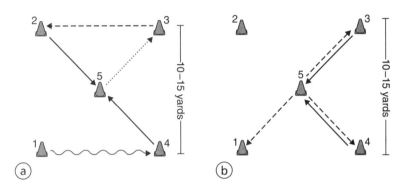

Attack and Retreat Drill

For this five-cone drill, the 5-yard (4.6 m) midway point between each pair of outside cones needs to be marked. The athlete starts in an athletic position outside cone 1. On a cue, the athlete faces outside the box and shuffles 5 yards (4.6 m) toward cone 2. At the 5-yard (4.6 m) mark, he or she plants one foot and sprints to cone 5 and then returns to the same 5-yard (4.6 m) mark by backpedaling. Then the athlete continues to face inside the box and shuffles to cone 2, faces outside the box, shuffles to the 5-yard (4.6 m) mark between cones 2 and 3, plants one foot, sprints to cone 5, and then backpedals back to the 5-yard (4.6 m) mark. The athlete then faces inside

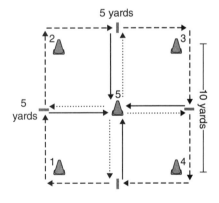

the box and shuffles to cone 3, turns to face outside the box, shuffles to the 5-yard (4.6 m) mark between cones 3 and 4, plants one foot, sprints to cone 5, backpedals back to the 5-yard (4.6 m) mark, and then faces inside the box while shuffling to cone 4. At cone 4, the athlete faces outside the box and shuffles to the 5-yard (4.6 m) mark between cones 1 and 4, plants one foot, sprints to cone 5, and backpedals back to the 5-yard (4.6 m) mark. To finish the drill, the athlete faces inside the box and shuffles past cone 1.

Drills With Six or More Cones

Drills can continue to be made more complex by using more cones and requiring the athlete to move to and around them using a variety of footwork combinations and body positions. Often, drills with six or more cones require a larger area for setup.

Pro-Agility Race

This test variation allows athletes to compete with one another by simply setting up another set of cones and having the athletes face one another. This partner drill is set up in the same manner as the pro-agility shuttle (see page 87); however two rows of three cones are set up about 3 yards (2.7 m) apart from each other. On a cue, one athlete will perform the pro-agility shuttle in the traditional manner by starting to the right, while the other athlete will start by sprinting to the left. The athletes will complete the drill as quickly as possible in an attempt to beat their opponent.

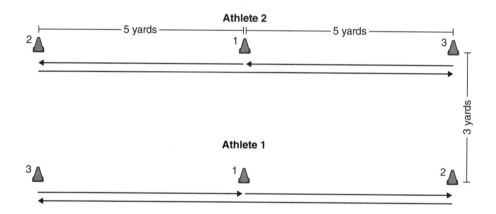

S Drill

Two lines of cones are set up in a zigzag or offset pattern with 4 cones in one line and 3 cones in a second line that is 10 yards (9.1 m) away from the first line. Within each line, the cones are 3 yards (2.7 m) apart. The athlete begins by standing facing cone 1 (the first cone in the first row of cones). On a cue, the athlete turns toward cone 2 and sprints to the left side of cone 2, cutting clockwise around it, and then sprints toward the right side of cone 3, cutting counterclockwise around it. The athlete continues to sprint toward each cone; cutting clockwise around the second line of cones and cutting counterclockwise around the first line of cones until the athlete passes cone 7.

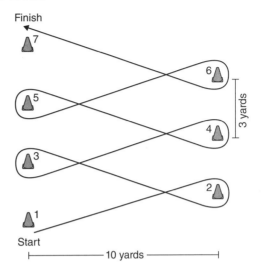

Snake Drill

A straight line of six cones is set up, spaced 2 to 3 yards (1.8-2.7 m) apart. The athlete begins by standing to the left of cone 1 (facing the line of cones) and, on a cue, sprints to the right of cone 2, to the left of cone 3, to the right of cone 4, to the left of cone 5, and to the right of cone 6. At cone 6, the athlete continues around it until he or she is facing the line of cones at which time the athlete sprints (weaves) back through the cones. The drill is complete when the athlete runs past cone 1.

CHAPTER 7

Quickness Drills

Jay Dawes

For athletes to excel in their sport, superior movement abilities are not enough. Many coaches have witnessed athletes who are both fast and agile when performing change of direction (COD) speed drills yet fail to achieve their true potential because they have poor decision-making skills. Thus, to optimize performance athletes should train their perceptual and decision-making ability as well as their physical skills.

Chapter 6 includes a wide variety of drills designed to improve an athlete's general athleticism and ability to change direction. Using these drills as part of a comprehensive agility and quickness program is paramount for developing proper movement technique, coordination, dynamic balance and body control. However, since most sports occur in an ever-changing and often chaotic environment, incorporating sport-specific drills that require both perceptual and decision-making skills may better prepare athletes for competition. These drills are commonly referred to as *open agility*, *quickness*, or *reactionary* drills (1, 3, 7). For the purpose of this chapter, these terms will be used interchangeably.

Open agility drills should be incorporated in such a way as to help bridge the gap between practice and competition. These drills require the athlete to anticipate, read, and respond to various environmental stimuli and select the correct movement patterns to perform the task accurately and efficiently (3, 8). The purpose of this chapter is to help the coach and the athlete understand how they can adapt closed agility drills to make them more reactionary. The chapter will also present several open agility drills to provide readers with a variety of drills that can be easily used or modified to meet the needs of a particular sport.

CHANGE OF DIRECTION SPEED DRILL ADAPTATION

After athletes become proficient at performing basic COD speed drills, they are ready to progress to those that are more chaotic and unpredictable, similar to what they will experience in their sports. With a few small adaptations, virtually any COD speed drill can be modified to enhance an athlete's cognitive and decision-making skills. The following are examples of ways to progress many of the COD speed drills in chapter 6 to be reactive (quickness) drills by incorporating temporal (time), spatial (space), and universal (both temporal and spatial) constraints. This can be done by adding a variety of auditory, visual, and mixed cues to COD speed drills.

▸ **Auditory cues.** The coach may periodically give an auditory (sound), cue, such as *switch, change,* or *stop,* while the athlete is performing the drill. At this cue, the athlete should immediately and accurately respond to the coach's command. For instance, while an athlete is running forward, the coach gives the *back* command. The athlete responds by immediately decelerating and backpedaling toward the starting line. Additional auditory cues and *distracters* (i.e., information in which no response is warranted) may be added to agility drills to help the athlete focus on task-relevant auditory information. For example, a football coach might use a snap count to signal the beginning of a drill. Keep in mind that reaction time is typically delayed when more auditory cues are added, because the athletes must decipher among and respond to multiple stimuli. For this reason, coaches should limit possible response cues and distracters to two or three options.

▸ **Visual cues.** During competition, athletes must constantly scan the field for teammates, opponents, a ball or puck, a referee, or a coach's signals from the sidelines. For this reason, incorporating different types of visual stimuli and cues may help athletes identify task-relevant game cues more quickly during competition. These cues may be as simple as a coach or teammate pointing to a marker to prompt an immediate change in direction or a signal for the athlete to sprint forward and catch a dropped ball. They may also be as complex as reading an opponent's movements and responding accordingly.

▸ **Mixed cues.** Both auditory and visual cues may be combined to challenge even the most advanced athletes. For example, a football athlete randomly tosses a ball to the right or left side of a teammate running forward. As soon as the runner catches the ball, the coach calls out a number between 1 and 3. Each number corresponds to a cone. After catching the ball, the athlete runs to the specified cone to complete the drill. Initially, the runner must visually track the trajectory of the ball in order to receive it. Next, the athlete must listen for the coach's auditory cue to know where to run to complete the drill or play.

By including these different types of stimuli within basic COD speed drills the athlete can start developing the targeted reactionary skills needed to enhance on-field performance. As with any drill, the more contextually specific it is, the greater the likelihood the athlete will be able to apply it in a game or practice situation. For example, there are numerous products that use light systems that provide a generic reactionary stimulus for athletes to respond to. Typically, these systems have several displays that will randomly light up, signaling the athlete to respond in a certain way. These types of systems may help an athlete develop general reactionary and visual skills, but since they do not provide a contextually specific stimulus (e.g., movement of other players or ball movement) their transferability to competitive situations is questionable (5, 6, 10). Once athletes consistently demonstrate good body control and technique, they can use these drills in a comprehensive agility-training program to improve their reaction time. This sort of program may help athletes perform sport-specific tasks during competition more quickly because they have developed better visual search patterns, anticipation, and speed of recognition (2, 8, 9).

Table 7.1 provides a list of the quickness drills and games included in this chapter.

Table 7.1 Quickness Drills and Games

Drill name	Page number
QUICKNESS DRILLS	
Shift sprints	136
Reactive sprint to backpedal drill	137
Wave drill	137
Shuffle reaction ball drill	137
Ball drops drill	138
Shuffle and forward sprint reaction ball drill	139
Triangle drill	139
Quickness box	140
Reactive Y drill	141
Number drill	142
Get up and go	143
Shadow drill	144

(continued)

Table 7.1 Quickness Drills and Games *(continued)*

Drill name	Page number
QUICKNESS DRILLS	
Coverage drill	145
Gap drill	145
Containment drill	146
GAMES FOR IMPROVING QUICKNESS	
Red light, green light	147
Knee tag	148
Heads or tails	149
Sharks and minnows	150
Everybody is "it"	150
Twenty-one	151
Team keep-away	151
Ultimate	152

QUICKNESS DRILLS

This section presents several sample agility and quickness drills. As previously mentioned, the only limit to what types of drills can be used are the coach's imagination. The basic reactive concepts discussed in these drills can be easily adapted to meet the specific needs of the athlete, the sport, and the training environment.

Shift Sprints

This drill develops first-step quickness and improves the ability to accelerate and decelerate. The athlete starts at one of two cones placed 20 yards (18.3 m) apart. On the coach's *go* signal, the athlete begins jogging back and forth between the two cones at an intensity of about 60%. When the coach calls *two*, the athlete speeds up to approximately 75 to 80% of full speed. When the coach calls *three*, the athlete runs between the cones at full speed. The athlete should continue running between the cones for the entire duration of the drill (25-30 seconds).

To ensure that the athlete does not anticipate a specific speed, the coach should call out signals randomly, mixing it up rather than repeatedly progressing through the speeds in the same order. For example, the coach may go from 1 to 3, followed by 2, or from 2 to 1 to 3. This keeps the drill unpredictable, forcing the athlete to focus intently on the coach's voice and the auditory cues being provided.

Reactive Sprint to Backpedal Drill

This drill improves the ability to accelerate and decelerate while running forward and backward, such as when covering an opponent in a variety of sports. Begin this drill by placing two cones 10 yards (9.1 m) apart. The athlete begins by standing in an athletic position at cone 1. On the *go* signal, the athlete runs forward toward cone 2. When the coach says *switch,* the athlete immediately decelerates and changes directions, backpedaling to cone 1.

Wave Drill

Identifying visual signals from a teammate or a coach during competition is an important skill. This drill enhances reactive quickness with visual cues. Two cones are placed 10 yards (9.1 m) apart. The athlete should stand in an athletic position at cone 1, and the coach should stand just beyond cone 2. On the *go* command, the athlete begins chopping the feet, taking small steps in place, and watching for the coach to give a visual signal for a directional change. To signal the athlete to run forward, the coach raises both arms overhead. The signal to run forward is always first. Once the athlete has reached the middle of the cones, the coach can change up the signals. To signal the athlete to backpedal, the coach drops both arms to the sides. The coach may also extend the arms directly in front to signal the athlete to stop in the current position, chop the feet, and wait for the next cue. The drill should last 8 to 10 seconds.

Shuffle Reaction Ball Drill

This drill improves lateral movement transitions and hand-eye coordination. Two cones are set up about 5 yards (4.6 m) apart. The athlete stands between the cones. The coach stands in front of the athlete and throws a ball toward either cone. The athlete must shuffle to the side to catch the ball and then toss it back. As the athlete's reaction time and movement patterns improve, the coach may increase the distance between the cones or the speed of the throws.

Coach

Ball Drops Drill

This drill is excellent for improving response to visual stimuli and first-step quickness. The athlete and the coach stand approximately 5 yards (4.6 m) away from each other. The coach has a racquetball (or any ball that bounces). The athlete assumes an athletic position. The coach holds the ball out to the side at shoulder height and then randomly drops it. As soon as the coach releases the ball, the athlete sprints toward it and catches it before it bounces twice. The athlete should catch the ball in a good athletic stance. The athlete may not dive for the ball to make up for poor reaction time.

Variations

The coach and the athlete can use the following variations to make the drill more challenging.

- Increase the distance between the athlete and the coach.
- Have the athlete start from different stances (three-point stance, on a knee, on the belly, starting to one side, and so on).
- The coach holds a ball on each side and drops only one. This requires the athlete to be aware of multiple focal points.
- The coach holds two balls and assigns a number to each (or uses differently colored balls). Then, the coach drops both simultaneously while calling out a number (or color) to indicate which ball the athlete should attempt to catch.
- Add specificity by using the ball athletes will use in their sports; for example drop a football or rugby ball for athletes in these sports.

Shuffle and Forward Sprint Reaction Ball Drill

This is similar to the shuffle reaction ball drill, but it requires the athlete to move forward as well as side to side when reacting. One cone is placed in each corner of a square with sides about 5 yards (4.6 m) long. The athlete stands between two cones on one side of the square. The coach stands facing the athlete on the opposite side of the square, just outside the boundary. The coach throws a ball toward any of the four cones. The athlete reacts by shuffling to the side or moving forward to catch the ball, and then tosses it back to the coach. As the athlete's reaction time and movement patterns improve, the coach may increase the distance between the cones or the frequency of the throw.

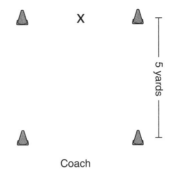

Triangle Drill

This drill improves fundamental quickness skills and reaction time by using an auditory stimulus. Three cones, numbered 1 through 3, are placed in a triangular pattern. The athlete stands in an athletic position at cone 1. The coach stands to the side and calls out a number that corresponds to one of the two cones in front of the athlete (see photo). The athlete immediately sprints to the chosen cone. Variations of this drill include the athlete facing away from the cones (forcing the athlete to turn and open the hips) or beginning in a push-up position with hands flat on the ground and arms extended. This forces the athlete to quickly stand up and sprint forward toward the selected cone.

Quickness Box

This drill is good for improving quickness in confined spaces. Four cones are set up to create a square with sides approximately 3 to 5 yards (2.7-4.6 m) long. The cones are numbered 1 through 4. The athlete assumes an athletic position in the center of the square (*a*) and waits for the coach to call out a number. When the coach signals, the athlete runs, backpedals (*b*), or shuffles as needed to touch the cone either with the closest hand or with the one specified prior to starting the drill. After touching the cone, the athlete sprints back to the starting position and waits for the coach to call the next number. The athlete repeats this drill for approximately 10 seconds per set for two or three sets.

Reactive *Y* Drill

This drill teaches athletes to adjust their stride and foot placement to transition quickly into other movement patterns. Four cones are set up in a *Y* pattern (*a*). The two cones forming the top of the *Y* and the base cone should be placed about 10 yards (9.1 m) from the middle cone. The base cone is 1, the middle cone is 2, and the top cones are 3 and 4. The coach stands just beyond cone 2. The athlete assumes an athletic position at cone 1. On the coach's signal, the athlete sprints to cone 2. When the athlete reaches it, the coach gives a directional cue (*b*) to signal which of the three cones (1, 3, or 4) the athlete should sprint to next. The directional cue can be a visual cue, such as pointing, or an auditory cue, such as calling a number. The coach may modify this drill by having the athlete backpedal or side shuffle to the designated cone.

Variation

To increase the sport-specificity of this movement, this drill can be performed by having one athlete follow a teammate, then when the leader reaches the first cone he or she will decide whether to sprint toward cone 3 or cone 4. The athlete who is in pursuit should react to the movement of the leader and attempt to tag the leader before he or she reaches the selected cone.

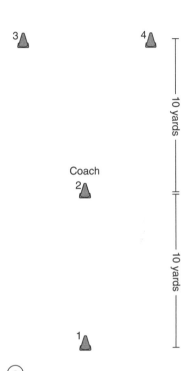

Number Drill

Six cones are positioned in two lines approximately 10 yards (9.1 m) apart. Each cone in the line should be approximately 10 yards (9.1 m) away from the next. The coach should number the cones 1 to 6, with cones 1 through 3 in line 1 and cones 4 through 6 in line 2. The athlete should begin by standing between cones 1 and 4. When the coach calls out a number, the athlete should sprint to the corresponding cone and stand by it while chopping the feet in place until the coach calls out the next number. The athlete continues this drill for up to 10 seconds, changing directions two to four times before resting.

Variations

The coach can call out a series of numbers, generally no more than 3, and require the athlete to move through this pattern as quickly as possible. Upon hearing the final number called, the athlete should execute the pattern. Several rows of cones can also be used and athletes can perform this drill as a race. Adding competition can increase the temporal stress of this drill as well as improve athlete motivation. The coach may also enhance the difficulty by using three sets of differently colored cones and randomly calling out either a number or a color for the athletes to respond to.

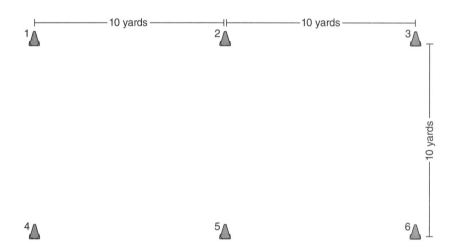

Get Up and Go

This drill will use the same setup displayed in the Number Drill (although the photos only show 4 cones, 6 are used). The athlete starts by lying on the belly behind and between cones 1 and 4 (*a*). When the coach calls out a number, the athlete sprints to the corresponding cone (*b*) and drops down into a push-up position (or plank position with arms extended) at the new cone (*c*). As the drill continues, the athlete runs to the cone in the opposite line as designated by the coach's cue. The athlete continues this drill for up to 10 seconds, changing directions two to four times before resting.

Shadow Drill

This drill teaches athletes to read an opponent's movement patterns. Two cones are set up 10 yards (9.1 m) apart from one another. Two athletes stand facing each other in the center of the cones. One athlete assumes the role of the leader. The other athlete must shadow the leader by mimicking the leader's actions.

Variation

Use the six-cone drill configuration used in the Number Drill (see page 142), with one athlete (the offensive player) positioned between cones 3 and 6 and another athlete (the defensive player) positioned between cones 1 and 4. With the midline of the drill's space dividing the players' movement squares (i.e., a line running between cones 2 and 5), the offensive player is allowed to use the entire square as the defensive player attempts to mimic the offensive player's movement pattern.

Coverage Drill

This drill teaches athletes to read the movement patterns of multiple opponents at the same time. Four cones are set up in a square, with sides 10 yards (9.1 m) long. One athlete starts in the center of the square. A second athlete lines up between a pair of cones and faces the athlete in the center. A third athlete lines up between the pair of cones to the left or right of the second athlete. On the *go* signal, the athletes along the perimeter of the square begin shuffling between the two cones on their sides of the square. The athlete in the center attempts to stay in alignment with (or squared up to) both athletes as they move between the cones. As the perimeter athletes move, the athlete in the center must adjust the position within the square as needed so they can keep both perimeter athletes in his field of vision. The athletes should perform this drill for approximately 10 seconds. After a 20- to 30-second rest, the athletes rotate to the left or right so that one of the perimeter athletes moves to the center. The drill must continue until each athlete has been in all three positions.

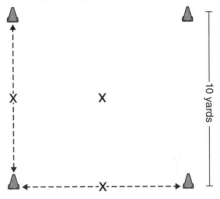

Gap Drill

This drill helps athletes find an opening to evade their competitors, such as in rugby or football. Four cones are set up approximately 1 yard (0.9 m) apart in a straight line to create three gaps, numbered 1 to 3. An athlete moves approximately 10 yards (9.1 m) away and assumes an athletic position facing the cones. On the *go* signal, the athlete sprints forward. At the 5- to 8-yard (4.6-7.3 m) mark, the coach calls a gap number, and the athlete runs through the designated gap.

Containment Drill

This drill helps athletes improve sport-specific quickness and the ability to read and react to an opponent's movement patterns. Four cones are placed in a large square, with sides approximately 15 to 20 yards (13.7-18.3 m) long (*a*). The defensive athlete lines up between two cones on one side of the square, which becomes the end zone. The offensive athlete lines up between the cones on the opposite side of the square. On the *go* signal, the offensive athlete attempts to evade the defensive athlete (*b*) and get into the end zone as quickly as possible. Although some physical contact will occur during this drill, athletes should not be overly aggressive or violent, since this behavior increases risk of injury. In fact, the athletes should be told specifically to minimize contact with one another. If athletes are involved in contact sports, the defensive athlete protecting the end zone can use blocking pads to increase sport specificity and to minimize risk of injury. The goal of this drill is for the defensive athlete to prevent the offensive athlete from getting into the end zone. This drill should be limited to 10 seconds or less and allow at least 30 to 60 seconds of recovery between sets.

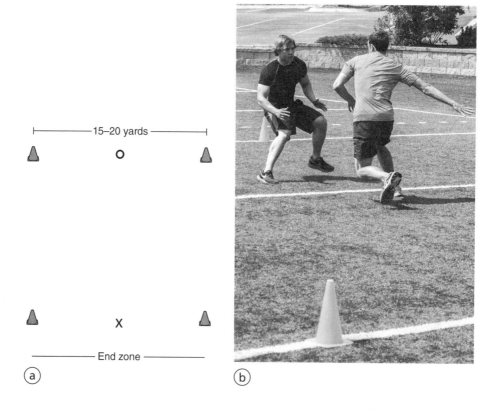

GAMES FOR IMPROVING QUICKNESS

Games that incorporate quickness skills are a fun way to increase athletes' motivation and enthusiasm for training. The quickness games in this section also help athletes develop their situational-movement skills and body awareness.

Red Light, Green Light

This game improves quickness and teaches athletes how to accelerate and decelerate effectively. Two cones are placed 40 yards (36.6 m) apart. Athletes should stand by one cone and the coach should stand by the other. On the *green light* command, the athletes sprint forward as far as possible before the coach yells *red light!* On this command, the athletes immediately stop in place. When the coach calls *green light* again, the athletes resume sprinting toward the second cone. The coach continues to call out commands until an athlete passes the second cone.

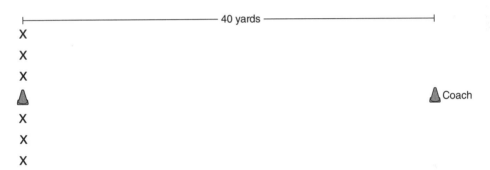

Knee Tag

This game improves sport-specific speed and quickness for combative athletes, such as wrestlers or mixed martial artists. It also helps them learn to read and appropriately respond to their opponents' movements. Four cones are set up in a square, with sides 2 yards (1.8 m) long. Two athletes stand approximately 3 feet (0.9 m) apart in the center of the square, face each other, and assume an athletic stance. At the whistle, one athlete attempts to touch the opponent's knees (see photo). (Note that the athletes should not both attempt to tag the knee at the same time for safety reasons.) The opponent should dodge as needed to avoid being touched. The first athlete scores a point each time he or she tags the opponent's knees. Athletes should perform the game for approximately 15 to 30 seconds and then switch roles. The game can be repeated multiple times. However, athletes should rest for 30 to 60 seconds between bouts. After both athletes have had equal opportunities to score, the one who has earned the most points wins.

Heads or Tails

This game develops first-step quickness and improves reaction time. Two cones are placed 20 to 40 yards (18.3-36.6 m) apart, and another cone is placed halfway between them. At the center cone, two athletes face each other with their hands outstretched and their fingertips touching directly over the cone (*a*). The athletes then assume an athletic position, dropping their hands down to their sides. The coach designates one athlete as *heads* and the other as *tails*. The coach flips a coin and calls out which side of the coin is facing up. The designated athlete turns (*b*) and attempts to sprint past the rear cone before being tagged by the other athlete (*c*). Points are given to any athlete who makes it to the scoring zone without being tagged or to any athlete who tags the fleeing runner before the designated safe area. Athletes should repeat the game 6 to 12 times.

Sharks and Minnows

The purpose of this game is to improve situational awareness and to teach athletes to read an opponent's body movements. Four cones are set up to create a playing area that measures approximately 20 yards by 40 yards (18.3 m by 36.6 m). One or two athletes assume the role of shark (defensive athletes) and position themselves in the center of the playing area. The remaining athletes or minnows (offensive athletes) line up on either end of the playing area. This game tends to work best with at least 6 but no more than 20 minnows. The size of the playing area will largely determine the number of athletes. On command, the minnows attempt to sprint from one end of the playing area to the other without being tagged by the shark(s). A minnow who is tagged by a shark switches role with that athlete.

Variation

Multiple sharks can be added to increase the agility demands of this activity and to challenge athletes to maneuver around multiple opponents.

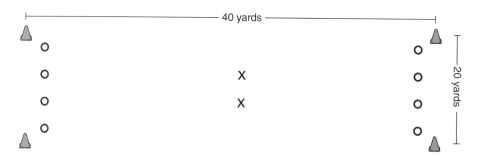

Everybody Is "It"

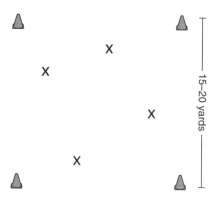

This game helps improve situational awareness and teaches athletes to read an opponent's body movements. Four cones are set up in a square, with sides approximately 15 to 20 yards (13.7-18.3 m) long. Three or four athletes should spread out over the designated playing area. On the *go* command, these athletes attempt to tag as many of the other athletes as possible without being tagged themselves. An athlete who is tagged must immediately perform a preassigned task or movement, such as five jumping jacks or push-ups, before returning to the game. If a dispute arises about which athlete was tagged first, both athletes must perform the assigned task. Athletes should play this game for 15 to 20 seconds, resting for 45 to 60 seconds between sets.

Twenty-One

This game improves quickness, situational awareness, and strategic thinking. It works best with
two or three athletes and should be performed
in a large open space. The game begins when the
coach randomly tosses a reaction ball (see photo)
into the air somewhere within the playing area.
Athletes must allow the ball to bounce at least
once before attempting to catch it. However,
the athlete who catches the ball receives a point
for each bounce of the ball prior to the catch.
For example, if an athlete catches the ball after
it has bounced twice, that person receives two
points. Once points are awarded, the athletes
should return to the starting area and wait for
the next throw. The first athlete to accumulate
21 points wins the game.

Team Keep-Away

This game improves quickness, situational awareness, and teamwork. Four cones are
set up to create a playing area of 30 by 30 yards (27.4 m by 27.4 m), which works well
for a group of 8 to 10 athletes. For more athletes, the coach may expand the playing
area to accommodate the additional athletes. Athletes divide into two equal teams
and spread out over the playing area. The coach starts the game by blowing a whistle,

starting a stopwatch, and passing a ball (e.g.,
a football, basketball, rugby ball, or soccer ball)
to one of the teams. The athletes in possession
of the ball pass it among themselves while
trying to prevent the other team from gaining
possession. An athlete who gains possession
of the ball must pass it within five seconds or
automatically forfeit it to the opposing team.
Athletes may grab, intercept, or strip the ball
as necessary to gain possession. The game is
played for a predetermined amount of time,
usually one to three minutes. The team in possession of the ball when time runs out, or the
team that has the ball longest, wins.

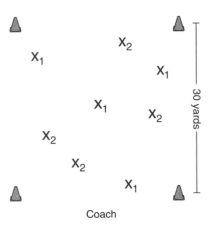

Variation

A variation of Team Keep-Away is called Three Passes. This game is performed in the
same manner as Team Keep-Away but when a team makes three consecutive passes in
a row, it scores a point. Once a point is scored, the scoring team is required to set the
ball down where the third pass was completed, and the other team takes possession.

Ultimate

This game, a modified version of Ultimate Frisbee, is great for developing situational awareness and teamwork. The rules to this game are similar to those of football. However, limited physical contact is allowed and the receiving athlete's role is slightly modified. Athletes should play this game in a large, open area at least the size of a basketball court. They may use a Frisbee or a ball (e.g., a football, basketball, rugby ball, or soccer ball). Athletes divide into two equal teams, and each team goes to its side of the playing area. One team begins the game as the offense and the other team begins as the defense.

The game starts when a designated athlete on the defensive team puts the ball into play by throwing it to the offensive team's side of the playing field. When an athlete on the offensive team catches or picks up the ball, he or she must remain stationary and throw the ball to another athlete on the team. This process is repeated to move the ball down the playing area toward the opponent's goal line. Teams score a point when one of their players crosses the opponent's goal line and catches the ball in the air. If a throw is intercepted or if a point is scored, the defensive team becomes the offensive team.

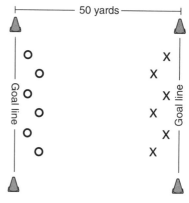

CHAPTER 8

Agility and Quickness Program Design

Ian Jeffreys

Agility and quickness development presents one of the great challenges to the strength and conditioning coach as its application will be context specific. Agility and quickness performance encompasses numerous different capacities, such as perceptual, cognitive, motor skill, and physical. Agility is also interlinked with the technical requirements of performance. Thus, it is clear that planning and implementing effective agility and quickness development is complicated.

Further adding to this complexity is the fact that there are two potentially contradictory elements at play: agility is both a physical- and a skill-based capacity, and developing each of these requires a different approach (6). Ultimately, agility and quickness expression is often at high intensities and so developing the ability to effectively apply the required quality of these capacities requires a degree of work at these high intensities. Given the high level of fatigue generated by this type of activity, there will always be a limit to the amount of high-intensity training an athlete can perform in any given time period. At the same time, agility and quickness are skills and therefore require an extensive amount of repetition to develop and refine the required movements. There is a great contradiction at the heart of programming effective agility, however; coaches need extensive practice to develop the skills, but there is a natural limit to the amount of high-intensity work an athlete can perform. Balancing these two requirements will therefore always be a challenge.

The author would like to acknowledge the significant contributions of Joel Raether and David Sandler to this chapter.

PROGRESSIVE DEVELOPMENT

Given that agility and quickness have high-skill related components, logically they should be subjected to a progressive skill-development program (2, 6). It is here that thinking like an educator can be extremely useful. Educational programs are built around developing a syllabus, which takes students from where they are now to where they need to be. This syllabus is broken down into content that is delivered at specific stages of development. Given that agility performance is skill-based and ultimately comprises several patterns that lead progressively to performance in the sport, it is logical to think that this educational process can provide a systematic approach to developing agility.

CONTEXT IS EVERYTHING

Agility and quickness are quite unique in that they are intricately linked with performance and, ultimately, the quality of an athlete's agility and quickness is determined by whether the athlete can successfully undertake the task required in a game (4, 6). Unfortunately, the majority of agility definitions lack a context-specific application that determines how effective it is in helping the athlete achieve the sport-related task (6). In deciding upon appropriate programming, it is therefore crucial to carefully consider the context in which an athlete will need to be agile.

In generating context specificity, the process of reverse engineering is extremely useful (8). Reverse engineering involves starting with the sport being played and working backward from that to determine the precise agility and quickness requirements of the sport and the athlete's position within the sport. This is radically different from starting with the definitions of agility and quickness and working forward to the game (6). Reverse engineering can ensure that whenever movements are developed, they address context-specific requirements of the game in question. The key question in the reverse engineering process is, "What is the athlete trying to achieve?" This allows the phases of the game to be identified, and the tasks that the athlete needs to be able to achieve to be successful can also be identified (4). These tasks can then be broken down into the movement patterns that the athlete will need to master to successfully undertake these tasks (4). These movements then become the focus of the agility-development program. This process ensures that, whenever movements are developed, they retain the necessary context-specificity to ensure they maximize the transfer from training to performance. Failure to do this may result in exercises that may bear little, if any, resemblance to the way they are deployed in sport. As a result, the exercises will have little beneficial effect on performance and, possibly, develop movement capacities that are at odds with (or could be detrimental to) the way in which the movements are deployed in the sport.

CLASSIFYING MOVEMENTS

An effective educational process identifies the basic skills required to master the subject. Similarly, an effective agility and quickness program should be based on identifying the basic movement patterns that are required to perform the sport-related tasks encountered in a game (3, 4, 6). Given the variety of sports and the range of tasks performed within these sports, identifying basic skills can be a challenge. Through reverse engineering, however, several generic requirements become clear, such as the ability to start motion, to accelerate rapidly, to decelerate to perform a skill, and to change direction to create space (6). These requirements can, in turn, be broken down into discrete movement patterns that, if mastered, can form the basis of effective agility performance in a wide range of sports (see table 8.1). While some differences will exist between sports, targeted movement patterns provide an appropriate structure around which to develop an effective agility and quickness program.

At the heart of the target classifications are the target functions, which aim to determine what athletes are trying to achieve (3, 6). At any given time, athletes are likely to be attempting either to start movement or to change the direction of movement (termed *initiation movements*), trying to move at maximal velocity (*actualization movements*), or waiting in transition to anticipate, react, or manipulate themselves in relation to a sport-specific stimulus (*transition movements*). Although agility training often focuses on initiation and actualization movements, far less emphasis is placed on transition movements. Often when these are trained they are taught incorrectly, with the emphasis on movement speed rather than on control. Athletes' ability to start and move at maximal velocity often depends on being in the correct position to enable effective subsequent movement.

Table 8.1 identifies the movement aims and the associated target movement patterns within each target function (initiation, transition, and actualization) that collectively develop a movement syllabus (6). This forms the basis of the development program, with these movement patterns established, then refined, and then progressively applied in increasingly sport-specific scenarios. When combined with the application of effective skill-based practices, the movement syllabus creates a very powerful system around which to develop an effective agility and quickness program.

PUTTING THE MOVEMENT SYLLABUS INTO ACTION

Effective agility training balances the requirements of the drills and the ability of the athlete. In this way, the level of challenge needs to be modulated so

Table 8.1 Target Classifications of Movement Patterns in Sport

Target function	Movement aim	Target movement pattern
Initiation	Start to the front	Acceleration pattern
	Start to the side	Cross step
	Start to the rear	Drop step
	Change direction (linear or lateral)	Cut step or plant step
Transition	Static wait	Athletic position
	Semi-static transition (jockeying)	Jockeying action
	Move to the side	Side shuffle
	Move to the rear	Backpedal
	Track the attacker diagonally	Cross-step run
	Decelerate	Deceleration pattern
	Controlled movement to the front	Chop steps in an athletic position or adjustment steps
Actualization	Accelerate	Acceleration movement patterns
	Move to top speed	Kick from a rolling start, maximum speed pattern
	Maintain a high speed with subtle directional changes	Curved running

that it is in a virtual sweet spot between being too easy, which can result in boredom, or too hard, which can result in anxiety and subsequent disengagement (6). A session designed for an elite athlete should look different from a session for a beginner. For this reason, a sport-specific agility program should include a progression in movement challenge and complexity as athletes move through their stages of development. In the initial stages, athletes can benefit from closed drills in which the movement is preplanned and the athlete is free to concentrate solely on the movement pattern at hand. The speed of these drills can be controlled and they often consist of single movement patterns (e.g., shuffling). In this stage, coaches should develop athletes' ability in all the identified movement patterns to ensure that there are no weak links in movement ability (6). Open drills can then be progressively introduced, to provide context and a stimulating environment (6).

As athletes develop, their coaches should start to combine the athletes' movement patterns in ways typically used in their sport. For example, backpedal drills can conclude with sprints to the rear, to the side, or forward. These combinations are commonly seen in numerous sports. As athletes develop, coaches can also deploy drills that are increasingly open. Here, athletes should respond to a range of stimuli, which become *sport generic* (i.e., movements that apply to numerous sports) and then increasingly sport specific (6, 14). For example, athletes can initiate incorporating backpedaling into a sprint drill. Next, they can change direction in response to a coach's signal, and then in response to another athlete's movement. These types of drills can include great variety in terms of distances, speeds, directions, and stimuli. In this way, the movement patterns progressively reflect the specific applications faced in sport.

The following list shows the stages of movement ability and application for game-speed development (6). As athletes demonstrate competency at one stage, they can progress to the next stage. This process can also be applied to agility.

1. Develop general and stable fundamental movement patterns.
2. Develop movement combinations, moving from closed drills to open drills.
3. Develop sport-generic movements in increasingly game-related contexts.
4. Perform sport-specific movements in a game context.

QUALITY IS VITAL

Practice makes permanent. This is a crucial message for any agility program. If athletes are to develop effective agility, they must perform each drill with the appropriate technique (4, 6). They must always remember that the drill is merely a means to an end, and that end is enhanced agility in competition. If they perform the drill poorly, they will not develop optimal agility. Therefore, coaches should always emphasize technique during exercises.

The movements outlined in table 8.1 provide an ideal reference for athletes to assess their performance of each movement. The results can form the start of an agility-development program. Where deficiencies are seen, these areas can be the focus of training to bring these movements up to standard. From there, coaches can develop each movement pattern along the following continuum, which moves from basic, closed drills to sport-specific movements that display high levels of agility. With this structure, coaches can develop sport-specific agility for each movement pattern in table 8.1 in the following manner.

1. Develop individual movement patterns.
2. Add variation (distance and direction).
3. Develop movement combinations.
4. Move to increasingly open situations.
5. Add sport-specific requirements.

Coaches can then structure agility-development programs to ensure that all movement patterns are developed within a given time frame. This may be weekly or biweekly.

CHARACTERISTICS OF EFFECTIVE SKILL DEVELOPMENT SESSIONS

Agility is a highly effective skill; therefore, agility programming should be based upon a sound grasp of the fundamentals of skill development. But the knowledge of how best to develop skills is still emerging, and so definitive statements as to the best ways of developing skills cannot be made. There do appear to be reliable mechanisms, however, by which the amount of skill development can be enhanced, such as through the effective selection and appropriate structuring of exercises.

Cognitive Involvement

It appears that skill development is enhanced when the athlete is cognitively involved with the session. High levels of cognitive involvement seem to link the parts of the brain responsible for automating with those involved in solving problems. The use of open drills, where athletes have to solve problems, is an effective way of maximizing this involvement (10, 11, 12).

A session should involve activities at the *edge of the athlete's capacity*. There appears to be a sweet spot between challenge and skill development (6). If all exercises are easy, athletes are not sufficiently stretched to develop their skill capacities. On the other hand, if the exercises are too advanced and challenging, athletes may not be actively engaged mentally because their chances of success are very low. It is therefore important to structure sessions so that the activities push the athletes toward the edge of their current capacity. It is important that the coach has ways of progressing agility exercises to achieve the optimal level of challenge. Employing degrees of freedom is especially useful in terms of progression. A *degree of freedom* can be thought of as a factor that an athlete has to consider and control when performing an exercise (6). All agility and quickness exercises can be thought of as lying on a continuum between closed and open. By adding a simple variant, coaches can add a degree of freedom, which in turn adds an additional cognitive factor, which in turn provides an additional challenge. Degrees of freedom can be added to all of the target movements, progressing them from predominantly closed to increasingly open and ultimately to sport-generic and sport-specific activities (6).

Ensuring Variation

Skill development appears to be enhanced when practices are variable; that is, when various aspects of the exercise change over subsequent repetitions (11). Again, the use of open drills is a way of achieving variance, but even relatively closed drills can have a degree of variance by altering starting positions, movement combinations, and so on. In a similar vein, random allocation of drills where, rather than all the exercises of the same drill being performed simultaneously they are interspersed with other exercises, appears to enhance skill development (6, 9, 10). These methods possibly achieve this by increasing the amount of cognitive involvement required to perform the exercises successfully.

External Focus

Getting athletes to use an *external focus* (focusing on the results of an action) rather than an *internal focus* (focusing on the body actions themselves) appears to enhance skill development (6, 12). Open and task-based drills are highly effective at naturally generating an external focus. However, even closed drills can foster an external focus if appropriate coaching cues are deployed (5, 11, 13).

Repetition

Perhaps the biggest factor of all is repetition as skill development comes through extensive, quality repetition. Therefore it is crucial that movements be repeated regularly throughout an athlete's training. Training should systematically ensure that the movements required to play the game are repeated consistently within any given training period (1).

STRUCTURING AN EFFECTIVE AGILITY DEVELOPMENT SESSION

Any effective agility session must start with a clear objective that should relate to the specific movement skills that are to be developed. The type of objective will depend upon the sport and the ability of the athlete. With beginner athletes, the objective may be to develop a single movement capacity, such as deceleration. As an athlete achieves these objectives, they can become more complex, such as the ability to create space. Ultimately, the objective will become more sport-specific, such as defending the key in basketball.

Throughout the planning process, this objective should guide all decisions for that training session. Once the objective is identified, the optimal session structure by which the objective will be achieved needs to be decided. This structure will be dictated by theoretical and logistical issues with the latter that include the time and resources available. It is always important to ensure that logistical issues are considered and that planning does not become simply a theoretical process. Unless a plan can be executed in context, it will be impossible to appropriately apply an effective agility development program, no matter how theoretically sound it is.

Once this overarching structure is established, the best exercises to achieve the objectives can be identified and then structured so as to provide an appropriate session flow. These exercises should be selected to ensure that they directly address the objective and provide the appropriate level of challenge for the athlete.

Because agility training is best carried out when an athlete is in a non-fatigued state, it is ideally performed at the start of a session (6). Similarly, the duration of agility drills should be short (3-5 seconds) to ensure that appropriate quality of movement, both in terms of technical performance and the quality of output, is maintained throughout the exercise (6). Similarly, rest periods should be sufficient to ensure a high quality of performance in the subsequent repetition. In some circumstances, drills can be extended, or rest periods reduced, where the aim is to develop the ability to maintain technique and quality under fatigue. Typically, this is only carried out with athletes who have a good level of movement competency.

When working with initiation and actualization applications (see table 8.1), the intensity of movement needs to be high. This ensures that the capacities reflect the game-like application and provide a sufficiently intense stimulus to produce the required physical adaptation. However, this is not to say that all agility movement must be of high intensity. Movements of lower intensity, especially transition-type movements can be performed to assist with the development of the appropriate skill patterns required for high performance. In this way, agility movements can attain the degree of repetitions needed to develop the required motor skills. Typically, intense movements should be limited to no more than two sessions per week. Less intense activities can be performed more frequently, however, since they induce less neural and physiological fatigue yet can help develop the skill capacities required. Similarly, the emphasis on skill development means that some form of agility training should always be present in an athlete's program, and it is here that the warm-up approach outlined later in this chapter is crucial.

Coaching Is Key

The systematic and strategic process described in this chapter should ensure that each session has the maximum chance of achieving its objectives. But the ultimate effectiveness of each session, and of the program as a whole, will be dictated by the quality of coaching delivered during any session. No matter how well selected, a drill alone will be effective only if the athletes perform the exercise in an appropriate manner. It is here that the ability to observe performance, to evaluate performance in relation to a technical model, and to provide appropriate feedback and instruction to bring the athlete's performance toward that model become critical. The importance of effective coaching can never be overstated in any agility and quickness development program.

Need for a Quality Warm-Up

Earlier in this chapter, the great challenges of balancing the need for skill development with controlling the overall volume of intense work was highlighted. It is here that the RAMP (raise, activate, mobilize, and potentiate) warm-up system is a powerful tool for the strength and conditioning coach (3, 7, 10). The warm-up is characteristically performed any time an athlete trains, and so provides a time-efficient method by which skill application can be applied without the need for any additional training time. In the RAMP warm-up system, the first phase involves raising physiological parameters, such as heart rate, body temperature, and so on. While this can be achieved by general means, achieving it by the systematic application of movement patterns allows them to be developed during every training session, thus contributing not only to the warm-up for that session but also to the development of involved movement skills and, ultimately, to agility performance (3, 6, 7, 10). Additionally, the potentiation phase, consisting of progressive increases in exercise intensity in preparation for the upcoming session, is an ideal opportunity to develop these movements further and to apply them in increasingly sport-specific contexts. These phases can be targeted to specific aspects of performance such as acceleration or direction change, or even to very sport-specific capacities such as creating space. This means that agility development can be achieved through targeted warm-ups and not only through dedicated agility sessions (6, 7, 10).

CONCLUSION

Agility and quickness are complex sporting skills that include both physical and cognitive components. As a result, only a progressive skill-development program will effectively improve agility and quickness. The educational model of a syllabus can be applied to developing agility: the coach can identify the basic movement patterns that are required to perform the sport and then design a program to establish, refine, and apply the movement syllabus in light of the specific sport and the ability of the athlete.

Sport-Specific Agility and Quickness Training

This chapter includes some of the most effective drills for each of the featured sports from the contributors' experiences. As with any training program, drills should be selected based on the athlete's specific sport, position, training age, skill level, specific areas in need of improvement, and coach–athlete constraints.

Table 9.1 provides a list of the sports included in this chapter.

Table 9.1   Sport-Specific Training for Agility and Quickness

Sport	Page number
Baseball and softball	165
Basketball	172
Combat Sports	179
Cricket	182
Field Hockey	189
Football (American or gridiron)	194
Ice Hockey	198
Lacrosse	201
Netball	203
Rugby	211
Soccer	217
Tennis	223
Volleyball	225
Wrestling	227

The authors would like to acknowledge the significant contributions of Al Biancani, Michael Doscher, Todd Durkin, Greg Infantolino, Katie Krall, and Mike Sanders to this chapter.

Athletes and coaches can easily adapt these drills or substitute others from chapters 6 and 7 based on their level of performance, training background, yearly training cycle, and training goals. As the athlete progresses, the coach should to develop or modify these drills based on the demands of the particular sport. The rate of progression should be determined by the athletes' ability to complete the correct pattern or movement, as well as by their physiological abilities such as strength. Furthermore, coaches should base progression on an athlete's overall body control, awareness, and technique when performing an activity or drill.

▶ *BASEBALL AND SOFTBALL*

Javair Gillett

To develop an effective agility program for baseball and softball it is important that the coach have an intricate knowledge of the game and the movements performed on the field. These sports require a unique combination of physical abilities, skills, and mental processes to be successful. Most decisions in baseball and softball must be made under significant time constraints. For this reason, baseball and softball athletes must have not only good physical skills and abilities but also good situational awareness and reaction time in order to execute a successful movement strategy quickly and accurately. As such, agility training drills should be specific to the movements associated with the sport and ultimately transition from drills that are preplanned and structured to drills that are performed in a randomized and variable learning environment.

Agility drills should be designed to meet the basic movements required on the field and can be made more specific to meet the needs of infielders, pitchers, outfielders, and catchers. Regardless of the athlete's position, defensive movements most often include quick initial accelerations as well as abrupt directional changes in the midst of running. Vision and eye movement are also integral components of performance for any fielder. For all positions, it is important that agility drills incorporate visual tracking and upper-body reaching tasks. High speed, multiplanar footwork drills can improve body control and positioning and assist in more precise visual tracking of the ball in flight. Agility drills involving fly balls should incorporate quick adjustments of the feet along with coordinated rotational motions of the hips and shoulders. Agility drills more specific to retrieving ground balls should also incorporate upper-body reaching in forehand and backhand fielding positions. In the forehand portion of a drill, the athlete takes an open step laterally with one foot while turning the body and lunging, and reaches toward the ground with the glove hand. In the backhand portion of a drill, the athlete turns the body, pivoting on one foot and taking a step across the body with the other foot while lunging and reaching with the glove hand.

PROGRAM DESIGN

The ultimate goal in baseball- and softball-specific agility program design is to progress to position-specific drills and mimic movements in a randomized, variable environment. Agility programs should be designed to meet the specific needs of the position. Infielder and pitchers' movements frequently involve quick lateral shuffles for short distances and crossover steps into sprints covering various distances. Outfielders will cover the greatest distances and most often require changes in body position, often while moving at the high speeds. Catchers' movements are very different from any other position on the field, so agility drills specific for that position should simulate blocking balls in the dirt and retrieving balls at short distances at various angles. Locomotive agility drills for the batter can focus on movements called for after contact. Base-running agility drills should simulate the turns that need to be made when rounding the bases and emphasize starting and stopping ability while within the base paths.

While position-specific agility drills should be practiced daily during the season, an in-depth off-season baseball- and softball-specific agility program can be introduced into a well-rounded strength and conditioning program two times per week. During preseason, the frequency of agility programs should increase and be performed three times per week, thereby increasing the total volume of this specific work. Further, drills should use between a 1:5 and a 1:20 work-to-rest ratio (1). Since most drills should involve short distances and last less than 5 seconds, a 1:20 work-to-rest ratio will be sufficient for a full ATP-PC recovery. As the season approaches, rest times should mimic game situations in which the athlete is usually afforded about 20 seconds of rest between pitches.

When determining the appropriate volume for agility programs, it is important to take into account the drills used, distance covered, and most importantly, the directional change demands and intensity. For example, a short but high-speed 180-degree turn (as in a rundown) will offer a different mechanical demand than a longer distance arc-like turn (as in rounding first base). Magrini and colleagues (1) suggest a total volume of 300 to 600 meters (328.1-656.2 yd) per session. For COD drills, 4 or 5 repetitions are suggested to be performed in each direction for appropriate learning to take place on either side. For high-frequency plyometric drills, the athlete should commit to performing the drill as fast as possible for up to 5 or 6 seconds. Many drills will offer a directional component (e.g., moving either right vs. left, up vs. back, or up left vs. up right) so equal attention is devoted and should be included in the total volume. It is advised that total volume be summed by using total repetitions performed in all directions. General-purpose drills should be performed for at least 2 or 3 sets whereas position-specific drills should be practiced over 4 or 5 sets. Performing a general-purpose drill allows athletes an opportunity to maintain good fundamental movement skills indicative of overall athleticism, whereas position-specific drills allow them to become better specialized at their specific position. Note that catchers require a unique set of skills that separate them from any other position on the field. Therefore, for transfer to occur, variable agility drills need to be designed to fit a catcher and practiced regularly.

GENERAL-PURPOSE DRILLS

Multiplanar Hip Hops and Pops

Hip hops and pops place an emphasis on body control and COD when the body's center of mass suddenly changes. Rotational hip hops and pops add hip rotation with shoulder disassociation. In all variations the athlete should attempt to keep the head and shoulders still. A more advanced version can be performed on one leg.

Linear Hip Hoppers

Begin facing forward with both feet behind a line. Hop forward and backward on both feet over the line.

Lateral Hip Hoppers

Begin facing sideways with both feet next to the line. Hop laterally on both feet over the line and back.

45-Degree Hip Poppers

Begin facing forward with both feet behind a line. Hop on both feet and rotate the hips 45 degrees to move one foot in front of the line while keeping the other foot behind the line. When the feet contact the ground they should land parallel to each other and at the same time. Quickly switch the feet and try to put the foot in front of the line in the same exact spot every time.

90-Degree Hip Poppers

Begin facing sideways with one foot on one side of the line and the other foot on the line. Hop on both feet and rotate the hips 90 degrees to move the foot that is off the line onto the line. The foot that begins on the line should land back on the line. Then quickly hop back into the starting position. When the feet contact the ground they should land parallel to each other and at the same time. Keep the head and shoulders facing perpendicular to the line at all times. Perform this drill rotating both to the right and to the left.

180-Degree Hip Poppers

Begin facing backward with both feet on the line. Before starting, rotate the shoulders so that they are perpendicular to the line. Hop with both feet and rotate the hips 180 degrees so that both feet land back on the line facing the opposite direction. When the feet contact the ground they should land parallel to each other and at the same time. Keep the head and shoulders facing perpendicular to the line at all times. Perform this drill rotating both to the right and to the left.

Hip Poppers with a Catch

Perform the desired hip hop or pop drill for 3 to 5 seconds and then throw a ball for the athlete to catch in the air. The ball should be thrown in different places around the drill area in order to force the athlete to make random bodily adjustments. This helps mimic the demands of the game.

Arm Slides with Reach

Diving for a ball or sliding headfirst into a base is difficult to safely replicate in a controlled environment. Agility drills involving falling onto the ground and reaching can assist in creating a knowledge and confidence for hitting the ground, simultaneously improving dynamic stability and building reactive strength in the core and shoulder complexes. COD principles for the upper body are explored here. To create a more universal environment, add a target and vary the distance and/or direction of the reach in random and reactive fashion.

Arm Slides with Reach

In a quadruped position with hands on a slider on the ground, have the athlete slide one arm along the ground extending it out in front of the body while falling forward. As in a traditional push-up exercise, use the other arm to assist in bracing and stopping the fall, preventing the chest from touching the ground. To add a level of difficulty, begin upright in the kneeling position and fall forward allowing the one arm to land, slide, and extend toward a target while the other arm assists in bracing and stopping the fall. Pop right back up into the upright and kneeling starting position or pop back up into a standing position.

INFIELDER- AND PITCHER-SPECIFIC DRILLS

Forehand and Backhand Lunge Pick-Ups

Elite baseball and softball players initially slow their hands, limit head movement, and visually track the ball deeper to allow themselves more time to decide and adjust their hand movement as the ball closes in. Incorporating upper-body reaching in forehand and backhand agility drills can help the athlete acquire the necessary skills that reinforce proper sequencing and timing in a game highly reliant on visual tracking and upper-body reaching movements.

Lunge Pick-Up

Traditional pick-up drills are performed by sliding laterally 2 or 3 times in both directions while fielding a ball on both ends.
- **Phase 1.** Initially perform this drill in the absence of catching a ball. Turn the body pivoting on one foot and lunge with a forehand reach, then return to the starting position. Then pivot and turn the body moving one foot across the body, lunge with a backhand reach, and then return to neutral. Once proper technique is acquired, speed up the execution of the drill by moving the feet and getting into and out of the lunge as quickly as possible.
- **Phase 2.** Pick three different locations on both sides and alter the landing zone of each step (8, 9, 10 o'clock to the left and 2, 3, 4 o'clock to the right). Speed up the movement as long as accuracy and control are maintained.

- **Phase 3.** Instead of pivoting from the starting position, quickly switch the feet while hopping and turning the body simultaneously. Drop into the lunged position and reach with the glove hand and touch the ground.
- **Phase 4.** The athlete should react to a ball hit by the coach. The athlete must decide either to use the forehand or the backhand lunge to reach to field the ball.

Foot Fire Switches

Traditional foot fire drills are preplanned agility drills that act as a high-frequency plyometric to improve ground contact time and foot quickness. The foot fire switch drill adds a temporal component and becomes more baseball- and softball-specific by incorporating additional tasks often used in the game while catching, exchanging, and throwing a ball, as in turning a double play.

Foot Fire Switch

Begin by gazing ahead with the hands in a receiving position while chopping the feet in place for 3 to 5 seconds. On a *go* command, the athlete reacts quickly, turns the body 90 degrees, switches the feet to a throwing stance (perpendicular to the original foot placement), and initiates a crow hop. For the right-handed thrower, the right foot lands on the ground first, hopping into position directly underneath the body while the left foot swings slightly outside of shoulder-width, landing immediately after the right foot. At this point, the athlete's body weight should be primarily distributed on the right foot underneath the body. Repeat the drill for the desired amount of repetitions. For more specificity, add a glove to the drill and react to a thrown ball instead of a verbal *go* command, allowing the athlete to track and successfully exchange the ball to the throwing hand.

OUTFIELDER-SPECIFIC DRILLS

Zigzags

These drills mimic going back toward a fly ball overhead at a slight angle. Disassociating the hips and shoulders allows the athlete to turn the hips toward the direction of the run while keeping the line of sight on the ball. Ultimately the goal is to create an unplanned, variable environment.

Zigzag Over-the-Shoulder

Begin by running forward to each cone by rotating the hips toward the next cone. At each cone, plant and push off using one foot to change direction without coming to a complete stop. Keep the head and shoulders facing forward while the hips rotate to allow the athlete to run forward.

Zigzag with a Catch

The coach stands at the starting point and after 2 to 4 cuts are made throws a ball into the air and the athlete tracks it down to make the catch. For an added reactive component, the coach can also point in which direction the athlete needs to turn before throwing the ball into the air.

Y Drills

These drills provide variations in an environment that often involves a quick decision, body control, and one swift cut while in pursuit of the ball.

Y Forward Approach

Starting at the top of the *Y* formation, either on the left or the right side, sprint to the middle cone and make an abrupt cut toward the bottom cone. On approach to the bottom cone sweep the ground with either a forehand or a backhand and crow hop through the cone to simulate fielding a ground ball and exchanging it to throw.

Y Backward Approach

Starting at the bottom of the *Y* formation in a neutral position facing forward, turn either to the left or the right and sprint to the middle cone. Then make an abrupt cut to the top of the *Y* position, either to the left or to the right. In phase 1 of this drill, the cut at the middle cone should be performed in the same direction as the initial turn. In phase 2 of the drill, the cut at the middle cone can be made going in the opposite direction of the middle cone. To add a level of difficulty, the coach can point to the direction of the initial turn and then throw a ball into the air so that the athlete has to make a cut at the middle cone and pursue a ball over the shoulder.

CATCHER-SPECIFIC DRILLS

Catcher's Pop-Up Agility

The catcher's pop-up drill can begin with the catcher envisioning the ball has already been blocked in the dirt.

The catcher begins in a kneeling position with the head down and the hands tucked into the body just above the ground. Standing in front of the catcher, the coach or a teammate tosses a ball in close vicinity to the catcher so the athlete can look up and still see where the ball contacts the ground. The catcher listens for the ball to hit the ground and immediately reacts, pops up quickly onto two feet, and retrieves the ball as quickly as possible. In a more advanced version of the drill, the catcher will need shin guards. The catcher starts in the crouch position and waits for the coach or a teammate to point in either to the right or to the left. Reacting to the point, the catcher moves in the corresponding direction and drops to the knees. After pointing, the coach or teammate drops a ball in close vicinity to the catcher. The catcher then immediately pops back up onto two feet and retrieves the ball.

Catcher's Bunt Agility

The catcher's bunt agility drill is a variable drill aimed to improve a catcher's response and movement time when moving from the crouch position to fielding a bunt.

The catcher starts in a crouch position and waits for the coach or a teammate, standing behind the catcher, to toss a ball out in front of the catcher so that it rolls a short distance away (between the baselines). While looking straight ahead, the catcher remains alert and uses vision and auditory cues to locate the ball and retrieve it as quickly as possible. To add a level of difficulty after tossing the ball, the coach can yell out a base for the catcher to throw to after fielding the ball.

BASE RUNNING-SPECIFIC DRILLS

Zigzag Weaving Drills

Zigzag weaving offers a setting for athletes to improve body control while running the bases. Lateral acceleration and deceleration technique is explored here, and since distance determines velocity in short explosive shuttling, each COD should become more difficult as the distance of the run increases. To add a temporal component, the coach can remove the cones and instead point or yell *switch* to initiate each subsequent change in direction.

Snake Weave (Inside Foot Cut)

In this variation, the athlete will run forward and turn tightly around the cones in an arc-like fashion rather than making abrupt, sharp-angled cuts. Allow the inside foot to plant just outside each cone. The larger the arc the easier it will be to execute this specific weave. Making this turn on flat ground is difficult and will require the athlete to explore different speeds to steer around each cone without slowing down.

Pickle

Five cones are set up 5 yards (4.6 m) apart in a straight line. To begin, the torso should be facing forward while the hips rotate to allow the athlete to run backwards by facing sideways, similar to when stealing a base, then turn and sprint to the right from cone 1 to cone 2. The athlete then turns to the left and sprints back to cone 1. In similar fashion and without stopping, the athlete sprints back and forth between cone 1 and 3, and back to cone 1 again. Next, the athlete sprints from cone 1 to cone 4, returning again to cone 1 and finally to cone 5 and back to cone 1 to complete the drill.

▶ *BASKETBALL*

Javair Gillett

Basketball players must be able to coordinate movement in various directions at a high rate of speed, with abrupt stops and starts, often with a basketball in hand. Additionally, they must be able to execute all of these skills while under the pressure of an offender or a defender. In order to be successful, it is imperative that the athlete has quick and accurate decision-making skills and good peripheral awareness.

PROGRAM DESIGN

An effective basketball-specific agility program will include purposeful exercises to adapt to these perceptual, cognitive, motor, and physical demands. For transfer to the court, agility drills need to progress to full-speed basketball-specific actions in an unplanned, variable environment.

Basketball can be broken down into brief segments of acceleration, deceleration, and multidirectional cutting activities. The length of a modern basketball game will vary based on level of play but will typically last 40 to 48 minutes, split evenly into quarters and halves with each possession lasting a maximum of 24 to 30 seconds (2). It has been noted that a basketball player may perform more than a thousand changes of movement during a game, with athletes changing positions about every 2 seconds throughout the duration of a game (1, 2). Stoppage times will vary in lengths and occur as a result of turnovers, timeouts, fouls, and so forth. Although a regulation basketball court is 94 feet (28.7 m) long, an athlete will rarely, if ever, travel that full length in a straight line. Furthermore, movement speeds and efforts will vary within each possession. For elite-level high school athletes, high-intensity activities only make up 14 to 18% of all movements, with significant drops in intensity occurring over the course of a game (2). Also, high-intensity movement requirements are significantly higher for guards as compared to centers due to the requirements of their position (2). Based on this evidence it seems logical that basketball-specific agility drills should last 5 to 30 seconds. Within these time periods, agility drills at various distances and intensities should be used to better replicate the stop-and-go nature of the sport and manage fatigue.

An agility training session can also be designed to simulate the segmentation of a basketball game. Total resting time makes up approximately 30% of the activity in a basketball game (2). As a result, work-to-rest ratios can vary between 1:1 for highly intense efforts of longer duration (30 seconds) and 1:20 for highly intense efforts of shorter duration (5 seconds). Furthermore, it is suggested that basketball-specific agility training sessions use contrasting rest periods (e.g., stand, walk, jog, and run) to better mimic the demands of the game.

The total volume of agility training should be position-specific and based on the total minutes an athlete will be required to play in a game. Teixeira and colleagues (4) found that a shuttle run involving three changes of direction were superior in improving anaerobic qualities to a shuttle run only using one COD.

The frequency of agility training sessions per week should also vary depending on the time of year, the volume of basketball practice, and live game activity. Also, Teixeira and colleagues (4) found that two training sessions per week of performing various shuttle runs is sufficient to show significant improvements in performance. For adaptations to occur, a higher number of training sessions should take place during the off-season, when the volume of practice and live game play is lower. Two agility sessions per week seems sufficient as it is assumed that a well-balanced program will also include strength and power training along with other forms of conditioning throughout the week. Emphasis should be placed on the athlete's position and the specific movements required on the court. These agility drills should also have an offensive or a defensive focus. In most cases, offensive-minded drills should incorporate a basketball. Movements for centers and forwards differ greatly from those of guards and therefore might include more rebounding and other drills closer to the rim staying around the lane. On the other hand, drills for guards may include more dribbling over greater distances while moving across the court and around the perimeter.

Lane Agility

The focus in the initial phases of training might be on the acquisition of proper movement mechanics and transitions in a preplanned setting. In basketball, the most basic movements on the court will be linear accelerations and decelerations, backpedaling, and lateral sliding. The lane agility drill is performed in the same pattern as the four corners drill described in chapter 6 (see page 125), but instead of creating a box, the setup is around the paint (the rectangular area on the court contained within the key that encompasses the middle of the floor underneath the basket). It also differs from the four corners drill in that upon reaching the last cone the athlete will repeat the pattern going the opposite direction (thereby going around the paint twice).

Half-Moon

The half-moon drill is a multidirectional agility drill that works well for movement technique and preplanned COD. It also offers many variations and can be easily modified to include different transitions and movement (shuffling, crossover step, 90-180-degree turns, and so on). In this example, cones are set 5 yards (4.6 m) apart and the athlete starts between the cones set at 3 o'clock and 9 o'clock. At the starting point, the athlete is always facing the cone at 12 o'clock. The athlete runs forward to the cone at 12 o'clock. When the athlete reaches the cone, the right foot should be slightly in front of the left foot. The athlete touches the cone with the right hand and then backpedals to the starting point. The athlete will then repeat this action, in a clockwise manner (thus, after reaching the cone at 3 o'clock, the next cone to run to is the cone at 9 o'clock), sprinting to each cone and then backpedaling to the starting position.

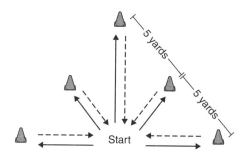

Star Closeout

The star closeout drill is a preplanned, basketball-specific agility drill useful when working on proper defensive closeout technique while moving in multiple directions. The proper approach in a closeout drill is for the athlete to widen the stance and drop the hips to lower the base of support very quickly. The athlete will also take a few short, choppy steps to decelerate before coming to a complete stop. In this drill, the athlete always returns to the starting point, which is called the *nail*. Five cones are set up in a star formation 5 to 10 yards (4.6-9.1 m) apart, with the nail directly in the middle of the star. If the drill is not performed on a basketball court, the cone at 12 o'clock will represent the top of the key. Starting at the nail, the athlete runs to the cone at 12 o'clock and comes to a stop with proper closeout form. In this first approach, when the athlete comes to a complete stop the right foot should be slightly in front of the left foot and the right hand should reach high in front of the body. This stance at a complete stop would mimic the defender preventing the offensive player from moving left. The athlete then naturally turns and quickly runs back to the starting position facing forward. Next, the athlete runs to the same cone at 12 o'clock but comes to a complete stop with the left foot slightly in front of the right foot and the left arm outstretched high in front of the body. Again, the athlete naturally turns and quickly runs back to the nail. The athlete then runs to the cone at 2 o'clock and comes to a complete stop with the left foot slightly in front of the right foot and returns to the nail. The athlete then runs to the cone at 10 o'clock and comes to a complete stop with the right foot slightly in front of the left foot and returns to the nail. Still facing 12 o'clock, the athlete turns and runs to the cone at 5 o'clock and comes to a complete stop with the left foot slightly in front of the right foot and returns to the nail. Finally, the athlete turns and runs to the cone at 7 o'clock and comes to a complete stop with the right foot slightly in front of the left foot and returns to the nail.

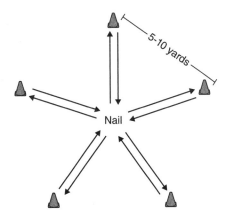

L Nail

The *L* nail drill is another preplanned, basketball-specific agility drill useful on both the offensive and defensive ends of the court. In this drill, cones are set up in an *L* shape; the distance can vary depending on the desired training effect. In this example, cones will be set 5 to 6 yards (4.6-5.5 m) apart and the drill will be explained emphasizing movement in the right direction (follow the same protocol to the left). Cone 1 will be the starting point, set at the free throw line, cone 2 will be placed just above the top of the key or 3-point line, and cone 3 will be placed to the right of cone 2. Multiple movement progressions will be used in this drill setup. An advanced variation will improve basketball-specific footwork by setting screens at cone 2 and exploring the use of drop steps. Another advanced variation is to combine the four phases into one single drill, giving it a more physiological and mechanical conditioning training effect.

- **Phase 1.** The athlete sprints from cone 1 to cone 2, comes to a stop with the right foot slightly in front of the left foot, and then backpedal sprints to cone 1.

- **Phase 2.** The athlete sprints from cone 1 to cone 2, slides to the right to cone 3, sprints back to cone 2, and then backpedal sprints to cone 1.

- **Phase 3.** The athlete sprints from cone 1 to cone 2, slides to the right to cone 3, drop steps (turning inward), and sprints to cone 1.

- **Phase 4.** The athlete sprints from cone 1 to cone 2, drop steps (turning inward) and slides to cone 3, sprints back to cone 2, and then drop steps (turning inward) to sprint back to cone 1.

V Cut

The *V* cut drill is a preplanned, basketball-specific agility drill that emphasizes the pick-and-roll and dive actions associated on the offensive end of the court and is most common for front court players (i.e., centers and forwards) who most often perform these actions. In this drill, cones are set up in a *V* shape and the distance can vary depending on the desired training effect. In this example, cones will be set 5 to 6 yards (4.6-5.5 m) apart and the drill will be explained emphasizing movement in the right direction (follow the same protocol to the left). Set cone 1 at the left wing, cone 2 at the top of the key or three-point line, and cone 3 under the basket. The athlete sprints from cone 1 to cone 2 and cuts off the left leg straight to cone 3. Then the athlete sprints back to cone 2, plants on the left leg, and pivots, turning inward toward the basket, and then slides back to cone 1. To vary the drill, add a screen at cone 2 and perform different rolling patterns.

Linear Cone Agility

The linear cone agility drill is a preplanned drill that creates practice repetition and offers many different variations in one setup. Two straight lines of cones are set up the length of the court in a straight line toward the basket, creating a lane boundary to stay within. Cone 1 is on the baseline, cones 2 and 3 are aligned with the free throw line, cones 4 and 5 are on the half-court line, cones 6 and 7 are aligned with the far free throw line, and cone 8 is on the far baseline.

The width of the lane can vary but it should be narrow and focus on improving the athlete's initial 1-2-3 step agility. The athlete starts at one end of the court on either the left or the right line of the cones. For this example, the athlete will start at cone 1 on the left side at one end of the court and on the other end of the court cone 1 will be on the right side. Up-the-court movements will be practiced moving to the right whereas coming back down-the-court movements will be practiced moving left.

- **Linear cone drill station 1.** *Slide step (front and hedge)*: The athlete sprints forward and, at cone 2, explosively slides laterally to the right to cone 3, runs back to cone 2, and then sprints up to cone 4 to repeat the same movement again at each cone up the court. On the way back down the court, all movements will focus on moving laterally to the right. In this drill, the athlete should visualize hedging laterally to stay in front of a defender.

- **Linear cone drill station 2.** *Crossover step (catch up)*: The athlete sprints forward and, at cone 2, explosively rotates the hips and sprints to cone 3, laterally slides back to cone 2, and then sprints to cone 4 to repeat the same movement again at each cone up the court. On the way back down the court, all movements will focus on moving laterally to the right. In this drill, the athlete should visualize an attempt to catch up to an offender who has already passed by.

- **Linear cone drill station 3.** *Figure eight (through screen)*: The athlete sprints forward and, at cone 2, explosively rotates the hips and sprints to cone 3, and then sprints around that cone making a very tight turn. The athlete then sprints back to cone 2 and turns up to cone 4 to repeat the same figure-eight movement at each cone up the court. On the way back down the court, all movements will focus on moving laterally to the right. In this drill, the athlete should visualize moving around a screening offender in an attempt to stay with the person being guarded.

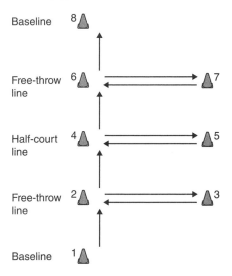

Tennis Ball Drops with a Dribble

Elite point guards are typically known for their agility, excellent dribbling and passing skills, and a low turnover rate. At some point in training, basketball-specific agility drills must include a basketball and have game-speed perceptual and cognitive components for successful transfer to occur. Along with accuracy and time to completion, practice drills should improve anticipatory skills and minimize response time. Tennis ball drops is a common drill that is used by athletes in a variety of sports because it offers an unplanned, variable component to agility. Tennis ball drops with a dribble becomes even more basketball-specific. In this drill, a coach tosses a tennis ball into the air and the athlete tries to catch the tennis ball after one bounce while dribbling a basketball. Once the ball is caught, the athlete has to toss the ball back to the coach accurately and prepare for another ball to be tossed. Creating a more fixed environment (e.g., catching only with the right hand) can change the difficulty of the drill.

Diamond Scoring

The diamond scoring drill is a variable basketball-specific drill aimed to improve agility while dribbling and shooting accurately. Cones are set up in a diamond shape with cone 1 at the top of the key or three-point line. Cones 2 and 3 are placed around each elbow along the free throw line. Cone 4 is placed just in front of the rim under the basket (restricted area arc). In this drill, the athlete is instructed to openly choose how to control the dribble of the ball as the entire task is completed.

The athlete starts at the top of the key or three-point line and begins dribbling. The first task is to make one lateral or backward move (creating space from the defender), pick up the ball, and shoot. The coach or teammate immediately returns the ball to the athlete, who dribbles to cone 2 and then takes another quick lateral or backward step, picks up the ball, and shoots. The athlete then proceeds with a dribble to cone 3 and takes an off-balance shot. Finally, the athlete dribbles to cone 4 and chooses to go either left or right to finish with a layup. In this drill, the only knowns are the target and the spots at which each shot will occur. Without a defender, specific ball handling and shooting styles can be controlled. Against a defender the athlete will have to successfully navigate the way to each spot in an ever-changing environment.

▶ *COMBAT SPORTS*

Loren Landow

A combat athlete can be defined as an individual who participates in a fighting sport, such as mixed martial arts, tae kwon do, or boxing. Although the importance of agility training for field and court sports is clear, the benefit of including agility drills in the training program for a combat athlete may not seem to be significant. In reality, though, there is great value in applying agility-based exercises to combat sports, because good footwork and the ability to change direction quickly to avoid or set up an attack on an opponent over short distances is critical (2).

When training the combat athlete, it is important to consider the difference between footwork training and agility training. In this context, *footwork training* refers to exercises that improve pure foot speed and coordination (i.e., training ladder, dot drills, line drills), while *agility training* encompasses drills that focus on the athlete's ability to maneuver around obstacles. Both of these types of training may be useful in developing balance, awareness, and general reaction skills (2). There are multiple ways to approach these training areas. Sport-specific drills can be used to enhance skills that pertain to the chosen discipline, whereas general skill development provides a good foundation of athleticism that may augment sport-specific abilities. Put simply, as combat athletes become more skilled at body control and awareness, they will most likely become more well-rounded fighters.

PROGRAM DESIGN

The drills featured in the following section are just a few options that can be used to develop a combat athlete's athletic ability. Both the coach and the athlete should keep in mind that the goal with this type of training is not to pursue an endless variety of drills; rather, improvements are stronger when the number of different exercises is limited and each drill is mastered. They must consider how each drill fits into the overall development plan. Creativity is encouraged but coaches should avoid randomly using drills without having a clear purpose for their selection. Instead, coaches should make sure that athletes complete each repetition using good athletic positions (as dictated by their sport), with appropriate weight distribution and good body control. The speed of each drill may be increased as the athlete progresses, but not to the point of sacrificing technique. Ultimately, it is important to focus on understanding how the various movement and resistance training modalities can properly fit into the overall goal of optimizing performance in combat sports.

FOOTWORK DRILLS

Rhythm and timing are critical components of footwork and are therefore vital to movement mastery. These temporal patterns can be trained via relatively simple drills, such as jumping rope, line hops, and agility ladders. There are additional benefits to footwork training, specifically the ability for athletes to potentially discover any side dominance or imbalance and to develop additional confidence in a leg that may currently be lacking. Footwork drills may also be helpful in rehabilitating lower-limb injuries and restoring coordination in the injured limb (1).

In and Out

The athlete begins in an athletic position with knees flexed and feet slightly narrower than hip-width. A partner or coach will initiate a command to move the feet in and out from outside the shoulders to inside the hips as quickly as possible while maintaining hip level in the athletic position. Time the drill for 8 to 10 seconds, followed by a 30-second rest period. Repeat for 6 to 8 repetitions.

Hip Rotation

The athlete starts at one end of the agility ladder, facing the first square from the side in an athletic position with the feet at hip-width. He or she rotates the hips 45 degrees back and forth to alternately move each foot inside the square with the other foot outside the square, and so on down the length of the ladder. Time the drill for 8 to 10 seconds with 30 seconds of rest and perform 3 to 6 repetitions.

Line Hop

The athlete starts in a position with the feet spaced narrowly and knees slightly flexed. He or she hops back and forth over the line with both feet as quickly as possible. Perform for 8 to 10 seconds with a 30-second rest interval for 3 to 6 repetitions.

Medicine Ball Toe Touch

The athlete stands (with a slight flex in the knees) in front of a medicine ball that is placed on the ground. He or she raises one foot and taps the top of the medicine ball while the other foot remains on the ground, and then immediately switches the feet to touch the other foot on top of the ball. The athlete quickly alternates feet to touch the top of the ball while rotating around it either clockwise or counterclockwise. As drill proficiency improves, the coach or partner may command the athlete to change directions during rotation. Complete the drill for 8 to 10 seconds, resting for 30 seconds between efforts for 3 to 6 repetitions.

AGILITY DRILLS

In order to be agile, combat athletes must be able to blend footwork and speed skills. Agility development requires putting these components together in order to maneuver around obstacles with skill and efficiency. Combat sports are also highly dependent on reaction ability. For this reason, agility is a key factor in the athlete's overall development. These drills may require some time to learn, but as the athlete acquires the proper motor skills for each task, drill complexity may be manipulated for additional conditioning or improved reactiveness.

Partner Reactive Shuffle

A pair of athletes begin by facing each other in an athletic position with their knees slightly flexed and feet outside the hips. One partner will attempt to mirror the other as he or she shuffles from side to side, following the shuffle pattern as closely as possible. The drill requires the athletes to maintain a proper low athletic position in order to achieve optimal balance and COD. Time the drill at a high intensity for 8 to 10 seconds with 30 seconds of rest between each round for 3 to 6 repetitions, switching leader and mirror roles each time.

Lateral Hurdle Run

Arrange four cones or low hurdles in a line, spaced about 18 inches (0.5 m) apart. The athlete stands at one end of the line facing out to the side and then moves laterally down and back over each cone or hurdle with a knee punch action. Move back and forth down the line continuously for 10 seconds, then rest for 30 seconds. Repeat the drill 4 to 6 times, facing alternate directions for each repetition.

Lateral Speed Shuffle

Arrange seven cones in a line, spaced about 2 to 3 feet (0.6-0.9 m) apart. The athlete starts at one end of the line in an athletic position and then quickly shuffles back and forth to weave between the cones, attacking around each cone laterally while moving slightly forward until reaching the end of the line. Maintain a good wide base with the feet and face the same direction throughout the drill. The athlete must alternate the starting side for 4 to 6 repetitions, with 30 seconds of rest between efforts.

▶ CRICKET

Simon Feros

Cricket is a bat-and-ball game that comprises two teams of eleven players, played on a grass oval with a rectangular pitch at its center. Each team bats and bowls for one or two innings (depending on game format). The objective of the batting team is to score as many runs as possible, while the goal of the bowling and fielding team is to dismiss each batter and reduce the number of runs scored. The team that wins is the one that has scored the most runs.

In cricket, batters react to a delivery from the bowler (pace or spin). The speed of the delivery influences the reaction and movement times available for the batter to decide whether to hit the ball or not, and to make the necessary postural adjustments in response to this decision (e.g., feet, trunk, head, and arms). A delivery with a late change in trajectory, either via a swing or a deviation from the cricket pitch, often requires a quick adjustment from the batter to successfully play a defensive or attacking stroke.

To successfully score a run (or multiple runs) from a delivery, the batter who struck the ball will run to the bowling end of the cricket pitch, while their batting partner will run to the batting end of the cricket pitch. This represents a 17.7-meter (58 ft) run and can involve a 180-degree turn if another run is to be performed. The intensity of the run depends on the game context and the trajectory and speed of the ball in relation to the nearest fielders. A maximal intensity run typically occurs when the batters perceive urgency to get to the other end to prevent themselves from being run out by the fielding team. This requires quick acceleration and sometimes a quick deceleration and a 180-degree turn (if another run is to be performed). Indeed, speed into and out of the 180-degree turn is critical for a quick transition between runs (2) and run-making ability (1).

The fielding team comprises specialist fielding positions, all with various reactive and skill requirements. Arguably the most specialized position is the wicketkeeper, who is responsible for receiving the ball that has passed the batter, and for running to the batter's end of the pitch to possibly affect a run out from a return throw from another fielder. A wicketkeeper predominantly starts in a semi-crouched position when standing back to a pace bowler but is in a deep squat position up to the cricket stumps when a spin bowler is operating. From these standing positions, wicketkeepers make an adjustment to foot position (often lateral) to receive the ball optimally. Sometimes a quick adjustment is required, where reaction ability is paramount. An example is when the batter edges the delivery, causing a quick deflection from the bat in a different trajectory.

Generally speaking, the closer the fielder is positioned to cricket pitch, the greater the reactivity component required to successfully catch or stop the ball. If the ball happens to pass the infielder, then usually this fielder performs a rapid turn (usually 180 degrees, but it can vary) to chase the ball. In some cases, the fielder also has to sprint 5 to 50 meters (16.4-164 ft) to chase the ball, pick up the ball, and throw to either end of the cricket pitch. This means that fielders require not only reactivity but also a quick COD, acceleration speed, maximum speed, and deceleration ability to successfully minimize the number of runs scored, or to cause a run out.

Bowling a cricket ball can be thought of as a closed-skill motion. However, bowlers take the role as fielders as soon as the ball has been released from the hand. A batter can strike the ball toward the bowler requiring a quick reaction and adjustment of body position to catch or stop the ball. Pace bowlers typically find this task more difficult than spin bowlers, as at the time when the ball is struck by the batter, the pace bowler is still in the follow-through phase. Nevertheless, both pace and spin bowlers require a fast deceleration and a quick application of force to change body direction, and to ultimately meet the anticipated trajectory of the oncoming delivery.

PROGRAM DESIGN

As a large variety of movement patterns exist across a cricket match (and respective game formats), and that there are different movement requirements for specialist positions, the ability to develop cricket-specific drills targeting reactivity, quickness, agility, and COD ability can certainly appear overwhelming to the coach. However, by analyzing the targeted movements of batters, bowlers, and fielders (including wicketkeepers), coaches can classify cricket movements and put them into a basic structure for building an effective program to develop reactivity, quickness, agility, and COD ability.

In order to break down cricket movements, it is useful to determine what batters, bowlers, and fielders are trying to achieve, and the game-like situations they will encounter. Coaches can effectively carry this type of analysis using target classifications. At any given time, cricketers are likely attempting either to start a movement or to change the direction of movement (i.e., initiation movement), trying to move with maximal acceleration or maximal velocity (i.e., actualization movement), or waiting in transition to react to a cricket-specific stimulus (i.e., transition movement). Tables 9.2, 9.3, and 9.4 identify key movements within each movement classification for batters, bowlers, and fielders (respectively). The information provided can help coaches perform a qualitative assessment of each movement pattern to identify the cricketers' strengths and weaknesses. Where deficiencies are

Table 9.2 Movement Patterns in Cricket Batters

Movement type	Movement aim	Target movement pattern
Initiation	Lift back or front foot off the ground prior to ball release and place it elsewhere with body weight on the balls of the feet	Start in a quarter-squat position, follow with a brief transition to a single-leg squat position, and then return to a quarter-squat position
	Move front foot, back foot, or both, after ball release to ensure that the head (or majority of body weight) is near the anticipated striking point	Forward/backward/diagonal quarter-lunge position (sometimes a crossover step or side shuffle is also performed)
	Change direction (180-degree turn)	Low and wide plant step with contralateral trunk flexion and rotation to transition to acceleration
Transition	Static wait for the ball to be released	Weight evenly distributed on both feet in a quarter-squat position
	Static wait to decide on a run	Weight slightly on the front foot with the cricket bat either in one hand or in two hands
	Dynamic transition (side shuffling)	Side shuffle in a quarter-squat position
	Decelerate to a COD	Deceleration pattern added with specific COD mechanics
Actualization	Accelerate	Acceleration movement patterns

Table 9.3 Movement Patterns in Cricket Bowlers

Movement type	Movement aim	Target movement pattern
Initiation	Change direction (linear or lateral) in response to incoming ball struck by the batter	Cut step or plant step in any direction
Transition	Dynamic wait for ball strike	Faster and more forceful deceleration in bowling follow-through is required to be better positioned to react and adjust to ball strike
Actualization	Accelerate	Acceleration movement patterns (linear or curvilinear)

Table 9.4 Movement Patterns in Cricket Fielders

Movement type	Movement aim	Target movement pattern
Initiation	Start to the front	Acceleration pattern
	Start to the side	Cross step
	Start to the rear	Drop step
	Change direction (linear or lateral) in response to incoming ball struck by the batter	Cut step or plant step in any direction
Transition	Dynamic wait for ball strike	Walking toward the batter as the bowler is running in to bowl (as the ball is about to be struck, the fielder gets in a wide quarter-squat position to enable a quick push from either foot in any direction)
	Moving to the side	Side shuffle
	Moving to the rear	Backpedal
	Deceleration into COD	Deceleration pattern added with specific COD mechanics
Actualization	Accelerate	Acceleration movement patterns (linear or curvilinear)
	Move to top speed	Maximum speed pattern

seen in a pattern, cricketers can do specific drills to bring these particular movements to a minimum standard. However, strong patterns need to be reinforced and practiced because they can be a strength that the cricketer brings to the team. From this analysis, coaches can develop each movement pattern along the following continuum, which moves from basic, *closed drills* (i.e., drills in which the movement is preplanned and the athlete is free to concentrate solely on the movement pattern at hand) to random sport-specific movements that display high levels of reactivity, quickness, agility, and COD. With this structure, coaches can develop cricket-specific agility for each movement pattern. It is important to keep in mind that the requirements of the exercise and the ability of the cricketer will influence the intensity and frequency of the movement patterns trained.

The next section describes drills for developing reactivity, quickness, COD, and agility for batters, bowlers, and fielders. All of the drills should be preceded by a dynamic warm-up and can be conducted during skills training and in the warm-up prior to the game. Performing the drills on short-cut grass, in cricket-specific attire (e.g., spiked shoes, batting gear) is important for performance and injury prevention (e.g., fielder sliding techniques). The drills can be used to create an agility training session for cricket players. Because everyone is expected to bat and field during a game, at least two drills from batting and two from fielding should be performed in any given training session. Specialist bowlers are encouraged to complete the two bowling-specific drills first, followed by the batting and fielding drills with the rest of the group. To develop reactivity, quickness, COD, and agility, these drills should be performed three days a week in the off-season and two to three days a week in preseason. During the cricket season, reactivity, quickness, COD, and agility should be maintained by performing these drills one or two days a week. A 1:3 work-to-rest ratio should be used to ensure that proper technique can be maintained and to ward off the negative effects of fatigue when performing drills.

BATTING-SPECIFIC DRILLS

Drop and Run

This drill requires batters to bunt the ball to their feet and immediately accelerate for a quick run. Beginners can do this drill with a ball that is rolled to them along the ground. The next progression is to have the ball thrown to them at a slow to moderate speed. Advanced cricketers should try this drill against pace bowlers and to bunt the ball within a 5-meter (5.5 yd) radius to allow a run with the particular field setting.

React and Adjust

This drill requires the pace bowler to bowl the ball from 75% of the cricket pitch length. The batter is required to react to the trajectory of the delivery and make a quick adjustment in footwork and body position to decide to defend or attack the ball. Defensive movements include blocking the ball on the front or back feet or safely evading the ball.

Run a Three (Closed-Skill Version)

This drill involves the batter striking the ball in the net environment, and to run a three. This includes three 17.7-meter (19.4 yd) runs and two 180-degree turns with quick deceleration into the turn and quick acceleration out of the turn. The batter is encouraged to hold the bat in the preferred hand (rather than in both hands), and to turn to the stronger side, as this has been shown to result in a faster running between wickets (2).

Run a Three (Open-Skill Version)

This drill involves the batter striking the ball in a simulated game environment, and to run a three if appropriate to do so without being run out. Although turning to the stronger side at the end of each run will result in faster running between wickets (2), it is important for the batter to turn to the side to see the fielders so a quick decision can be made whether to take another run or not. Repeated practice at turning to the weaker side will eventually eliminate this weakness.

BOWLING-SPECIFIC DRILLS

Quick Deceleration

This drill simply involves the bowler following through over a shorter time and distance, and getting set in a quarter-squat position, ready to change direction if required. Spin bowlers will find this drill easier to do than pace bowlers. Caution is required for the pace bowlers, as decelerating too quickly may lead to injury. After the ball is released, the pace bowler typically runs through to about half the distance of their run-up. A 25- to 50% reduction in follow-through distance should suffice for pace bowlers (reduction depends on run-up speed at delivery).

Quick Deceleration and Catch

This drill involves the bowler doing the quick deceleration drill but now being required to catch a ball toward the end of the follow-through. This drill is excellent for improving reactivity and quickness. For novice cricketers, a coach can throw the ball slower, in a preplanned direction known to the bowler, and release the ball when the bowler has finished the follow-through. To make this drill more difficult, the ball can be thrown faster, farther away from the bowler, in a random direction, or earlier in the follow-through. Bowlers can train their backpedaling ability by catching a ball thrown overhead. To train the bowlers' ability to anticipate the ball being struck to them, they should bowl the ball to the batter and watch the batter's footwork and downswing of the bat. This means that the bowler is encouraged to keep the eyes on the batter even in the follow-through (where the trunk is often flexed, laterally flexed, and rotated to the side of the nonbowling arm).

FIELDING-SPECIFIC DRILLS

Deflect and Catch

This drill involves four or more cricketers (even number required), standing in a small circle arms-width apart from each other. Two balls are thrown underhand simultaneously by two athletes directly facing each other. The objective of the throw is to try to make the balls contact each other in midtrajectory. This will cause the balls to deflect and present an opportunity to be caught by anyone in the circle. The smaller the circle or the faster the throws, the greater the reactivity and quickness required. Note that this drill can result in finger injuries if performed with a cricket ball, so a tennis ball is advised. To make this drill more cricket-specific, an underhand throw can be made to the batter, where an attempt can be made to deflect the ball to an arc of fielders.

Jump, Turn, Land, and Throw

This drill involves the fielder picking the ball up and throwing it to the nonstriker's end of the cricket pitch. It simply comprises a pickup, jump, turn, and a landing that is side-on to the wickets at the nonstriker's end. Upon landing, the fielder should be in the early cocking phase of the throw so that the ball can be released quickly.

Split Step and Multidirectional COD
(Open-Skill Version)

This drill involves a simulated match, where the fielder walks in with the bowler toward the batter and performs a small jump just prior to striking the ball. Upon landing with both feet approximately shoulder-width apart and body weight evenly distributed, the fielder should rapidly change direction in response to the trajectory of the incoming ball. This could involve either a forward acceleration, a backpedal, a crossover step, a drop step, or a side shuffle.

Split Step and Multidirectional COD
(Closed-Skill Version)

This drill can be performed by having a coach throw the ball in a predetermined direction (e.g., in front, overhead, left or right), with a specific movement solution to practice in response (e.g., a crossover step) to particular ball trajectories.

▶ *FIELD HOCKEY*

Farzad Jalilvand

Field hockey is an intermittent sport that requires athletes to execute a wide variety of motor skills, such as acceleration, deceleration, and multiple CODs throughout a match (8, 9). A typical (i.e., high school or college) match consists of two 35-minute halves with a 5- to 10-minute break between the two. In contrast, elite-level international competitions are divided into four 15-minute quarters with 2-minute breaks after the first and third quarters and a 10-minute break at the half.

Success in the sport of field hockey depends on the ability to perform repeated agility tasks and acceleration efforts during a game (4, 5, 8, 10). According to observational research, a typical field hockey match consists of more than 500 CODs, with a new pattern employed about every 8 to 11 seconds (6). These efforts are coupled with multiple sprints lasting from 1.8 to 3.1 seconds, and generally up to 20 meters (21.9 yd) per bout (7). These repeat sprint efforts may occur as often as 6 or 7 times per minute (1) with approximately 20 to 60 sprints per game (7).

A few fundamental concepts should be considered before developing an agility and quickness training program for field hockey players. For instance, many spend a good majority of the game in a semi-crouched position while dribbling, defending, and contesting for the ball because of the short size of the field hockey stick. From a performance standpoint, transitioning from the semi-crouched position (athletic position) to sprinting or changing direction effectively requires mastering the basic movements such as the crossover step, open step, shuffling, and sprinting while using good body mechanics (2, 3). Furthermore, since the athletes are required to carry a hockey stick, velocity may be reduced compared to when an athlete is running without an implement (11). Therefore, it is important to use the implement as a progression when training to provide the greatest transfer of skill to the field and to practice.

PROGRAM DESIGN

In training for physical preparation, it is important to train movement patterns from the least complex to the most complex. This allows the coach to help athletes develop specific physical traits in a systematic and logical fashion. The specific training targets that use this hierarchy model include

1. developing the necessary qualities of COD speed, quickness, and agility to maneuver an open playing field and execute sport-specific tasks (i.e., receive, carry, distribute, or contest the ball),

2. develop first-step quickness to evade opponents and invade the opposing team's territory, and

3. develop the ability to read and react to specific situations, opponents, and teammates in practice scenarios and games.

This purposed hierarchy model for improving field hockey specific agility has three phases focused on specific training goals arranged in a systematic and progressive manner. Each of these phases represents a distinct training season and each phase is designed to enhance the next. Throughout these phases it is important to monitor the acute training variables (i.e., intensity, volume, and frequency) as training progresses from off-season through preseason and in-season. These variables also aid in tracking accumulated load (e.g., total sprint distance), which can help determine the athlete's levels of fatigue. Finally, when training for quickness and agility, quality of movement always overrules quantity and, therefore, should take precedence regardless of the training season. Table 9.5 provides sample training parameters specifically for agility, COD speed, and quickness for each season.

Off-Season

In the off-season, the priority is foundational work aimed at developing the basic subcomponents of agility and quickness. The intensity of training during this phase should be lower than during the phases to follow. During this phase a greater emphasis should be placed on volume and technique in order to develop good movement patterns. The following are the major training goals that should be emphasized during the off-season.

Table 9.5 Sample Season-Specific Agility and Quickness Training Guidelines for Field Hockey

Variable	Off-season		Preseason		In-season	
Intensity	Low to moderate		High		Maximal	
Volume	Accelerations of ≤500 meters (547 yd) of total distance	COD speed drills (5-25 repetitions per drill)*	Accelerations of ≤1,000 meters (1,094 yd) of total distance	COD speed and agility drills (≤25 repetitions per drill)*	**Variable accelerations	**Variable COD and agility drills
Frequency (per week)	2-3		2-3		1-2	
Work-to-rest ratio	1:12-1:20	1:4-1:20	1:12-1:20	1:4-1:20	Variable	

*COD speed distances should be within the context of accelerations.
**Depends upon athlete fatigue, space, and competition schedule.

1. **Improve braking ability via the use of deceleration drills.** These drills should be emphasized to improve the athlete's capacity to absorb ground reaction forces by using good body mechanics both with and without a hockey stick. Deceleration drills focus on stopping in both the athletic position and a staggered stance (e.g., right or left leg).

2. **Focus on movement quality and COD technique.** The athlete should be taught to maintain an athletic position while creating optimal length tension relationships between muscle groups to perform the next movement task. Good body mechanics should be emphasized when executing lower intensity preplanned lateral and cutting drills. Athletes should be taught how to apply force appropriately in multiple directions via the use of drills that emphasize transitional movements (e.g., lateral shuffles, angled cuts, chop steps).

3. **Incorporate acceleration drills that emphasize low and intermediate velocities.** Teaching athletes to use good acceleration mechanics when sprinting helps develop a solid foundation of movement skills to support more intense and complex movements as the athlete progresses.

Preseason

The target goals for preseason should build on the skills and abilities developed in the off-season. The preseason phase is characterized by higher intensities and more complex movement tasks when compared to the off-season. Additionally, the volume of training during this phase is slightly less than during the previous phase to offset the increase in intensity level. In addition to continuing to refine the skills developed in the off-season, the following are areas that should be considered when implementing an agility and quickness training program during the preseason.

1. **Emphasize acceleration across a wide range of velocities in conjunction with preplanned COD speed drills.** During this stage, emphasis should be placed on teaching the athlete to transition from deceleration to acceleration in multiple directions at the appropriate speed and intensity based on the scenario or situation presented.

2. **Incorporate COD speed drills with sharper cuts and smaller ankle, knee, and hip angles.** Smaller angles increase the intensity of most drills because of the potential for greater eccentric loading.

3. **Introduce open drills.** Incorporating basic perceptual and decision-making tasks that require elements of visual scanning, pattern recognition, auditory stimuli, and kinesthetic cues help athletes begin to learn how to apply new skills in a manner that is contextually specific to their sport.

In-Season

During the late preseason and into the in-season, higher-intensity drills performed as quickly as possible and similar to competition events should be incorporated. The following are considerations to help bridge the gap between training and actual game performance.

1. **Incorporate perceptual and decision-making skills into COD speed and agility drills.** Drills aimed at incorporating perceptual and decision-making skills that require the athlete to react and perform to either visual or auditory stimuli help prepare for competition.

2. **Perform bouts of maximal linear and multidirectional acceleration.** Minimizing the time between deceleration and acceleration should be emphasized in order to minimize the time between movements. Greater rest should be allowed when maximal linear and directional acceleration drills are performed, since they can be very fatiguing. Because it is important to perform these as quickly as possible, ample rest should be allowed between bouts to minimize the effects of fatigue.

The following drills focus on basic COD speed abilities that are appropriate to perform in the initial stages of the off-season and that can be progressed through each subsequent phase by using the modifications previously discussed.

Crossover to Accelerate

Place five cones 5 meters (5.5 yd) apart over a 20-meter (21.9 yd) distance. The athlete assumes an athletic position facing the first cone. The athlete will assume this position until the coach blows a whistle to initiate the drill. Once the whistle is blown, the athlete will rotate the hips, pivoting and pushing off the inside foot to accelerate 5 meters (5.5 yd). On reaching the line, the athlete needs to transition down to the athletic position facing the opposite direction from the starting position. The athlete will need to stick this position until a whistle is blown again. Repeat over the full distance or until an equal amount of repetitions have been made for each foot if a distance greater is used.

Linear Acceleration-Deceleration
(with or without Hockey Stick)

Place seven cones 10 meters (10.9 yd) apart over a 60-meter (65.6 yd) distance. The athlete assumes an athletic position or a two-point stance at the starting cone. The coach will initiate the drill by blowing a whistle. The athlete will accelerate for 10 meters (10.9 yd). On reaching the line, the athlete needs to decelerate across another 10 meters (10.9 yd)—to the 20-meter (21.9 yd) line—without stopping completely. Once the line is reached, the athlete will transition to acceleration as fast as possible. Repeat over the remaining 30 meters (32.8 yd). The deceleration zones can be made shorter to increase the complexity of the drill.

Pull-Back to Triple Threat

This drill is designed to introduce the athlete to visual scanning and anticipation. Specifically, it enforces getting the athlete into a triple-threat shooting, passing, and dribbling position with the ball in response to a defender's movement. One athlete dribbles forward against a defender who is backpedaling. While backpedaling, the defender sporadically attempts to stick tackle the offensive player. The offensive player must anticipate and react to the defensive maneuver and perform a pullback to get into the triple-threat position and attempt to go around the defender. The defender must then change direction and get into a defensive position. This drill is repeated over a distance specified by the coach.

FOOTBALL
(AMERICAN OR GRIDIRON)

Loren Landow

American football is a team sport that consists of two teams of 11 players. The primary goal of this sport is for the offense to advance the ball downfield into the other team's end zone by running or passing. The primary role of the defensive players is to halt this progression. The offense must advance at least 10 yards (9.1 m) in four downs of play or they lose possession of the ball, and the other team's offense is given an opportunity to score.

According to Gleason and colleagues (1), through the observation of practice and gameplay, it is evident that the agility-related demands of the game vary by position. For example, a quarterback must perform a wide range of movements ranging from quick, low-velocity pivots during a handoff, to positioning the feet to throw a pass, to quick multidirectional movements when scrambling to avoid a tackle. Offensive linemen must perform quick forward accelerations and fast reactive footwork to get into a position that will allow them to move a defensive lineman in the direction they wish to open a gap for their backfield (i.e., halfbacks, fullbacks, quarterbacks), to penetrate the line of scrimmage and gain yardage, or hold off the defensive players from interfering in a pass attempt. Skill players, such as receivers, often run relatively predetermined routes, and attempt to evade the defense in order to be in a good position to receive a pass, whereas a defensive linebacker provides extra pass protection, and may also serves as an extra pass rusher in a blitz.

PROGRAM DESIGN

Agility training for American football should emphasize a system for developing movement strategies. Teaching athletes how to transition from a frontal plane movement to a linear movement is a logical first step. This requires a transition—also known as a *bridge*—in the transverse plane. Transverse plane motions are, at their essence, a bridge into acceleration from COD. An example would be a linebacker who shuffles, decelerates, and then accelerates. The athlete is attempting to get back into proper acceleration mechanics, and the efficiency of transitioning from one movement to another will largely be determined by how well these movement patterns have been learned. In other words, the speed and efficiency of this transition are dependent on how well the neuromuscular system has been trained to execute a movement task so that it can be performed with good form and technique. This concept is also often referred to as *automaticity*. Regardless, the movement pattern the athlete chooses in order to change direction depends on the base of support relative to the center of mass. Foot position, whether narrow, wide, or somewhere between, determines weight distribution, which subsequently determines movement strategy.

To teach these movement transitions, a systems-based strategy for multidirectional training is recommended. This system should be based on locomotion in all planes of motion, and how they blend together in a situational manner. Multidirectional movement is highly contextual, and athletes must be taught the various circumstances in which to implement various skills. For example, a receiver might make a cut with perfect foot placement in the frontal plane, but with the center of mass drifting over the outside foot. The result is an off-balanced athlete. If, however, the athlete has been taught how to select the optimal movement based on effective weight distribution, joint alignment, and target location, there is a greater opportunity for success.

The process of teaching multidirectional movement skills often begins with a focus on mastering linear locomotion and deceleration first, since an athlete cannot learn to change direction into acceleration if he or she does not understand proper acceleration mechanics. Next, frontal plane motion is addressed. This includes movements such as shuffles and crossover run, and the ability to decelerate within the frontal plane. Finally, some attention should be shifted to the transverse plane bridging movements. Once these key movements in each plane are mastered, the athlete should be taught to blend these movements together to create seamless transitions between them.

Progressing Sagittal Locomotion and Deceleration

For acceleration drills, a coach should focus on helping the athlete understand how to hold posture with a slight forward lean and execute the *punch-drive piston* mechanics required to accelerate efficiently and effectively. This punch and drive action is characterized by punching or driving the knee forward and then driving the foot back and downward into the ground to create forward propulsion. Wall drills should be used early and often, followed by resisted marches, A-skips, resisted sprints, and finally short sprints without resistance. Common movement errors during acceleration drills typically stem from the athlete coming out of an accelerative position and getting too much heel lift on the rear leg, instead of punching the knee and toe forward while maintaining a dorsiflexed ankle position. This movement fault reduces the athlete's mechanical advantage from the knee and the hip based on the angle of the shank hitting the ground. An emphasis on posture can correct this fault over time and improve multidirectional movement.

When training deceleration, a simple low-speed forward and backward locomotion of 5 yards (4.6 m) involving continuous decelerations in both directions can be very effective. This progresses to a similar drill, where the athlete jogs out 5 yards (4.6 m) and adds a torque component into the deceleration, rotating 90 degrees to make a turn, then rotating back to the original position into a backpedal and subsequent backward deceleration. This movement creates a bridge between transverse and frontal plane movements. The athlete's feet should be flat when the athlete stops, and the shins should be parallel to each other with the majority of the weight distributed over the inside foot, rather similar to a hockey stop on ice skates.

These drills allow the athlete to learn proper acceleration and deceleration in the sagittal plane, while introducing the frontal and transverse work that is to come. Using such a sequence helps athletes solidify skills in a logical order without overloading them with complex tasks. From here, the coach can focus more on shuffles and crossover runs in the frontal plane, then add transverse plane *bridges* to acceleration.

Training Frontal Plane Movement and Transverse Bridging

Although the exact movements of a specific drill might not occur on the field, designing an athlete's training program to start with closed, frontal plane drills can create the accumulated stress needed to create an adaptation. The specific adaptation in this case is the development, or *neuromuscular grooving*, of ideal starting and stopping mechanics in the frontal plane.

An example of a drill to aid in the development of proper mechanics during transverse plane bridges is a shuffle of 5 yards (4.6 m) followed by a deceleration "hockey stop" stick and hold. The majority of the athlete's weight should be on the inside foot to transition more efficiently back to the opposite direction. The transition can occur in any plane (e.g., moving into a shuffle, crossover run, acceleration) but during the athlete's early stage of performing these drills, it is likely best to keep movement tasks simple.

From a shuffle and stick, the athlete can progress to a shuffle down and back with a stick at the end, and then ultimately to a reactive continuous COD shuffle. This same type of progression can also be used with a crossover run.

These frontal plane drills, along with the aforementioned sagittal plane drills, should be the foundational movements emphasized by coaches for American football. The various transverse plane bridging movements should only be added once acceleration and deceleration in the sagittal and frontal planes are mastered. From there, the coach's creativity is the only limitation in terms of how to construct environmental demands that challenge the athlete to solve movement problems with a difficulty level that matches individual athlete competence. Once a coach understands the general guidelines and framework of movement, he or she can use creativity to build a drill based on different positions.

Table 9.6 provides three sample training sessions for American football.

Table 9.6 Sample Agility and Quickness Training Sessions for American Football

Drill	Distance	Sets	Repetitions	Rest period
SESSION 1: FRONTAL AND TRANSVERSE PLANE DRILLS				
Shuffle and stick	5 yards (4.6 m)	4	4 per side	30 seconds
Shuffle right and stick	5 yards (4.6 m)	4	5 per side	30-45 seconds
Shuffle left and stick	5 yards (4.6 m)	4	5 per side	30-45 seconds
Carioca: small step with rotation	20 yards (18.3 m)	4	2 per side	45-60 seconds
Carioca: knee punch with rotation	20 yards (18.3 m)	4	2 per side	45-60 seconds
SESSION 2: FRONTAL PLANE REACTIVE DRILLS				
Lateral shuffle and stick	5-8 yards (4.6-7.3 m)	2	4 per side	60 seconds
Lateral shuffle reactive (start on first clap, decelerate and pause on second clap, etc.)	5-8 yards (4.6-7.3 m)	2	4 per side	90 seconds
Continuous lateral shuffle reactive (multiple claps; change direction and shuffle in opposite direction with each clap)	5-8 yards (4.6-7.3 m)	2 (10 seconds per set)	4 reps	45-60 seconds
Box drill		2	3 per side	2 minutes
SESSION 3: REACTIVE CHANGE OF DIRECTION DRILLS				
Sprint to shuffle	Sprint 10 yards (9.1 m) then shuffle 5 yards (4.6 m)	1	4	30-45 seconds
Partner mirror	Shuffle 5 yards (4.6 m) then sprint 10 yards (9.1 m)	2	4	60 seconds between reps; 3 minutes between sets
Reactive Y	5-10 yards (4.6-9.1 m) between cones	1	4	60-90 seconds

▶ ICE HOCKEY

Mark D. Stephenson

Ice hockey is an invasion sport, where one team is trying to invade another team's territory (8). Ice hockey is played on skates on ice for three 20-minute periods. The 60-minute game is played five-on-five in a confined space. Because the playing area of the ice is relatively small, agility becomes a critical skill (4).

A typical game is very dynamic and involves exposure to intermittent high-intensity activity, typically in 30-second shifts. Both high-velocity collisions and unpredicted COD are common (5). In addition to reacting to other players, athletes must also be able to react to the unpredictability of the puck. This demand for agility requires the athlete to be able not only to accelerate and decelerate repeatedly but also to change direction intermittently while remaining in motion (3, 5).

Since ice hockey is played on a different surface, training that takes place on a field is often referred to as *dry-land* or *off-ice* training. Implementing agility drills in the dry-land or off-ice setting first and then moving to on-ice training is a typical and proper progression. Drills are performed in this sequence to ensure that the movement techniques are refined and then transferred, based on the performance demands of the sport. On-ice agility drills are often reserved for in-season training because of the cost of ice time. Proper progression of agility drills involves starting with closed agility, ensuring proper body mechanics and tactical execution. Once the foundation of closed agility skills is established, progression to open agility can begin. After advancing to open agility, adding a cognitive component can increase the difficulty of the drill.

PROGRAM DESIGN

Reactive agility requires decision-making (9). Athletes are often required to assess the situation, process the information, decide what to do, then execute the appropriate action or actions. This process can be described simply as *perceive, process, and react*. Both the perceptual and decision-making components of agility are trainable and should be incorporated into agility training programs (6). Incorporating cognitive aspects into the training drills will help develop the ability to perceive, process, and react and perform agility movements in a game-specific context.

COGNITIVE AGILITY DRILLS

Both open and closed agility drills can become advanced drills by simply adding a cognitive aspect to the drill. Having the athlete perform a simple math calculation while performing an agility drill will increase the workload. If the coach makes the answer become a stimulus for another movement aspect of the drill, the workload increases further.

For example, prior to a drill, the coach informs the athlete that, while sprinting in a planned direction, he or she will be given a single-digit multiplication problem, and an odd number answer will require the athlete to move to the left and an even number answer requires the athlete to move to the right (figure 9.1).

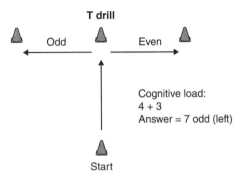

Figure 9.1 Using the *T* drill as a cognitive agility drill.

REACTIVE AGILITY DRILLS

Reactive agility incorporates some type of stimulus that results in a COD or a change of technical skill such as sprinting, lateral shuffling, or backpedaling. This can be auditory, such as a whistle or a voice command, or visual, such as a movement of a person (figure 9.2).

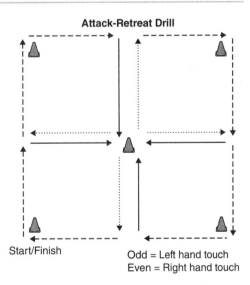

Figure 9.2 Using the attack-retreat drill as a reactive agility drill.

COACHING IMPLEMENTATION

The complexity of these drills is dependent on the athlete's skill level and tactical maturity. Incorporating decision-making within the agility drills should progress from simple to complex. If a coach observes that the athlete is repeatedly having difficulty properly executing the task, then the cognitive load should be simplified until he or she can demonstrate an ability to execute the task regularly. Also, it is in the best interest for the coach to have a scripted problem sheet. This will allow the drills to go on without delays or interruptions that may occur if the coach is trying to think of a new problem. Here's an example.

Simple Complexity

$4 + 4 = 8$

$6 \times 3 = 18$

Moderate Complexity

$3 + 6 - 4 = 5$

$8 \times 3 - 7 = 17$

High Complexity

How many siblings do you have?

How many paternal cousins, minus 3?

Table 9.7 provides two sample training sessions for ice hockey.

Table 9.7 Sample Off-Season Agility and Quickness Training Sessions for Ice Hockey

Drill	Repetitions	Rest period
DAY 1		
M Drill	8	1:5**
Hourglass drill	8	1:5**
Pro-agility*	10	1:5**
60-yard (54.9 m) shuttle	8	60 seconds
DAY 2		
X Drill	8	1:5**
Attack and retreat*	8	1:5**
T Drill*	5 per side	1:5**
150 yard (137.2 m) shuttle (25 yd [22.9 m] per shuttle)	6	60 seconds

*Modify this drill; instead of touching the hand to the line, a foot touch is used instead. For safety reasons, athletes should not touch the ice with the hand.
**Work-to-rest ratio

▶ *LACROSSE*

Mark D. Stephenson

Like ice hockey, lacrosse is considered to be an invasion sport, with one team trying to penetrate another team's domain (1). Although lacrosse is played on a relatively large open field (120 yards [109.7 m] × 60 yards [54.9 m]), the majority of the 60-minute game is played six-on-six in a space of 60 yards (54.9 m) × 60 yards (54.9 m). Because the field of play is so short, agility is a critical skill for the success of the lacrosse athlete (2).

Lacrosse is a game that involves exposure to intermittent high-intensity activity, collisions, and COD, and requires components of both open and reactive agility (2). In lacrosse, agility requires the athlete to accelerate and decelerate linearly on a repeated, almost continuous, basis in multiple directions at varying speeds and intensities (1).

It is beneficial for the athlete to perform agility drills while holding a lacrosse stick. Lacrosse requires catching and throwing and also ball control by cradling. Incorporating these skills during agility training may be useful after the athlete has demonstrated good form and technique without a stick. These simulated stick skills should be position-specific for the athlete. For example, during the attack and retreat drill, the defensive athlete should *spoke check* and attack, while midfielders should *hand check* at the same time as footwork is practiced. As the athletes become more efficient, have them cradle the ball while doing the drills and be sure they work on both strong- and weak-side cradling.

PROGRAM DESIGN

Many of the drills featured in chapters 6 and 7, both specific and general movement, can be easily applied to the game of lacrosse. The complexity of the training drills should be appropriate to the athlete's skill level and tactical maturity. The agility program should begin with learning basic agility patterns (e.g., acceleration, deceleration, cutting, running) before progressing to drills that are more lacrosse-specific.

Coaches can improve their athletes' reactive agility by incorporating cognitive aspects into the training drills to enhance their perceptual and decision-making skills (3) to better evaluate their circumstances, analyze the information, decide on what actions need to be deployed, and then perform the movements or actions to be successful. This can be accomplished in several ways.

- ▶ Add a reactive component by incorporating an auditory or visual stimulus that signifies a specific COD or a technical skill (e.g., sprinting, lateral shuffle, backpedal).

▶ Incorporate stick skills while performing the agility drill. These skills may include catching, throwing, and cradling. Incorporating ball handling skills with the stick increases the athletes' cognitive load because, in doing so, they must be attentive to the specific skills required to handle the stick, as well as executing proper movements within the drill. This is similar to what the athletes will be required to do in their sport.

▶ Have the athlete perform a simple math calculation while performing an agility drill to increase the cognitive workload and require the athlete to process the information quickly and respond accurately. For some examples, refer to the program design section for ice hockey (page 198).

Generally speaking, decision-making tasks within agility drills should progress from simple to more complex. Athletes should perform the drills without an implement (i.e., a stick) initially so they can focus on the proper footwork patterns and movements needed to execute the agility task. Once the athlete demonstrates basic movement proficiency in these drills, a lacrosse stick can be added. Finally, ball handling and catch and throw activities can be added for the most advanced level of both physical and mental agility for lacrosse. If a coach detects that an athlete cannot correctly execute a task, the cognitive load needs to be simplified or removed until the athlete can consistently perform the task correctly.

When designing an agility session, the coach should start the athletes with small-space drills and then progress to larger-space drills. The small-space drills require multiple quick CODs, which places a higher demand on the central nervous system than larger-space drills because of spatial and temporal constraints (3). It is also more effective to perform these drills while the central nervous system is not fatigued to ensure that technique is not significantly impaired.

Table 9.8 provides a sample training session for lacrosse.

Table 9.8 Sample Agility and Quickness Training Session for Lacrosse

DRILL	SETS	REPS	REST PERIOD
Modified T-test	1	4	60 seconds between reps; 3 minutes between sets
Pro-agility drill	2	2 per side	60 seconds between reps; 3 minutes between sets
Attack and retreat drill	2	4	60 seconds between reps; 3 minutes between sets
Number drill	2	4	60 seconds between reps; 3 minutes between sets

▶ NETBALL

Erin E. Haff

Netball is a sport derived from basketball, but it also has parallels to European handball and Ultimate Frisbee. Although the rules, the duration of the game, the equipment, and team numbers are similar to basketball, there are a few significant differences that change the rhythm and physical demands of the game. For example, there is no dribbling and no running with the ball, the ball must be passed within three seconds of reception, both the ball and the basket are somewhat smaller, there is no backboard, players are designated and restricted to certain areas of the court, and in defensive play the player's feet must be 3 feet (0.9 m) away from the offensive player with the ball.

The game relies on rapid acceleration, deceleration, and COD combined with short bouts of sprinting and lateral and vertical movements, all while catching and throwing a ball (6). Such explosive and forceful movements require near-maximum levels of muscular strength and power production, but positional and court restrictions prevent players from achieving true maximal velocity. The capacity to accelerate, change direction, and decelerate thus plays a critical role in performance (4) because it enables an athlete to better pursue and evade the opponent as well as react to the movement of the ball.

The most important performance skill capacities to develop in netball players include the following (5):

▶ fast and sharp COD movements inclusive of rapid decelerations and explosive accelerations,

▶ aerial CODs (i.e., the ability to turn fully in the air prior to landing),

▶ single-leg jumping ability,

▶ awareness of the ball, the teammate, and the opponents, and

▶ interception timing and accuracy.

It is also important to note that landing is a fundamental skill of many movements performed during the game (8). Thus, it is extremely important to train and reinforce this skill from a multitude of differing variations (e.g., jump directions, landing types).

Although the court is similar in width to that of a basketball court, it is slightly longer. Unlike basketball, netball positions have restrictions as to where positional groups are allowed on the court. The types of activity performed range from lower- to higher-intensity movements (i.e., standing, walking, jogging, shuffling, running, and sprinting) (figure 9.3). Netball players change activity, on average, every 4.1 seconds with very few work periods extending beyond 10 seconds, except for those performed by the

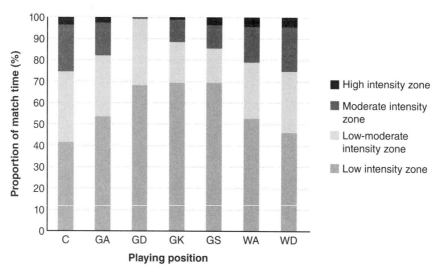

Figure 9.3 Relative time spent in each playing intensity zone during netball matches.

Note: The results represent the percentage of match time spent in each intensity zone, averaged over an entire season. C = center, GA = goal attack, GD = goal defense, GK = goalkeeper, GS = goal shooter, WA = wing attack, WD = wing defense.

Reprinted by permission from C.M. Young, P.B. Gastin, N. Sanders, L. Mackey, and D.B. Dwyer, "Player Load in Elite Netball: Match, Training, and Positional Comparisons," *International Journal of Sports Physiology and Performance* 11, no. 8 (2016): 1074 -1079.

goalkeeper and the defense players (3). Depending on the positional group (offensive, defensive, or midcourt), the total distance traveled in a 60-minute match will range from 3.8 to 8 kilometers (2.4-5 mi) and about 1 to 3 meters (1.1-3.3 yd) within a single movement with the ball. The average duration of work (for a high-level player) is less than 6 seconds across all positions (3). The average work-to-rest ratio that is most frequently performed across the three positional groups is 1:5 or greater, followed by 1:1 and 1:2 with the goalkeeper and the defense exhibiting, on occasion, the highest work-to-rest ratio of 5:1 (3).

PROGRAM DESIGN

Agility and quickness are key elements to training programs designed for any level of netball and should be continually addressed throughout the training year (table 9.9). Coaches should realize that until their athletes gain sufficient strength and conditioning to perform such movements effectively and consistently on their own, ball work skills should be done separately and only added gradually to agility and sprint drills, so as to avoid the breaking down of either skill.

Because of the highly specific roles of the various netball court positions, the need for an individualized component of training and conditioning, notably

Table 9.9 Sample Season-Specific Agility and Quickness Training Guidelines for Netball

	Off-season	Preseason	In-season
Types of drills Goals: • Progress from closed to open skills • Bilateral to unilateral movements and jump/landing abilities	Mixture of general movement patterns performed by all positions	Mixture of general movement patterns while establishing movement patterns specific to the position without, then with the ball	• Mixture of general movement patterns via shorter, more complex movements • Focus shifts to positional and game action movements
Focus Goals: • Strength endurance phase: proper technique and landing mechanics (single-plane) • Strength phase: eccentric and concentric strength (multiplane) • Power phase: reactive strength (multiplane)	• Build anaerobic fitness base • Establish proper and consistent movement technique	• Maintain anaerobic fitness and movement technique using a smaller percentage of training time compared to off-season • Include individual position drills to develop and instill game-action movement patterns (gradually incorporate the ball into the drills)	• Maintain anaerobic fitness and abilities of general movement patterns • Develop positional, game-action movement patterns with and without the ball
Frequency	• 3 times per week to establish a fitness base in conjunction with the resistance training program • Alternate days to allow for individual focus (strength and speed) and sufficient recovery	• 3-4 times per week in conjunction with the resistance training program • As there will be a focus shift from general to more individualized and some game-action movement patterns, individual (position) sessions may be added to the training week	• 3-4 times per week in conjunction with the resistance training program • Although total training duration may be shorter, high-intensity sessions need to be repeated to maintain fitness; this is recommended to complement skill and tactical development under stressful situations similar to the actual competitive environment (1)

(continued)

Table 9.9 Sample Season-Specific Agility and Quickness Training Guidelines for Netball *(continued)*

	Off-season	Preseason	In-season
Intensity	Depends on the focus and how it works in conjunction with the resistance training program	(Same as off-season)	Depends on the competition schedule and how it works in conjunction with the resistance training program
Duration	• About 30%-40% of the total time* • Need to establish the required fitness base in conjunction with the resistance training program • Main focus is to develop strength that will underpin fitness so resistance training takes precedence	• About 20%-35% of the total time* • Strength and fitness need to be maintained while adding specific position skills and team tactics (this addition will diminish the total time available in a session); emphasize quality over quantity	• About 10%-20% of the total time* • More time spent working positional and game action movements so agility and speed training is incorporated into these sport specific drills and movements
Work-to-rest ratio	Ranges from 1:1-1:5 depending on the focus and how it falls within the overall training scheme	(same as off-season)	(same as off-season)

Programming is for the general team and individual positions only.
*Depends on the athlete's training age, physical condition at the start of off-season, team style of play, and coaching strategies adopted (7).

during the competitive season, is warranted to maximize performance. For this, programs need to consider

▶ the type of activity,

▶ the number of repetitions per activity,

▶ the average time spent per activity,

▶ the total time spent performing each activity, and

▶ the relative contribution of each activity as it relates to match play.

For an in-depth analysis of these attributes for netball positions, see references (3) and (9). Style of play and team strategy will also play a significant role in determining distances, duration, and work-to-rest ratios for some of these programming needs.

SAMPLE AGILITY AND QUICKNESS TRAINING SESSION FOR NETBALL

Coaches and athletes can use a variety of the drills found in chapters 6 and 7. Several, if not all, are great for improving a netball player's agility and quickness via different means of delivery and directions. However, it is important to remember that the distance traveled, duration, and movement patterns (i.e., complexity) for each drill is determined by the degree of specificity for each position. Additionally, the athlete's training age and ability should always factor into these decisions.

Before each agility and quickness training session, athletes should complete a 10- to 15-minute dynamic warm-up session (table 9.10). Each drill is typically performed once, twice if moving laterally to address each side, and covers 15 to 20 meters (16.4-21.9 yd).

The sample sessions are aimed at preseason. Some of the drills are variations of the drills presented in chapters 6 and 7 that allow the coach or athlete to change the level of difficulty or make it more game-specific.

Table 9.10   Sample Warm-Up for Netball

Activity or drill	Description or explanation
Jog forward (variation: jog on the balls of the feet)	Prepares for impact and high-intensity agility drills
Jog backward (variation: jog on the balls of the feet)	Same as jog forward but with a varied direction
High skip forward	Exaggerated form; emphasizes a quick takeoff and landing to mimic plyometric drills
High skip backward	Same as high skip forward but with a varied direction
Lateral shuffle with arm circles	Prepares for drills that target a COD
Three micro steps to lunge (variation: use different lunge patterns)	Prepares for drills that target a COD in a multidirectional plane
Pogo (double leg bounce)	Prepares for impact with sprint and agility drills
Pogo (single leg bounce with assist)	Next level up in preparing for impact with sprint and agility drills
Pogo (single leg bounce)	Alternate 3 left, 3 right; repeat until the end of the line is reached
Straight leg shuffle	Prepares for impact drills; keep legs straight and feet dorsiflexed; touch off ground with the balls of the feet
High knee march	Emphasizes and enhances proper posture and movement techniques for sprinting

(continued)

Table 9.10 Sample Warm-Up for Netball *(continued)*

High knee (alternating legs)	3 left, jog 3-4 steps, 3 right; repeat until the end of the line is reached
High knee (single leg)	Alternate 3 left, 3 right; repeat until the end of the line is reached
Butt kick march	Emphasizes and enhances proper posture and movement techniques for sprinting
Butt kick (alternating legs)	3 left, jog 3-4 steps, 3 right; repeat until the end of the line is reached
Butt kick (single leg)	Alternate 3 left, 3 right; repeat until the end of the line is reached

Session 1

Dot

This drill increases speed, agility, balance, and coordination of an athlete's footwork as well as aiding in the overall stability of knees and ankles (see options and variations in chapter 6).

Quick Feet

This drill is good for practicing taking off for a pass and reinforcing correct landing mechanics (see variations in chapter 6). The athletes stand on the baseline or transverse line and jog lightly but quickly in place (i.e., the *quick feet* position). The coach points left, right, or straight up, and the athletes quickly turn or jump in that direction, then resume the quick feet position. Then the coach says *go* and the athletes push off using the foot they are on (without stepping back) to run a couple of steps forward. Variations of the drill have the athletes (upon landing) sprinting to a cone or marker 3 to 5 meters (3.3-5.5 yd) away or sprinting to receive a pass where the marker is located, performing an aerial rebound or catch and pass, or landing in the changed direction then sprinting to the marker and resuming the quick feet position until the next *go* command.

Zigzag

This drill is good for developing dodging and double-breaking skills. Use 6 to 10 cones to mark out a zigzag pattern with approximately 3 meters (3.3 yd) between them. Athletes sprint around the outside of the cones, shuffle around each cone to change direction, and sprint to the next one. Variations include alternate sprinting to and shuffling to each cone. The coach can make the drill more multidirectional by using forward and backward sprints, shuffling movements, or both, or by adding a grounded or aerial catch and pass at all or varying points of COD.

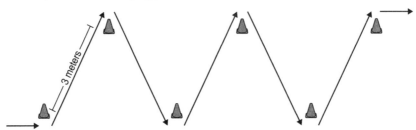

Session 2

Ladder

This drill is recommended for developing foot speed, agility, coordination, and body awareness from different multiplanar positions (see options and variations in chapter 6).

Shuttle Run

This drill can be used to develop the skill of driving, then recovering (see variations in chapter 6). Using half to three-quarters of the court, set up 3 to 4 cones to use in the shuttle run. All cones should be at least 5 meters (5.5 yd) apart. Athletes sprint to the first cone, sprint back to the start, sprint to the second cone, sprint back to the start, and so on. Variations include a side shuffle instead of sprinting, alternating between sprinting forward or backward and shuffling, varying the distances of the cones or incrementally lengthening or shortening them (i.e., 5 meters-10 meters-20 meters-10 meters-5 meters), and adding a pass on any or only on the final drive to encourage players to keep their eyes up and be ready for anything.

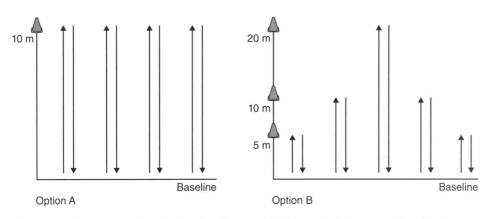

In comparison to option *A*, the shuttle run drill for netball incorporates varying intermittent distances and the cones serve to indicate the distances so athletes know where to turn around or change a movement pattern (option *B*).

Three- and Four-Cone Drills

For netball, variations to the three- and four-cone drills described in chapter 6 that create a greater distance between the cones (e.g., 5 to 7 meters [5.5-7.7 yd]) can be used separately or in conjunction with the shorter-distance drills found in that chapter (i.e., not all drills have to incorporate the greater distances).

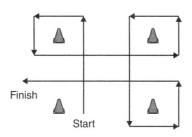

Place cones at 5 meters and 7 meters apart.

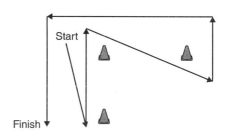

Place cones at 5 meters apart.

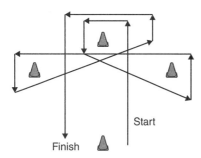

Vertical cones are 7 meters apart. Horizontal cones are 5 meters apart.

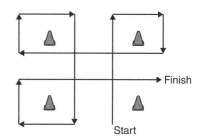

Place cones at 5 meters and 7 meters apart.

▶ *RUGBY*

Ian Jeffreys

Rugby union is an invasion game where the aim is to advance the ball into an opponent's dead ball area to score a try. It is played by two teams of 15 players and, at the senior level, over an 80-minute duration, divided into two halves of 40 minutes each. At junior levels, overall duration and the duration of halves is typically less, and dependent upon the players' age. Importantly, rugby is a collision sport, where high levels of physical contact are likely at any time, and momentum (mass × velocity) plays a critical role in these collision situations. Consequently, rugby players have to balance speed and agility application with optimal mass.

Rugby play consists of set piece play and dynamic phase play. Dynamic phase play can be thought of as the time between a set piece (scrum or lineout) and the ball becoming dead. Dynamic phase play itself can be broken into open play and breakdown play. During open play the ball is in the possession of the attacking side and is being run, passed, or kicked in an attempt to make forward progress toward the opposing try line. The defensive team will try to stop this forward progress by tackling the opposing player, with a tackle occurring when the ball carrier is held or brought to ground by one or more opponents, and at this point breakdown play occurs. When a player is tackled and cannot immediately pass the ball, both teams can attempt to gain possession through a tackle contest, ruck, or maul. When players are brought to the ground, they must immediately release the ball and a ruck is formed when one or more players from each team (who must remain on their feet), challenge the ball. If the tackled player is held off the ground, a maul can occur when one or more players from each team join the tackler and attempt either to drive the player forward or to take the ball from the tackler.

Importantly, the rules for the ruck and maul state that all players must enter both from behind the ball (i.e., from a position nearer their goal line than the back of the ruck and maul). This has important consequences for the movement requirements of the game that emphasize the importance of the gain line. When a tackle occurs in advance of the team's players, supporting teammates will be moving forward onto the ball. Defenders in this situation must first retire behind the tackle situation before they can enter the ruck or maul. As a result, an important emphasis in rugby is placed on getting over the *gain line* (an imaginary line halfway between two teams in set piece or dynamic phase play). Rugby tactics often involve methods by which teams can get over the gain line as rapidly and effectively as possible.

If the ball goes out of play, or if there is a minor infringement such as a forward pass or a knock on, or if the ball becomes unplayable in a ruck or maul, play stops and must be restarted by a lineout or scrum (set piece). *Lineouts* are the method by which players restart when the ball has gone out of play, whereas *scrums* are the other method of restarting after minor infringements or when the ball becomes unplayable.

Both the set pieces and breakdowns are highly technical and involve relatively static battles for the ball, and so movement plays a relatively small part in these phases of play. However, during *open play* (when the ball is away from these situations), effective movement is an important part of getting over the gain line and advancing the ball toward an opponent's try line.

Given the importance of the gain line, there will always be an emphasis on ensuring sufficient momentum for forward progress. Here, it is important to differentiate what are termed tight and wide situations, and these can be thought of on a continuum. *Tight situations* refer to those near to the set piece or breakdown, and tend to be heavily populated with players, both offensive and defensive, with each having little opportunity to move forward before a tackle situation is encountered. Consequently, there is little opportunity to generate high levels of speed. *Wide situations*, on the other hand, are situations where the ball has been moved (run, passed, or kicked) away from the initial breakdown situation. Greater space is available, and often players will have greater distance to run into, enabling them to achieve higher running speeds.

PROGRAM DESIGN

A trend in rugby is that teams have become excellent at keeping possession through multiple breakdown situations. Each time a team maintains possession of the ball after a break is considered a *phase of play*. In the modern game, the number of phases teams put together far exceeds what was historically the case. However, such is the quality of defense at the highest level that this is typically a battle between offensive organization and defensive organization during this phase of play.

Tables 9.11 and 9.12 show how rugby phases can be divided into organized phase play and broken phase play. Both of these can then be subdivided into offensive and defensive categories. What is important is to identify and understand the team's aims within each of these phases. This in turn will dictate the movement patterns required to achieve these aims, which should then guide the agility program for rugby.

Organized Phase Play

During offensive organized phase play a team is in possession of the ball, either from winning it in a set piece, or through maintaining it through subsequent phases of possession. The aim will be to try to get the ball over the gain line and generate forward momentum. How this is done will be dictated

Table 9.11 Phases of Play for Rugby Offense

Phase of play	Organized phase play		Broken phase play		
Context of play	Tight	Wide	Turnover	Line break	Kick
Agility and speed goals	• Generate momentum into contact • Disrupt defensive organization • Create and run into space	• Generate high speed • Disrupt defensive organization • Create and run into space	• Move ball away from where it is won • Move ball into space	• Move ball into space • Support on both sides	• Field ball • Consider options to counterattack • Get players into supporting positions
Agility and speed drills	• Accelerations from standing and low speed rolling starts • Direction changes	• Accelerations from rolling starts • Curved runs • Evasive direction changes	• Accelerations from standing and rolling starts • Attainment of high speed • Evasive and running to space skills	• Accelerations from standing and rolling starts • Attainment of high speed • Evasive and running to space skills	• Accelerations from standing and rolling starts • Adjustment of runs to provide support • Evasive and direction changes

Table 9.12 Phases of Play for Rugby Defense

Phase of play	Organized phase play		Broken phase play		
Context of play	Tight	Wide	Turnover	Line break	Kick
Agility and speed goals	• Generate momentum into contact • Bring defensive line forward rapidly • Adjust position to defend space • Make the defensive play	• Limit offensive options through position manipulation • Have fast line speed • Make the defensive play	• Recover defensive organization • Cover space • Limit offensive opportunities	• Scramble defense to limit space	• Provide an effective chase • Recover appropriate positions
Agility and speed drills	• Accelerations from standing and low speed rolling starts (linear and lateral) • Direction changes	• Rapid accelerations • Decelerations and position adjustments	• Accelerations from standing and rolling starts • Speed and direction adjustments	• Accelerations from standing and rolling starts • Attainment of high speed • Manipulative speed and direction adjustments	• Accelerations from standing and rolling starts • Adjustment of runs to provide support • Evasive and direction changes

by whether the team focuses on tight situations or wide situations as part of organized phase play.

In tight situations, space is at a premium, and players have little distance between them and the opposition. Therefore, players' ability to accelerate and generate momentum into a likely contact situation is a key facet of the game. Players who have the ability to generate momentum yet also possess deceptive COD capacity tend to be highly effective in these situations.

As the ball is moved toward more open situations, greater space is available and players can generate greater running speeds both on and off the ball. It is important for players to combine speed with effective deceptive capabilities to create space and the required movement control to make any required play (e.g., take and give a pass).

When one team is in offensive phase play, another will be in defensive phase play. Here the aim is to minimize open spaces by ensuring that all space is covered and bringing the defensive line forward as rapidly as possible to try to make a tackle over the gain line. The ability to accelerate forward rapidly and adjust to an effective defensive position is therefore essential. In tight situations, accelerations will be very short, while in open situations players will cover a greater distance and need to be able to manipulate themselves into effective defensive scenarios.

Broken Phase Play

Given the highly organized nature of phase play, attacking opportunities are often limited and the game becomes an extended gain line battle that is played over multiple phases. Situations where defensive organizational structures can be broken provide excellent attacking opportunities (called *broken play*). Offensively, these situations entail a line break or turnover ball (a situation where a team loses possession) or a potential counterattack after a kick, and all provide an important opportunity for attack.

From a line break there will be an emphasis on the breaking player to either run to space or to pass to a supporting player in space. The offensive team will try to provide supporting runners who must be able to achieve high speeds but also adjust their runs to the space opening up ahead of them. Maximum speed and an ability to adjust speed in relation to curving the run (and, consequently, adjusting the feet to maintain a supporting position) are central aspects of agility in rugby.

In turnover situations, the offensive team will try to make immediate use of the ball, as for a very short period of time the defense will be disorganized. The play will be largely dictated by how the turnover occurs. In tackle or ruck situations, the defense can often reorganize itself quickly and the opportunities for broken play may be limited. However, if the turnover occurs in wider play, for example from a dropped pass, this provides an excellent opportunity to attack. These situations often require an attempt to move the ball into open spaces and may even involve a kick into a space where a defensive play would normally have been. As a result, the skills associated with open field running (e.g., maximum speed, curved running, COD) are necessary.

Additionally, broken play can be initiated through a deliberate kick from the opposition. This will normally be fielded by one of the back three players, who will have to decide whether an opportunity presents itself to run the ball. If this is the case, the player receiving the ball will be required to run rapidly into space and needs to be able to avoid the oncoming tackler through appropriate evasive skills. Additionally, the other players of that team will have to recover rapidly into a position to support the runners.

The team losing a turnover is in a defensive broken-field situation and quite often their players will be out of position. Players' ability to shut down offensive opportunities and to return as rapidly to appropriate defensive positions becomes crucial. In situations where a deliberate kick has occurred, the team will have to chase the kick diligently, at an appropriate speed and in appropriate numbers to provide a defensive line against a possible counterattack. Additionally, some players will have to remain in a deeper position to field any counter kick from the opposition. If the transition is caused by a situation where the defensive line is broken, then defenders will be required to run greater distances to try to prevent the opposition from advancing the ball (a scramble defense). Here, the ability to run at greater speeds, and to run in curved patterns that react to the opposition's movements, is vital to success.

Based on this analysis, it is clear that rugby agility depends greatly on generating high speeds from both static and rolling starts, but also on the ability to achieve higher maximum speeds in open situations. Importantly, these need to exploit curved forms of running as well as purely linear methods. Critically, players with the ability to evade tackle situations through offensive feints, changes of speed, and CODs will be highly valued. Obviously, the relative importance of these movement skills will be largely dictated by whether players are engaged in predominantly tight or wide situations, which is, in turn, largely dictated by their playing position and the style of play adopted by the team. Thus, agility training can be targeted at the specific skills required of the team and the playing positions.

SAMPLE AGILITY AND QUICKNESS OPEN FIELD TRAINING SESSION FOR RUGBY

This session works on the ability to run effectively in an open field and combines maximum speed work with the ability to adjust in a curvilinear direction to enable the manipulation of field position, opposition position, and supporting player position.

Acceleration Runs (Fast, Faster, and Fastest)

Open play running in rugby requires the ability to accelerate from a fast rolling start. This drill develops this capacity.

Four cones are lined up 20 meters (21.9 yd) apart for an overall sprinting distance of 60 meters (65.6 yd). Athletes accelerate through the cones with the aim of running each section faster than the previous section. This replicates the running pattern for outside backs who typically have to accelerate from fast rolling starts. The drill is performed three times, with a slow walk back to the start to ensure full recovery.

Curved Running (Basic)

Space is at a premium in rugby and so open play running is seldom solely linear. The ability to curve runs to offensively make and exploit space and to defensively close down space is important. This drill develops the basic capacity to run a curved pattern but without losing running speed.

Six cones are lined up 10 meters (10.9 yd) apart (ideally the cones should be quite tall to facilitate running around them). Athletes run a curved pattern through these cones to develop the ability to reach and maintain high speeds in a curvilinear format. The drill is performed twice, with a walk back to the start to ensure full recovery.

Game Format Curve

This drill is a progression of the previous drill, and is intended to replicate a game-related curved running scenario such as a winger running at a full back and then curving into an outside line to run around the player. Game format curve drills should be set up so that a player becomes comfortable running in both directions. The drill is performed three times, with a walk back to the start to ensure full recovery.

Get Past

This drill also replicates a game-related curved running scenario, but this time an opponent is included in the drill to reproduce the type of situations a player will face in a game. Importantly, the player performing the drill should aim to attack the opponent via a curved run, but if it fails, the player should be able to use other movements to get past the opponent. The drill is performed three times, with a walk back to the start to ensure full recovery.

▶ *SOCCER*

Ian Jeffreys

Soccer is one of the most challenging sports for which to design an agility and quickness program because it consists of almost constant movement over two 45-minute periods. Given the amount of movement, agility becomes a central element in a soccer player's effectiveness. Training that improves this capacity has the ability to enhance soccer performance significantly, contributing to improvement in all elements of play.

A key factor in developing agility is that it is very context-specific. Although fundamental movement patterns do exist, the ultimate aim of training is to enable athletes to deploy these movements effectively in a game. To this end, it is useful to think of agility as game speed (not to be confused with linear speed). *Game speed* can be defined as a context-specific skill, in which athletes maximize their performance by applying sport-specific movements of optimal velocity, precision, efficiency, and control in anticipation of and in response to the key perceptual stimuli and skill requirements of the game (3).

This definition has a number of vital messages. The first is that movement requirements are specific to a given sport, often even to a given position. For example, a goalkeeper's movement requirements are different from those of a central midfielder. Secondly, effective game speed consists of an optimal velocity that should be judged not only by maximal velocity but also by its precision, control, and efficiency. These terms are essential in the context of soccer, where movements need to be maintained for a 90-minute period. Here, the ultimate aim of the game is to express soccer skills, rather than simply to move at maximal speed. Although maximal speed is an important variable, the ability to harness speed and agility is more important for maximizing soccer performance.

Since game speed and agility are context-specific, coaches must be able to break down the movement requirements of soccer to develop an effective program. Soccer movement is intermittent, with each game featuring between 1,200 and 1,400 changes of direction (2). These movements vary in speed and direction, with players changing directions about every 2 to 4 seconds (4). Typical sprinting activities span approximately 5 to 15 meters (5.5-16.4 yd) and occur once every 30 seconds on average (1, 3). The majority of playing time is spent in transitional phases, where speeds vary from walking to high-speed running. These transitional movements occur in many directions, including forward, sideways, and backward. Sprinting activities can be performed straight ahead; however, they often include some COD at the outset of the sprint or at some point during the sprint.

PROGRAM DESIGN

Given the vast range of movement requirements across 90 minutes of play, and the different requirements of playing positions, designing soccer-specific agility sessions may be daunting. However, by analyzing the target movement specifications of the sport, coaches can classify soccer movements and put them into a basic structure for building an effective agility program.

To break down soccer movements, it is helpful to determine what athletes are trying to achieve. Coaches can effectively carry this out using target classifications. At any given time, athletes are likely attempting either to start movement or to change the direction of movement (*initiation movements*), trying to move at maximal velocity (*actualization movements*), or waiting in transition to react to a soccer-specific stimulus (*transition movements*). Although agility training often focuses on initiation and actualization movements, far less emphasis is placed on transition movements. Often, when these movements are trained, they are taught incorrectly, with the emphasis on movement speed rather than on control. Athletes' ability to start and move at maximal velocity often depends on being in the correct position to enable effective subsequent movement. Table 8.1 on page 156 identifies the following key movements within each movement classification.

Effective agility training balances the requirements of the exercise and the ability of the athlete. Thus, a session designed for an elite athlete should look different from a session for a beginner. For this reason, a soccer-specific agility program should include a progression in movement challenge and complexity as athletes move through their stages of development. In the initial stages, athletes can benefit from closed drills that allow the speed of the drills to be controlled and often consist of single movement patterns (e.g., shuffling). In this stage, coaches should develop athletes' ability in all of the identified movement patterns for soccer to ensure that there are no weak links in movement ability. The following list provides the system for game-speed development, which shows stages of movement ability and application (3). As athletes maintain proper movement patterns at one stage, they can progress to the next level.

1. Develop general and stable fundamental movement patterns.
2. Develop key movement combinations, moving from closed to open drills.
3. Develop sport-specific movements in game context.
4. Perform sport-specific movements in game context.

As athletes develop, coaches should start to combine movement patterns in ways typical to soccer. For example, backpedal drills can conclude with sprints to the rear, to the side, or forward. These combinations are commonly seen in soccer. As athletes develop, coaches can also deploy drills that are increasingly open. Here, athletes should respond to a range of stimuli, which can become increasingly soccer-specific. For example, athletes can initiate incorporating backpedaling into a sprint drill. Next, athletes can perform a drill where they change direction in response to a coach's signal, and then in response to another athlete's movement. In this way, the movement patterns become increasingly more challenging in a way that progressively reflects the specific movement patterns found in soccer. These types of drills can include great variety in terms of distances, speeds, directions, and stimuli.

Quality Is Vital

Practice makes permanent. This is an important message for any soccer agility program. If athletes are to develop effective agility, then they must perform each drill with the appropriate technique. They must always remember that the drill is merely a means to an end, and that end is enhanced agility. If they perform the drill poorly, they will not develop optimal agility. Therefore, coaches should always emphasize technique during exercises.

The movements outlined in table 8.1 provide an ideal reference for athletes to assess their performance of each movement. The results can form the start of an agility development program. Where deficiencies are seen, athletes can do additional work to bring these movements up to standard. From there, coaches can develop each movement pattern along the following continuum, which moves from basic, closed drills to random sport-specific movements that display high levels of agility. With this structure, coaches can develop soccer-specific agility for each movement pattern in the following manner:

1. Develop individual movement patterns.
2. Add variation (distance and direction).
3. Develop movement combinations.
4. Move to increasingly more open situations.
5. Add sport-specific requirements.

Coaches can then structure agility development programs to ensure that all movement patterns are developed within a given timeframe. This may be weekly or biweekly.

Table 9.13 outlines a sample weekly structure that incorporates agility and speed work into warm-up protocols. This combination is a very time-efficient way to include speed and agility training within a training session, and it ensures the agility drills are performed when the athletes are not fatigued.

Table 9.13 Sample Program Week for Soccer Using Four Warm-Ups

Session number	Agility and speed-work focus	Drills and exercises
1	Starting and acceleration	• Starting mechanics (all directions) • Acceleration (varied directions, distances, static and rolling starts)
2	Deceleration and transition	• Mechanics of deceleration and jockeying • Jockeying and transition challenges • Challenges with applied offensive and defensive movement
3	Maximum speed	• Speed mechanics • Speed application (straight and curved runs) • Applied speed challenges
4	Direction change and applied agility	• Direction change development drills • Applied offensive and defensive movement challenges

SAMPLE AGILITY AND QUICKNESS TRAINING SESSION FOR SOCCER

The following is a sample session for developing COD speed and quickness. Athletes should begin with a dynamic warm-up to prepare the body for more vigorous activity. Chapter 3 provides a variety of dynamic warm-up drills to choose from.

The drills provided address the general guidelines regarding the common types of activities of an agility and quickness training session for soccer. Specific sessions should be designed based on the overall goal of the session and the type of athlete. In general, beginner (less trained) athletes will focus to a larger degree on the technical aspects of performance with a smaller emphasis on application. For advanced (better trained) athletes, the opposite will be the case with greater emphasis on the applied elements and less on the technical. For all athletes, focus should be on the quality of training rather than the quantity of drills performed. The aim is to enhance agility, and so focus should be on ensuring that technique and work quality are at a level commensurate with the athlete's abilities. Therefore, work-to-rest ratios should ensure that each subsequent repetition is started from a state of full recovery. Again, this will be dependent on the level of the athlete and their level of conditioning. In general, for sprint-type activities, walk-back recoveries are recommended. For agility-type activities, activity time should generally be in the 2- to 5-second range, with rest duration adequate to ensure that performance is maintained on each subsequent repetition. Repetitions vary depending upon their duration, but generally 4 to 8 repetitions of an activity are recommended. However, it is important to observe the session; if technique or work quality starts to deteriorate, this may be a sign that the athletes are fatiguing and an indicator that more work may not be beneficial.

Lateral Shuffle and Stick

Two cones are placed 5 to 10 yards (4.6-9.1 m) apart. The athlete begins in an athletic position facing cone 1. When ready, the athlete shuffles to cone 2 while keeping the hips low and the hips, shoulders, and torso parallel to the cones. When the cone is reached, the athlete immediately sticks the finish position. The feet should be almost flat, pointed forward, and wider apart than the knees. In turn, the knees should be wider than the hips. The athlete holds the position for a brief pause to make sure the position can be maintained in a stable manner. No additional movements should occur during the pause. Once stability is achieved, another movement can be started.

Proper finish position.

Lateral Shuffle and Pushback

Two cones are placed 5 to 10 yards (4.6-9.1 m) apart. The athlete begins in an athletic position facing cone 1. The athlete then moves laterally from cone 1 to cone 2. When the cone is reached, the athlete plants the outside leg and explosively pushes back to move in the opposite direction.

Lateral Shuffle Mirror

Two cones are placed 10 yards (9.1 m) apart. Between the cones, two athletes assume an athletic position facing each other. One assumes the role of the offense and the other of the defense. Moving only laterally between the cones, the offensive athlete tries to lose the defensive athlete, who in turn tries to stay with the offensive athlete. The drill should last between three and six seconds.

Run to Cone and Cut

Two cones are placed 5 yards (4.6 m) apart. The athlete assumes an athletic position next to cone 1 and faces cone 2. With a self-start, the athlete runs toward cone 2. When the cone is reached, the athlete makes a cut step and then accelerates in the opposite direction.

Coach's Signal Variation

For an open version of this drill (see photo), the coach stands 2 yards (1.8 m) behind cone 2. The athlete runs toward cone 2 as before, but before the cone is reached, the coach gives a verbal or a visual signal instructing the athlete to move in a certain direction. The athlete makes a cut step and accelerates in the given direction.

Run and Cut

For this drill (also known as a *get past*), two cones are placed 10 yards (9.1 m) apart. Two athletes perform the drill; one assumes an offensive role and the other assumes a defensive role. The offensive athlete starts at cone 1. The defensive athlete assumes an athletic position at cone 2. The drill starts with the first movement of the offensive athlete, who moves forward trying to get to the end of the zone (cone 2). The defensive athlete moves forward and then adjusts his movements as he or she tries to tag the offensive athlete. The depth of the zone can be adjusted as needed, based on how long the drill lasts, the skill level of the athletes, or the intended outcome of the drill.

Get to the Point

Two goals (or two pairs of cones) are placed 10 yards (9.1 m) apart. This drill is similar to the run and cut, but this time, the defender starts a few feet away from the offensive player, as in a game situation. On the coach's signal, the offensive player tries to cut and move either to the near post or to the far post. To add another element of game context, another player can deliver a ball to the offensive player on the cut toward the goal. The attacker tries to direct the ball into the goal and the defender tries to clear it (as in a game).

▶ *TENNIS*

Mark Kovacs

Tennis is a sport that has changed substantially over the last two decades as technology has developed and training has improved. The players who are the most successful are also the best all-around athletes. Agility and quickness are two of the most important physical components of success on the court. Training for tennis-specific quickness and agility is framed within the dimensions of movement, time, and distance covered during points. Tennis movement is highly situation-specific, and is performed in a reactive environment (3). Although all players have some consistent traits, tennis movement is highly specific to the position of the athlete on the court and the type of shot that has just been made by the opponent.

In competitive tennis, the average point is made in less than 10 seconds (1, 2). The recovery between points is usually between 20 and 25 seconds. Tennis players make an average of four directional changes per point (4, 6), but motion in any given point can range from a single movement to more than 15 directional changes during a long rally. In a competitive match, it is not uncommon for players to make more than a thousand directional changes (1).

Approximately 80% of all strokes are played within a distance less than 8 yards (7.3 m). Less than 5% of strokes are played that require more than 5 yards (4.6 m) between strokes (7). It is interesting to note that tennis players can cover about 1 to 2 feet (30-61 cm) more on their forehand side than on their backhand side (9). This information is very helpful when devising movement training programs for tennis, since athletes may need to train for slightly longer distances on the forehand side. These are important findings, since most quickness and agility programs for other sports focus on distances longer than those seen in tennis. Tennis players rarely achieve distances in which a traditional full-acceleration technique is reached. They never experience maximum velocity while running during the confines of a match.

Unlike many other sports, the majority of tennis movements are in a lateral direction. A study of professional players' movement found that more than 70% of movements were made from side to side, with less than 20% of movements in a forward linear direction, and less than 8% of movements in a backward linear direction (9). This is very important information because lateral acceleration and deceleration in the distances previously described are a major determining factor of success in tennis. Linear acceleration and agility are both separate and distinct biomotor skills. To optimize these skills, therefore, they should be trained separately (10), and later combined with sport-specific agility drills. One other area that can have an immediate effect on how fast athletes move in short distances is their reaction time. *Reaction time* can be defined as the time between when a stimulus is detected (visual awareness of the opponent's stroke or ball) and force is produced (8). Although reaction time does not correlate well with sprints that last longer than a few seconds, it does correlate very well to quick CODs over a short distance, which is typical of play in tennis (5).

Therefore, tennis athletes should train to improve reaction time along with other tennis movements, general acceleration and agility technique, strength, and power. In training, coaches should use a visual stimulus to help athletes develop visual reaction time. An auditory stimulus (whistle, voice, or hand clap) is less tennis-specific than a visual cue.

Rotation is a major component of tennis-specific movement, and as such movements that incorporate this skill should be used in quickness and agility drills. Many of the drills outlined in chapters 6 and 7 can be made more tennis-specific by adding rotation (through the use of medicine balls or tennis strokes) during many of the COD movements. For example, during each COD, the athlete can mimic a forehand or backhand groundstroke, or even a volley. Some particularly useful drills from chapter 6 include lateral line hop and the 180-degree traveling line hop from the line drills section as well as lateral shuffle, pro-agility race, *T* drill, and attack and retreat drill from the cone drills sections.

The following tips can be helpful when training for tennis-specific agility and quickness.

▶ The athlete should aim to progress toward performing tennis-specific reactive agility drills within the agility training program to maximize the transfer of training effect to on-court performance.

▶ Lateral training should make up the largest percentage of agility training time.

▶ Short distances that mimic the movement demands of tennis support an effective program.

▶ Coaches should track each player's movement patterns during competition and devise an individual program based on their data and observations.

▶ Athletes should add resistance to exercises only after they have perfected technique and movement mechanics.

▶ Deceleration training is important to help tennis athletes move more efficiently on the court, as well as to reduce the likelihood of injury.

Table 9.14 provides a sample training session for tennis.

Table 9.14 Sample Agility and Quickness Training Session for Tennis

Drill	Repetitions or time	Sets	Rest period
Lateral line hops	10 seconds	3	60 seconds
Lateral shuffle (forehand side)	5 repetitions	3	60 seconds
Lateral shuffle (backhand side)	5 repetitions	3	60 seconds
Modified T-test	5 repetitions	3	60 seconds
Attack and retreat	2 repetitions	3	60 seconds

Athletes should use a racket so that, during each COD, they can mimic specific racket skills (forehand, backhand, volley, etc.).

▶ *VOLLEYBALL*

Logan Lentz Kell and Doug Lentz

The sport of competitive indoor volleyball uses a player rotation design. The positions within the sport consist of one setter, two middle blockers, three outsider hitters, and a libero who is a backcourt defensive specialist. There are six athletes on the court during each point. A predominance of jumping in volleyball occurs in the front court with the performance of attacking spike jumps and defensive blocks. Based on the size of the court, and the number of players involved, the ability to change direction over relatively short distances (i.e., within a 3- to 5-meter [3.3-5.5 yd] radius) is essential. Additionally, setters must execute jump sets and there are defensive diving efforts displayed throughout a match (9, 10) that require excellent perceptual and decision-making skills.

Volleyball requires speed, agility, and upper- and lower-body muscular power to be successful (2, 10). In general, volleyball players must perform repeated maximal or near-maximal jumps, frequent CODs, and repeated overhead movements when blocking or spiking (4). Based on these demands, it would appear that a volleyball player's performance may be enhanced by improving technique for sport-specific and general movement skills, movement efficiency, and the ability to generate explosive power. For this reason, a training program aimed at improving agility for the volleyball athlete should address each of these areas.

Several studies have reported a significant relationship between speed, agility, and jumping performance (1, 5, 6, 7, 9). Since both jumping and COD ability are critical elements of this sport, incorporating jumps and landings in a volleyball-specific agility and quickness program makes logical sense. This approach allows both agility and power to be developed in the same training session.

When developing an agility training program for the volleyball athlete, there are several programming variables the coach should consider. As previously mentioned, the volleyball court dimensions are relatively small compared to other sports played on a court, such as basketball or netball. The coach should therefore look at the average distances traveled by a player and prescribe and adjust drills accordingly. For example, when comparing the standard T-test to the modified T-test, it appears that the modified version may more closely replicate the distance a volleyball player has to cover during a game. Additionally, the coach may also want to consider modifying the distances recommended for many of the tests and traditional agility drills featured in chapters 5, 6, and 7 to more appropriately meet the requirements and demands of volleyball players. Drills to improve foot speed and kinesthetic awareness that involve smaller dimensions (e.g., ladder drills, line drills, dot drills) may also be useful for improving quickness and movement time for the volleyball athlete.

PROGRAM DESIGN

The following is a sample training session for an indoor volleyball player. As a basic guideline this program should be performed 2 or 3 days per week, on nonconsecutive days. Based on observation and current best practices, some recommended training volumes (sets × reps) and rest intervals have also been included in this training session. The number of repetitions to be performed in this sample session are both fixed (i.e., a set number of reps) and flexible (the number of repetitions completed in a given timeframe). This strategy allows athletes and coaches to adjust the volume of work performed based on the individual athlete's capabilities. The work-to-rest ratios have been selected based on match play (short sets and longer rallies), and to primarily stress the phosphagen and glycolytic energy systems (3). However, coaches should also use their personal experience, monitor how their athletes are responding to each drill, and adjust the program according to the individual athlete's ability and fitness level.

Table 9.15 provides a sample training session for volleyball.

Table 9.15   Sample Agility and Quickness Training Session for Volleyball

Drill	Sets	Repetitions or time	Work-to-rest ratio
Forward and backward line hops	3	5 seconds	1:5
Lateral line hops	3	5 seconds	1:5
Scissors	3	5 seconds	1:5
Pro-agility*	3	5 repetitions	1:10
Modified T-test	3	5 repetitions	1:5
Modified ball drop drill**	3	5-10 repetitions	1:5-1:10
Shadow drill***	3	3 repetitions	1:12-1:20

*Modify this drill by adding a vertical jump at each line.
**The coach should toss the ball in the air rather than just drop it and require the athlete to dig the ball.
***Add sport-specific movements, such as jumping, spiking, or blocking to simulate match play.

▶ WRESTLING

Jason Barber

Wrestling is arguably one of the oldest known sports (3). Aside from technique, wrestling requires high amounts of mental drive, stamina, physical strength, flexibility, conditioning, speed, quickness, and agility. It is important to understand the differences in wrestling styles. International styles of wrestling include freestyle and Greco-Roman. Freestyle is similar in many aspects to what the United States knows as high school and collegiate wrestling, with some subtle variations. While Greco-Roman wrestling does not allow any contact with the legs at all, creating a very different requirement for technique and training, freestyle, collegiate, and folk style (high school) allow the participant to touch the legs, thus creating more options to score points. It is important to understand the differences in wrestling disciplines, as the agility considerations can be a bit different at the elite level.

Familiarizing themselves with each style of wrestling allows coaches to program more effectively for those disciplines. Almost all disciplines of wrestling at every level compete for 6 minutes total. In tournament competition the wrestler may have a maximum recovery time of just 10 minutes between wrestling matches.

Wrestling is a very demanding sport that places a large emphasis on the anaerobic energy system (3). Currently, there is no research that has investigated the average distances traveled during a wrestling match. However, a coach may be able to project (to a degree) how far the wrestler will need to travel during a match based on the size (28 feet [8.5 m] in diameter) of the wrestling mat. As the coach selects drills to enhance agility and quickness, he or she can modify those drills based on the defined space of the wrestling mat to develop spatial awareness for the athlete.

Wrestling entails that the participant moves forward, laterally, backward, and at an angle, so these movements should be addressed in training. Training agility and quickness is neurologically very demanding (4). For this reason, agility and quickness programming should be performed when the athlete is not significantly fatigued. One way to keep the athlete from performing drills under fatigue is to integrate agility and quickness into the wrestler's warm-up routine (4).

Because wrestling is a total-body sport, it is beneficial to incorporate upper- and lower-body agility and quickness drills, which can essentially warm the body up for practice. However, it is not recommended that agility and quickness drills be performed before anaerobic or aerobic conditioning (1). Performing these drills as conditioning can potentially lead to diminished training effects if speed and quickness are the desired outcomes (1).

PROGRAM DESIGN

For agility and quickness training, athletes should perform no more than five different drills that emphasize COD speed (specific to wrestling) (2, 5). These drills should be performed in rotation anywhere from two to three days per week, depending on the competitive season (2). Athletes should cycle through a variety of drills to reduce the monotony of training and to move the body in multiple directions. Coaches can program these drills with a set pattern or as reaction drills, in which wrestlers respond to a visual cue. The athletes' focus during these drills should be on the quality of repetitions, not the quantity. Coaches should terminate the drill when the athletes' exercise technique is compromised due to fatigue. Many of the agility and quickness drills from chapters 6 and 7 can be used in wrestling training programs. Line, dot, and ladder drills are particularly useful for developing footwork patterns and quick feet. Drills that require quick forward, backward, and lateral movements are beneficial for teaching proper body position, awareness, and control. Additionally, many of the cone drills featured in chapter 6 can easily be adapted for the wrestler by simply altering the distances used so they can be performed on a mat, or adding basic wrestling moves at each cone (e.g., shooting, knee slide, sprawl). The following are just a few examples of drills that are useful for wrestlers.

Agility Shuttle

This drill is great for developing explosiveness, foot speed, balance, quickness, and agility, which are all needed during a match. It also improves the ability to accelerate, decelerate, and perform movements in all directions. Ten cones are set up 3 feet (0.9 m) apart in a straight line. The athlete begins in an athletic position to the left side of cone 1, sprints to a point just past cone 2, then breaks down and shuffles to the right just past cone 2, backpedals to just behind cone 2, and then shuffles back to the left of cone 2 as shown in the figure. From there, the athlete sprints to cone 3 and then repeats the same pattern at this cone and at each of the remaining cones in the line. After completing this run, the athlete should rest one minute before the next attempt. The athlete will then repeat this drill, this time beginning to the right of cone 1. During the drill, the athlete's hips must stay low during each COD; the goal is to maintain balance and body control at all times. The body should not lean backward during the backpedaling or too far to the side during the shuffling.

Get Up and Go

In most matches, wrestlers find themselves on the mat on their back, side, or abdomen. The ability to recover quickly and to move into a position to come back at an opponent is key to success for wrestlers. This drill helps wrestlers develop quickness and agility while improving their ability to recover from being put on their backs or thrown to the mat. Between 15 and 20 numbered cones are set up around the wrestling mat to form a square. The cones should be 3 to 8 yards (2.7-7.3 m) away from the center of the mat. The athlete lies down in the center with the back on the mat. The coach gives a *go* command followed by a cone number. On the *go* command, the athlete rolls over, gets up as quickly as possible, and sprints to the designated cone. The athlete comes back to the center of the mat, lies down again, and repeats the drill (running to a different cone each time) for four to six reps, with a 45-second rest between runs. The athlete must maintain body control and balance when rolling over to get up from the mat and should eliminate wasted motion to improve the speed to get up and recover from being on the mat. For variety, the cone pattern can be varied.

SAMPLE AGILITY AND QUICKNESS TRAINING SESSION FOR WRESTLERS

The following are three sample agility training sessions for wrestlers, with exercises arranged sequentially from those that are simpler to those that are more complex. Start each session with a general and a specific wrestling warm-up lasting approximately 5 to 10 minutes. Based on the athletes' practice schedule and other training requirements, two 10- to 15-minute agility training sessions per week are typically well tolerated by an athlete, do not create significant fatigue, and can help improve overall speed and quickness (5).

Series 1: Foot Speed Drills

▶ Use the inner circle of the wrestling mat as the reference line for the line hop drills.

▶ Perform 1 or 2 sets as quickly as possible for 10 seconds.

▶ Allow 20 to 30 seconds of rest between sets (i.e., approximately a 1:2-1:3 work-to-rest ratio).

Drills:

1. Forward and backward line hop
2. Lateral line hop
3. Diagonal jump
4. Forward and backward single-leg line hop
5. Single-leg line hop

Series 2: Forward and Backward Movements

▶ Set up a series of 5 to 10 cones or hurdles (4-6 inches [10-15 cm] tall).

▶ Perform 2 or 3 sets of each drill.

▶ Allow a 1:5 work-to-rest ratio between repetitions and 15 to 30 seconds of rest between drills.

Drills:

1. High-knee running over cones or hurdles
2. Forward run (5 to 10 meters [5.5-10.9 yd]) then jump over cones or hurdles
3. Forward run with 180-degree jumps over cones or hurdles
4. Get up and go
5. Star drill
6. Snake drill (use a forward stance in motion with occasional shots weaving in and out of cones)

Series 3: Lateral Movements

▶ Set up a series of 5 to 10 cones or hurdles (4-6 inches [10-15 cm] tall).

▶ Perform 2 or 3 sets of each drill.

▶ Alternate leading with the right and left foot to ensure equal volumes of training for each leg.

▶ Allow 15 seconds of rest between sets (i.e., approximately a 1:5 work-to-rest ratio) and 15 to 30 seconds of rest between drills.

Drills:

1. Lateral high knee running over cones or hurdles
2. Lateral shuffle (5 meters [5.5 yd]) to jumps over cones or hurdles
3. Lateral weave in and out of the cones or hurdles using the snake drill set up
4. Lateral jump over cones or hurdles with a burpee between each jump

References

Introduction

1. Young, WB, James, R, and Montgomery, I. Is muscle power related to running speed with changes of direction? *J Sports Med Phys Fitness* 43:282-288, 2002.

Chapter 1

1. Aagaard, P. Training-induced changes in neural function. *Exerc Sport Sci Rev* 31:61-67, 2003.

2. Aagaard, P, Simonsen, EB, Andersen, JL, Magnusson, P, and Dyhre-Poulsen, P. Increased rate of force development and neural drive of human skeletal muscle following resistance training. *J Appl Physiol* 93:1318-1326, 2002.

3. Baker, D, and Nance, S. The relation between running speed and measures of strength and power in professional rugby league players. *J Strength Cond Res* 13:230-235, 1999.

4. Baker, D, and Nance, S. The relation between running speed and measures of strength and power in professional rugby league players. *J Strength Cond Res* 13:230-235, 1999.

5. Baker, D, Wilson, G, and Carlyon, R. Periodization: The effect on strength of manipulating volume and intensity. *J Strength Cond Res* 8:235-242, 1994.

6. Baldon, RM, Lobato, DFM, Carvalho, LP, Santiago, PRP, Benze, BG, and Serrao, FV. Relationship between eccentric hip torque and lower-limb kinematics: Gender differences. *J Appl Biomech* 27:223-232, 2011.

7. Bale, P, Mayhew, JL, Piper, FC, Ball, TE, and Willman, MK. Biological and performance variables in relation to age in male and female adolescent athletes. *J Sports Med Phys Fitness* 32:142-148, 1992.

8. Bangsbo, J. The physiology of soccer—with special reference to intense intermittent exercise. *Acta Physiol Scand Suppl* 619:1-155, 1994.

9. Barfod, KW, Feller, JA, Clark, R, Hartwig, T, Devitt, BM, and Webster, KE. Strength testing following anterior cruciate ligament reconstruction: A prospective cohort study. *J Strength Cond Res*, 2018. [e-pub ahead of print]

10. Beckham, G, Mizuguchi, S, Carter, C, Sato, K, Ramsey, M, Lamont, H, Hornsby, G, Haff, G, and Stone, M. Relationships of isometric mid-thigh pull variables to weightlifting performance. *J Sports Med Phys Fitness* 53:573-581, 2013.

11. Blackburn, JT, Mynark, RG, Padua, DA, and Guskiewicz, KM. Influences of experimental factors on spinal stretch reflex latency and amplitude in the human triceps surae. *J Electromyogr Kinesiol* 16:42-50, 2006.

12. Bompa, TO, and Haff, GG. Strength and power development. In *Periodization: Theory and Methodology of Training*. 5th ed. Champaign, IL: Human Kinetics, 261, 2009.

13. Bosco, C, Komi, PV, and Ito, A. Prestretch potentiation of human skeletal muscle during ballistic movement. *Acta Physiol Scand* 111:135-140, 1981.

14. Brechue, WF, Mayhew, JL, and Piper, FC. Characteristics of sprint performance in college football players. *J Strength Cond Res* 24:1169-1178, 2010.

15. Bronner, S, and Bauer, NG. Risk factors for musculoskeletal injury in elite pre-professional modern dancers: A prospective cohort prognostic study. *Phys Ther Sport* 31:42-51, 2018.

16. Brooks, T, and Cressey, E. Mobility training for the young athlete. *Strength Cond J* 35:27-33, 2013.

17. Buckthorpe, M, and Roi, GS. The time has come to incorporate a greater focus on rate of force development training in the sports injury rehabilitation process. *Muscles Ligaments Tendons J* 7:435-441, 2017.

18. Chaabene, H, Prieske, O, Negra, Y, and Granacher, U. Change of direction speed: Toward a strength training approach with accentuated eccentric muscle actions. *Sports Med*, 2018.

19. Chappell, JD, and Limpisvasti, O. Effect of a neuromuscular training program on the kinetics and kinematics of jumping tasks. *Am J Sports Med* 36:1081-1086, 2008.

20. Chelly, MS, Fathloun, M, Cherif, N, Ben Amar, M, Tabka, Z, and Van Praagh, E. Effects of a back squat training program on leg power, jump, and sprint performances in junior soccer players. *J Strength Cond Res* 23:2241-2249, 2009.

21. Cissick, JM. Means and methods of speed training, part I. *Strength Cond J* 26:24-29, 2004.

22. Cissick, JM. *Sport speed and agility.* Monterey, CA: Coaches Choice, 2004.

23. Comfort, P, Haigh, A, and Matthews, MJ. Are changes in maximal squat strength during preseason training reflected in changes in sprint performance in rugby league players? *J Strength Cond Res* 26:772-776, 2012.

24. Cronin, JB, and Hansen, KT. Strength and power predictors of sports speed. *J Strength Cond Res* 19:349-357, 2005.

25. Da Cruz-Ferreira, AM, and Fontes Ribeiro, CA. Anthropometric and physiological profile of Portugese rugby players—Part I: Comparison between athletes of different position groups. *Rev Bras Med Esporte* 19:48, 2013.

26. Davies, G, Riemann, BL, and Manske, R. Current concepts of plyometric exercise. *Int J Sports Phys Ther* 10:760-786, 2015.

27. Dawes, J, and Lentz, D. Methods of improving power for acceleration for the non-track athlete. *Strength Cond J* 34:44-51, 2012.

28. Dawes, JJ, Elder, C, Krall, K, Stierli, M, and Schilling, B. Relationship between selected measures of power and strength and linear running speed amongst Special Weapons and Tactics police officers. *J Aust Strength Cond* 23:23-28, 2015.

29. De Hoyo, M, Gonzalo-Skok, O, Sanudo, B, Carrascal, C, Plaza-Armas, JR, Camacho-Candil, F, and Otero-Esquina, C. Comparative effects of in-season full-back squat, resisted sprint training, and plyometric training on explosive performance in U-19 elite soccer players. *J Strength Cond Res* 30:368-377, 2016.

30. Deane, RS, Chow, JW, Tillman, MD, and Fournier, KA. Effects of hip flexor training on sprint, shuttle run, and vertical jump performance. *J Strength Cond Res* 19:615-621, 2005.

31. DeWeese, BH, and Nimphius, S. Program design and technique for speed and agility training. In *Essentials of Strength Training and Conditioning*. 4th ed. Haff, GG, and Triplett, NT, eds. Champaign, IL: Human Kinetics, 521-558, 2016.

32. Dos'Santos, T, Thomas, C, Jones, PA, and Comfort, P. Mechanical determinants of faster change of direction speed performance in male athletes. *J Strength Cond Res* 31:696-705, 2017.

33. Duthie, GM, Pyne, DB, Marsh, DJ, and Hooper, SL. Sprint patterns in rugby union players during competition. *J Strength Cond Res* 20:208-214, 2006.

34. Edwards, S, Austin, AP, and Bird, SP. The role of the trunk control in athletic performance of a reactive change-of-direction task. *J Strength Cond Res* 31:126-139, 2017.

35. Eke, CU, Cain, SM, and Stirling, LA. Strategy quantification using body worn inertial sensors in a reactive agility task. *J Biomech* 64:219-225, 2017.

36. Faigenbaum, AD, McFarland, JE, Keiper, FB, Tevlin, W, Ratamess, NA, Kang, J, and Hoffman, JR. Effects of a short-term plyometric and resistance training program on fitness performance in boys age 12 to 15 years. *J Sports Sci Med* 6:519-525, 2007.

37. Flynn, TW, and Soutas-Little, RW. Mechanical power and muscle action during forward and backward running. *J Orthop Sports Phys Ther* 17:108-112, 1993.

38. Garhammer, J, and Mclaughlin, T. Power output as a function of load variation in Olympic and power lifting. *J Biomech* 13:198, 1980.

39. Gjinovci, B, Idrizovic, K, Uljevic, O, and Sekulic, D. Plyometric training improves sprinting, jumping and throwing capacities of high level female volleyball players better than skill-based conditioning. *J Sports Sci Med* 16:527-535, 2017.

40. Greig, M, and Naylor, J. The efficacy of angle-matched isokinetic knee flexor and extensor strength parameters in predicting agility test performance. *Int J Sports Phys Ther* 12:728-736, 2017.

41. Hakkinen, K, Komi, PV, and Alen, M. Effect of explosive type strength training on isometric force- and relaxation-time, electromyographic and muscle fibre characteristics of leg extensor muscles. *Acta Physiol Scand* 125:587-600, 1985.

42. Ham, DJ, Knez, WL, and Young, WB. A deterministic model of the vertical jump: Implications for training. *J Strength Cond Res* 21:967-972, 2007.

43. Hamill, J, Knutzen, KM, and Derrick, TR. Linear Kinetics. In *Biomechanical Basis of Human Movement*. 4th ed. Philadelphia: Wolters Kluwer, 371-372, 2015.

44. Hanson, AM, Padua, DA, Troy Blackburn, J, Prentice, WE, and Hirth, CJ. Muscle activation during side-step cutting maneuvers in male and female soccer athletes. *J Athl Train* 43:133-143, 2008.

45. Harland, MJ, and Steele, JR. Biomechanics of the sprint start. *Sports Med* 23:11-20, 1997.

46. Harris, NK, Cronin, JB, Hopkins, WG, and Hansen, KT. Squat jump training at maximal power loads vs. heavy loads: Effect on sprint ability. *J Strength Cond Res* 22:1742-1749, 2008.

47. Harry, JR, Paquette, MR, Schilling, BK, Barker, LA, James, CR, and Dufek, JS. Kinetic and electromyographic sub-phase characteristics with relation to countermovement vertical jump performance. *J Appl Biomech*:1-26, 2018.

48. Hefzy, MS, al Khazim, M, and Harrison, L. Co-activation of the hamstrings and quadriceps during the lunge exercise. *Biomed Sci Instrum* 33:360-365, 1997.

49. Hewett, TE, Ford, KR, Myer, GD, Wanstrath, K, and Scheper, M. Gender differences in hip adduction motion and torque during a single-leg agility maneuver. *J Orthop Res* 24:416-421, 2006.

50. Hof, AL, Gazendam, MG, and Sinke, WE. The condition for dynamic stability. *J Biomech* 38:1-8, 2005.

51. Houck, J. Muscle activation patterns of selected lower extremity muscles during stepping and cutting tasks. *J Electromyogr Kinesiol* 13:545-554, 2003.

52. Hunter, JP, Marshall, RN, and McNair, PJ. Relationships between ground reaction force impulse and kinematics of sprint-running acceleration. *J Appl Biomech* 21:31-43, 2005.

53. Izquierdo, M, Hakkinen, K, Gonzalez-Badillo, JJ, Ibanez, J, and Gorostiaga, EM. Effects of long-term training specificity on maximal strength and power of the upper and lower extremities in athletes from different sports. *Eur J Appl Physiol* 87:264-271, 2002.

54. Jeffreys, I. Warm-up and flexibility training. In *Essentials of Strength Training and Conditioning*. 4th ed. Haff, GG, and Triplett, NT, eds. Champaign, IL: Human Kinetics, 317-350, 2016.

55. Jones, P, Bampouras, TM, and Marrin, K. An investigation into the physical determinants of change of direction speed. *J Sports Med Phys Fitness* 49:97-104, 2009.

56. Jones, PA, Thomas, C, Dos'Santos, T, McMahon, JJ, and Graham-Smith, P. The role of eccentric strength in 180° turns in female soccer players. *Sports* 5:42-53, 2017.

57. Kawamori, N, Crum, AJ, Blumert, PA, Kulik, JR, Childers, JT, Wood, JA, Stone, MH, and Haff, GG. Influence of different relative intensities on power output during the hang power clean: Identification of the optimal load. *J Strength Cond Res* 19:698-708, 2005.

58. Kawamori, N, Rossi, SJ, Justice, BD, Haff, EE, Pistilli, EE, O'Bryant, HS, Stone, MH, and Haff, GG. Peak force and rate of force development during isometric and dynamic mid-thigh clean pulls performed at various intensities. *J Strength Cond Res* 20:483-491, 2006.

59. Komi, PV, and Vitasalo, JH. Signal characteristics of EMG at different levels of muscle tension. *Acta Physiol Scand* 96:267-276, 1976.

60. Landry, SC, McKean, KA, Hubley-Kozey, CL, Stanish, WD, and Deluzio, KJ. Neuromuscular and lower limb biomechanical differences exist between male and female elite adolescent soccer players during an unanticipated run and crosscut maneuver. *Am J Sports Med* 35:1901-1911, 2007.

61. Landry, SC, McKean, KA, Hubley-Kozey, CL, Stanish, WD, and Deluzio, KJ. Neuromuscular and lower limb biomechanical differences exist between male and female elite adolescent soccer players during an unanticipated side-cut maneuver. *Am J Sports Med* 35:1888-1900, 2007.

62. Latt, E, Jurimae, J, Maestu, J, Purge, P, Ramson, R, Haljaste, K, Keskinen, KL, Rodriguez, FA, and Jurimae, T. Physiological, biomechanical and anthropometrical predictors of sprint swimming performance in adolescent swimmers. *J Sports Sci Med* 9:398-404, 2010.

63. Lentz, D, and Dawes, J. Speed Training. In *Training for Speed, Agility, and Quickness*. 3rd ed. Brown, LE, and Ferrigno, VA, eds. Champaign, IL: Human Kinetics, 27, 2015.

64. Leone, M, Comtois, AS, Tremblay, F, and Legier, L. Specificity of running speed and agility in competitive junior tennis players. *Medicine and Science in Tennis* 11:10-11, 2006.

65. Lin, JD, Liu, Y, Lin, JC, Tsai, FJ, and Chao, CY. The effects of different stretch amplitudes on electromyographic activity during drop jumps. *J Strength Cond Res* 22:32-39, 2008.

66. Lockie, RG, Schultz, AB, Callaghan, SJ, and Jeffriess, MD. The relationship between dynamic stability and multidirectional speed. *J Strength Cond Res* 30:3033-3043, 2016.

67. Luhtanen, P, and Komi, PV. Mechanical factors influencing running speed. In *Biomechanics VI-B*. Asmussen, E, and Jorgensen, K, eds. Baltimore, MD: University Park Press, 1978.

68. M., S, E., S, and U., S. *THIEME Atlas of Anatomy*. Second. New York, NY: Thieme Medical Publishers, 2014.

69. M., ZV, and Prilutsky, BI. Mechanics of active muscle. In *Biomechanics of Skeletal Muscles*. Champaign, IL: Human Kinetics, 2012.

70. Mackala, K, Fostiak, M, and Kowalski, K. Selected determinants of acceleration in the 100m sprint. *J Hum Kinet* 45:135-148, 2015.

71. McAtee, R. *Facilitated Stretching*. 4th ed. Champaign, IL: Human Kinetics, 2014.

72. McBride, JM. Biomechanics of resistance training. In *Essentials of Strength Training and Conditioning*. 4th ed. Haff, GG, and Triplett, NT, eds. Champaign, IL: Human Kinetics, 2016, pp. 19-42.

73. McBride, JM, Blow, D, Kirby, TJ, Haines, TL, Dayne, AM, and Triplett, NT. Relationship between maximal squat strength and five, ten, and forty yard sprint times. *J Strength Cond Res* 23:1633-1636, 2009.

74. McCormick, BT, Hannon, JC, Newton, M, Shultz, B, Detling, N, and Young, WB. The effects of frontal- and sagittal-plane plyometrics on change-of-direction speed and power in adolescent female basketball players. *Int J Sports Physiol Perform* 11:102-107, 2016.

75. McGinnis, PM. *Biomechanics of sport and exercise*. 2nd ed. Champaign, IL: Human Kinetics, 2005.

76. Mero, A, and Komi, PV. Force-, EMG-, and elasticity-velocity relationships at submaximal, maximal and supramaximal running speeds in sprinters. *Eur J Appl Physiol Occup Physiol* 55:553-561, 1986.

77. Mornieux, G, Gehring, D, Furst, P, and Gollhofer, A. Anticipatory postural adjustments during cutting manoeuvres in football and their consequences for knee injury risk. *J Sports Sci* 32:1255-1262, 2014.

78. Myer, GD, Ford, KR, McLean, SG, and Hewett, TE. The effects of plyometric versus dynamic stabilization and balance training on lower extremity biomechanics. *Am J Sports Med* 34:445-455, 2006.

79. Nagahara, R, Mizutani, M, Matsuo, A, Kanehisa, H, and Fukunaga, T. Association of sprint performance with ground reaction forces during acceleration and maximal speed phases in a single sprint. *J Appl Biomech* 34:104-110, 2018.

80. Nagahara, R, Takai, Y, Kanehisa, H, and Fukunaga, T. Vertical impulse as a determinant of combination of step length and frequency during sprinting. *Int J Sports Med*, 2018.

81. Naylor, J, and Greig, M. A hierarchical model of factors influencing a battery of agility tests. *J Sports Med Phys Fitness* 55:1329-1335, 2015.

82. Neptune, RR, Wright, IC, and van den Bogert, AJ. Muscle coordination and function during cutting movements. *Med Sci Sports Exerc* 31:294-302, 1999.

83. Newton, RU, Murphy, AJ, Humphries, BJ, Wilson, GJ, Kraemer, WJ, and Hakkinen, K. Influence of load and stretch shortening cycle on the kinematics, kinetics and muscle activation that occurs during explosive upper-body movements. *Eur J Appl Physiol Occup Physiol* 75:333-342, 1997.

84. Nicholas, CW. Anthropometric and physiological characteristics of rugby union football players. *Sports Med* 23:375-396, 1997.

85. Nuzzo, JL, McBride, JM, Cormie, P, and McCaulley, GO. Relationship between countermovement jump performance and multijoint isometric and dynamic tests of strength. *Journal of Strength and Conditioning Research* 22:699-707, 2008.

86. Opplert, J, and Babault, N. Acute effects of dynamic stretching on muscle flexibility and performance: An analysis of the current literature. *Sports Med* 48:299-325, 2018.

87. Patla, AE, Adkin, A, and Ballard, T. Online steering: Coordination and control of body center of mass, head and body reorientation. *Exp Brain Res* 129:629-634, 1999.

88. Peterson, MD, Alvar, BA, and Rhea, MR. The contribution of maximal force production to explosive movement among young collegiate athletes. *J Strength Cond Res* 20:867-873, 2006.

89. Pojskic, H, Aslin, E, Krolo, A, Jukic, I, Uljevic, O, Spasic, M, and Sekulic, D. Importance of reactive agility and change of direction speed in differentiating performance levels in junior soccer players: Reliability and validity of newly developed soccer-specific tests. *Front Physiol* 9:506, 2018.

90. Pruyn, EC, Watsford, M, and Murphy, A. The relationship between lower-body stiffness and dynamic performance. *Appl Physiol Nutr Metab* 39:1144-1150, 2014.

91. Ramachandran, S, and Pradhan, B. Effects of short-term two weeks low intensity plyometrics combined with dynamic stretching training in improving vertical jump height and agility on trained basketball players. *Indian J Physiol Pharmacol* 58:133-136, 2014.

92. Ellenbecker, T, Davies, G, and Bleacher, J. Proprioception and neuromuscular control. In *Physical Rehabilitation of the Injured Athlete*. 3rd ed. Andrews, J, Wilk, K, and Harrelson, G, eds. Philadelphia, PA: WB Saunders, 2012.

93. Santos, HH, Avila, MA, Hanashiro, DN, Camargo, PR, and Salvini, TF. The effects of knee extensor eccentric training on functional tests in healthy subjects. *Rev Bras Fisioter* 14:276-283, 2010.

94. Sarabia, JM, Moya-Ramon, M, Hernandez-Davo, JL, Fernandez-Fernandez, J, and Sabido, R. The effects of training with loads that maximise power output and individualised repetitions vs. traditional power training. *PLoS One* 12:e0186601, 2017.

95. Sayers, M. Running techniques for field sport players. *Sports Coach* 23:26-27, 2000.

96. Sheppard, JM, Dawes, JJ, Jeffreys, I, Spiteri, T, and Nimphius, S. Broadening the view of agility: A scientific review of the literature. *Journal of Australian Strength and Conditioning* 22:6-29, 2014.

97. Sheppard, JM, and Triplett, NT. Program design for resistance training. In *Essentials of Strength Training and Conditioning*. 4th ed. Haff, GG, and Triplett, NT, eds. Champaign, IL: Human Kinetics, 439-469, 2016.

98. Sheppard, JM, and Young, WB. Agility literature review: Classifications, training and testing. *J Sports Sci* 24:919-932, 2006.

99. Shumway-Cook, A, and Woollacott, MH. *Motor control: Theory and practical applications*. 2nd ed. Philadelphia: Lippincott Williams & Wilkins, 2001.

100. Siegel, JA, Gilders, RM, Staron, RS, and Hagerman, FC. Human muscle power output during upper- and lower-body exercises. *J Strength Cond Res* 16:173-178, 2002.

101. Sigward, S, and Powers, CM. The influence of experience on knee mechanics during side-step cutting in females. *Clin Biomech (Bristol, Avon)* 21:740-747, 2006.

102. Small, K, McNaughton, L, Greig, M, and Lovell, R. The effects of multidirectional soccer-specific fatigue on markers of hamstring injury risk. *J Sci Med Sport* 13:120-125, 2010.

103. Spiteri, T, Newton, RU, Binetti, M, Hart, NH, Sheppard, JM, and Nimphius, S. Mechanical determinants of faster change of direction and agility performance in female basketball athletes. *J Strength Cond Res* 29:2205-2214, 2015.

104. Spiteri, T, Nimphius, S, Hart, NH, Specos, C, Sheppard, JM, and Newton, RU. Contribution of strength characteristics to change of direction and agility performance in female basketball athletes. *J Strength Cond Res* 28:2415-2423, 2014.

105. Stone, MH, Sands, WA, Carlock, J, Callan, S, Dickie, D, Daigle, K, Cotton, J, Smith, SL, and Hartman, M. The importance of isometric maximum strength and peak rate-of-force development in sprint cycling. *J Strength Cond Res* 18:878-884, 2004.

106. Stone, MH, Stone, M, and Sands, W. *Principles and Practice of Resistance Training*. Champaign, IL: Human Kinetics, 2007.

107. Suchomel, TJ, Nimphius, S, and Stone, MH. The importance of muscular strength in athletic performance. *Sports Med* 46:1419-1449, 2016.

108. Swati, K, Ashima, C, and Saurabh, S. Efficacy of backward training on agility and quadriceps strength. *Human Physiology* 53:11918-11921, 2012.

109. Thomas, K, French, D, and Hayes, PR. The effect of two plyometric training techniques on muscular power and agility in youth soccer players. *J Strength Cond Res* 23:332-335, 2009.

110. Turner, AN, and Jeffreys, I. The stretch-shortening cycle: Proposed mechanisms and methods for enhancement. *Strength and Conditioning Journal* 32:87-99, 2010.

111. Van Hooren, B, Bosch, F, and Meijer, K. Can resistance training enhance the rapid force development in unloaded dynamic isoinertial multi-joint movements? A systematic review. *J Strength Cond Res* 31:2324-2337, 2017.

112. van Ingen Schenau, GJ, de Koning, JJ, and de Groot, G. Optimisation of sprinting performance in running, cycling and speed skating. *Sports Med* 17:259-275, 1994.

113. Verkhoshanski, Y. Perspectives in the improvement of speed-strength preparation of jumpers. *Yessis Rev of Soviet Phys Ed Sports* 4:28-34, 1969.

114. Vescovi, JD, and McGuigan, MR. Relationships between sprinting, agility, and jump ability in female athletes. *J Sports Sci* 26:97-107, 2008.

115. Viitasalo, JT, and Komi, PV. Effects of fatigue on isometric force- and relaxation-time characteristics in human muscle. *Acta Physiol Scand* 111:87-95, 1981.

116. Wallace, BJ, Kernozek, TW, and Bothwell, EC. Lower extremity kinematics and kinetics of Division III collegiate baseball and softball players while performing a modified pro-agility task. *J Sports Med Phys Fitness* 47:377-384, 2007.

117. Weber, K, Pieper, S, and Exler, T. Characteristics and significance of running speed at the Australian Open 2006 for training and injury prevention. *Medicine and Science in Tennis* 12:14-17, 2007.

118. Wilderman, DR, Ross, SE, and Padua, DA. Thigh muscle activity, knee motion, and impact force during side-step pivoting in agility-trained female basketball players. *J Athl Train* 44:14-25, 2009.

119. Wilson, GJ, Murphy, AJ, and Giorgi, A. Weight and plyometric training: Effects on eccentric and concentric force production. *Can J Appl Physiol* 21:301-315, 1996.

120. Wisloff, U, Castagna, C, Helgerud, J, Jones, R, and Hoff, J. Strong correlation of maximal squat strength with sprint performance and vertical jump height in elite soccer players. *Br J Sports Med* 38:285-288, 2004.

121. Yu, B, Queen, RM, Abbey, AN, Liu, Y, Moorman, CT, and Garrett, WE. Hamstring muscle kinematics and activation during overground sprinting. *J Biomech* 41:3121-3126, 2008.

122. Zatsiorsky, VM. Biomechanics of strength and strength testing. In *Strength and Power in Sport*. Komi, PV, ed. Oxford, UK: Blackwell Scientific, 439-487, 2003.

Chapter 2

1. Abernethy, B, Schorer, J, Jackson, RC, and Hagemann, N. Perceptual training methods compared: The relative efficacy of different approaches to enhancing sport-specific anticipation. *J Exp Psychol Appl* 18:143-153, 2012.

2. Abernethy, B, Zawi, K, and Jackson, RC. Expertise and attunement to kinematic constraints. *Perception* 37:931-948, 2008.

3. Annett, J. Motor imagery: Perception of action? *Neuropsychologia* 33(11):1395-1417, 1995.

4. Cox, RH. Sport psychology: Concepts and applications. 7th ed. New York: McGraw-Hill, 2012.

5. Farrow D, Young W, and Bruce L. The development of a test of reactive agility for netball: A new methodology. *J Sci Med Sport* 8:52-60, 2005.

6. Gabbett TJ, Carius J, and Mulvey M. Does improved decision-making ability reduce the physiological demands of game-based activities in field sport athletes? *J Strength Cond Res* 22:2027-2035, 2008.

7. Gorman, AD, Abernethy, B, and Farrow, D. Is the relationship between pattern recall and decision-making influenced by anticipation recall? *Q J ExpPsychol* 66:2219-2236, 2013.

8. Haider, H, Eberhardt, K, Esser, S, and Rose, M. Implicit visual learning: How the task set modulates learning by determining the stimulus-response binding. *Consciousness Cognition* 26:145-161, 2014.

9. Hertel, J, Denegar, CR, Johnson, SA, Hale, SA, and Buckley, WE. Reliability of the cybex reactor in the assessment of an agility task. *J Sport Rehab* 8:24-31, 1999.

10. Horstmann G. The psychological refractory period of stopping. *J Exp Psychol* 29: 965-981, 2003.

11. Krzepota J, Stepinski M, and Zwierko T. Gaze control in one versus one defensive situations in soccer players with various levels of expertise. *Perceptual and Motor Skills* 123:769-783, 2016.

12. McGarry T, Anderson, DI, Wallace, SA, Hughes, MD, and Franks, IM. Sport competition as a dynamical self-organizing system. *J Sport Sci* 20:771-781, 2002.

13. Memmert, D, Simons, DJ, and Grimme, T. The relationship between visual attention and expertise in sport. *Psychol Sport Exer* 10:146-151, 2009.

14. Neil, R, Hanton, S, Mellalieu, SD, and Fletcher, D. Competition stress and emotions in sport performers: The role of further appraisals. *Psychol Sport Exer* 12:460-470, 2011.

15. Pavely, S, Adams RD, Di Francesco, T, Larkham, S, and Maher, CG. Execution and outcome differences between passes to the left and right made by first-grade rugby union players. *Phys Ther Sport* 10:136-141, 2009.

16. Roca, A, Ford, PR, McRobert, AP, and Williams, AM. Identifying the processes underpinning anticipation and decision-making in a dynamic time-constrained task. *Cog Process* 12:301-310, 2011.

17. Roca, A, Ford, PR, McRobert, AP, and Williams AM. Perceptual-cognitive skills and their interaction as a function of task constraints in soccer. *J Sport Exer Psychol* 35:144-155, 2013.

18. Ryu, D, Kim, S, Abernethy, B, and Mann, DL. Guiding attention aids the acquisition of anticipatory skill in novice soccer goalkeepers. *Res Q Exer Sport* 84:252-262, 2013.

19. Schmidt, RA, and Lee, TD. *Motor Control and Learning: A Behavioral Emphasis.* 6th ed. Champaign, IL: Human Kinetics, 2018.

20. Schmidt, RA, and Wrisberg, CA. *Motor Learning and Performance.* 5th ed. Champaign, IL: Human Kinetics, 2013.

21. Schwab, S, and Memmert, D. The impact of sports vision training program in youth field hockey players. *J Sports Sci Med* 11:642-631, 2012.

22. Serpell, BG, Young, WB, and Ford, M. Are the perceptual and decision-making components of agility trainable? A preliminary investigation. *J Strength Cond Res* 25:1240-1248, 2011.

23. Sheppard, JM, Young, WB, Doyle, TL, Sheppard, TA, and Newton, RU. An evaluation of a new test of reactive agility and its relationship to sprint speed and change of direction speed. *J Sci Med Sport* 9:342-349, 2006.

24. Spiteri, T, Hart, NH, and Nimphius, S. Offensive and defensive agility: A sex comparison of lower body kinematics and ground reaction forces. *J Appl Biomech* 30:514-520, 2014.

25. Spiteri, T, McIntyre, F, Specos, C, and Myszka, S. Cognitive training for agility: The integration between perception and action. *Strength Cond J* 40:39-46, 2017.

26. Spiteri T, Newton RU, Binetti M, Hart NH, Sheppard JM, and Nimphius, S. Mechanical determinants of faster change of direction and agility performance in female basketball athletes. *J Strength Cond Res* 29:2205-2214, 2015.

27. Spiteri, T, Newton RU, and Nimphius, S. Neuromuscular strategies contributing to faster multidirectional agility performance. *J Electromyogr Kinesiol*, 25:629-636, 2015.

28. Steinberg, GM, Chaffin, WM, and Singer, RN. Mental quickness training: Drills that emphasize the development of anticipation skills in fast-paced sports. *J Phys Ed* 69:37-42, 1998.

29. Veale JP, Pearce AJ, and Carlson JS. Reliability and validity of a reactive agility test for Australian football. *Int J Sports Physiol Perf* 5:239-248, 2010.

30. Vickers, JN. *Perception, Cognition, and Decision Training: The Quiet Eye in Action*. Champaign, IL: Human Kinetics, 2007.

31. Weinberg, R. Does imagery work? Effects of performance and mental skills. *J Imagery Res in Sport and Phys Activity* 3:1932-1939, 2008.

32. Wheeler, KW, and Sayers, MGL. Modification of agility running technique in reaction to a defender in rugby union. *J Sports Sci Med* 9:445-451, 2010.

33. Williams, MA, Huys, R, Canal-Bruland, R, and Hagemann, N. The dynamical information underpinning anticipation skill. *Human Movt Sci* 28:362-370, 2009.

34. Wilson, MR, Wood, G, and Vine, SJ. Anxiety, attentional control, and performance impairment in penalty kicks. *J Sport Exer Psychol* 31:761-775, 2009.

35. Yarrow K, Brown P, and Krakauer JW. Inside the brain of an elite athlete: The neural processes that support high achievement in sports. *Nat Rev Neurosci*, 10:585-596, 2009.

Chapter 3

1. Armstrong, LE, and Pandolf, KB. Physical training, cardiorespiratory physical fitness, and exercise-heat tolerance. In *Human Performance and Environmental Medicine at Terrestrial Extremes*. Benchmark Press, 199-226, 1988.

2. Arnheim, DD, and Prentice, WE. *Principles of Athletic Training*. 10th ed. New York: McGraw-Hill, 2000.

3. Asmussen, E, Bonde-Peterson, F, and Jorgenson, K. Mechanoelastic properties of human muscles at different temperatures. *Acta Physiol Scand* 96:86-93, 1976.

4. Barengo, NC, Meneses-Echavez, JF, Ramirez-Velez, R, Cohen, DD, Tovar, G, and Bautista, JEC. The Impact of the FIFA 11 + training program on injury prevention in football players: A systematic review. *Int J Environ Res Public Health* 11(11):11986-12000, 2014.

5. Baumgarten, M, Bloebaum, RD, Ross, SDK, Campbell, P, and Sarmiento, A. Normal human synovial fluid: Osmolality and exercise-induced changes. *J Bone Joint Surg Am* 67-A:9, 1985.

6. Bergh, U, and Ekblom, B. Influence of muscle temperature on maximal strength and power output in human muscle. *Acta Physiol Scand* 107:332-337, 1979.

7. Brown, LE, Ferrigno, V, eds. *Training for Speed, Agility, and Quickness.* 3rd ed. Champaign, IL: Human Kinetics, 4, 2015.

8. Enoka, RM. *Neuromechanics of Human Movement.* Champaign, IL: Human Kinetics, 2002.

9. Enoka, RM. *Neuromechanics of Human Movement.* 4th ed. Champaign, IL: Human Kinetics, 305-309, 2008.

10. Gray, SC, Deviton, G, Nimmo, NA. Effect of active warm-up on metabolism prior to and during intense dynamic exercise. *Med Sci Sports Exerc* 2091-2096, 2002.

11. Hedrick, A. Flexibility, body weight, and stability ball exercises. In *Resistance Training Program Design.* 2nd ed. Coburn, JW, and Malek, MH, eds. Champaign, IL: Human Kinetics, 251-286, 2012.

12. Kim, DJ, Cho, ML, Park, YH, and Yang, YA. Effect of an exercise program for posture correction on musculoskeletal pain. *J Phys Ther Sci* 27(6):1791-1794, 2015.

13. Jeffreys, I. Motor learning - applications for agility, part 1. *Strength Cond J* 28:72-76, 2006.

14. Jeffreys, I. Warm-up revisited: The RAMP method of optimizing warm-ups. *Professional Strength and Conditioning* 6:12-18, 2007.

15. Jensen, J, Rustad, PI, Kolnes, AJ, and Lai, Y-C. The role of skeletal muscle glycogen breakdown for regulation of insulin sensitivity by exercise. *Front Physiol* 2:112, 2011.

16. Malliou, P, Rokka, S, Beneka, A, Mauridis, G, and Godolias, G. Reducing risk of injury due to warm up and cool down in dance aerobics instructors. *J Back Musculoskelet Rehabil* 20:29-35, 2007.

17. McArdle, WD, Katch, F, and Katch, VL. *Exercise Physiology: Energy, Nutrition and Human Performance.* 5th ed. Baltimore: Lippincott Williams & Wilkins, 2001.

18. Milanovic, Z, Sporis, G, Trajkaric, N, James, N, and Samija, K. Effects of a 12 week SAQ training programme on agility with and without the ball among young soccer players. *J Sports Sci Med* 12(1): 97-103, 2013.

19. Mills, M, Frank, B, Goto, S, Blackburn, T, Cates, S, Clark, M, Aguilar, A, Fava, N, Padua, D. Effect of restricted hip flexor muscle length on hip extensor muscle activity and lower extremity biomechanics in college-aged female soccer players. *Int J Sports Physiol Perf* 10(7): 946-954, 2015.

20. Moon, JH, Lee, JS, Kang, MJ, Kang, SW, and Kim, HJ. Effects of rehabilitation program in adolescent scoliosis. *Ann Rehab Med* 20:424-432, 1996.

21. Moriyama, H. Effects of exercise on joints. *Clinical Calcium* 27(1): 87-94, 2017.

22. Oksa, J. Neuromuscular performance limitations in cold. *Int J Circumpolar Health* 61(2): 154-162, 2002.

23. Oksa, J, Rintamaki, H, Rissanen, S, Rytky, S, Tolonen, U, and Kim, PV. Stretch-and H-reflexes of the lower leg during whole body cooling and local warming. *Aviation, Space, and Environmental Medicine* 71(2): 156-161, 2000.

24. Sawka, MN, Wenger, CB, Young, AJ, and Pandolf, KB. Physiological responses to exercise in the heat. *Institute of Medicine (US) Committee on Military Nutrition Research*, 1993.

Chapter 4

1. Arendt, E, and Dick, R. Knee injury patterns among men and women in collegiate basketball and soccer: NCAA data and review of literature. *Am J Sports Med* 23:694-701, 1995.

2. Balyi, I, and Hamilton, A. *Long-Term Athlete Development: Trainability in Childhood and Adolescence: Windows of Opportunity, Optimal Trainability*. Victoria, Canada: National Coaching Institute British Columbia and Advanced Training and Performance, 2004.

3. Beaulieu, ML, Lamontagne, M, and Xu, L. Lower limb muscle activity and kinematics of an unanticipated cutting manoeuvre: A gender comparison. *Knee Surg Sports Traumatol Arthosc* 17:986-976, 2009.

4. Behringer, M, Vom Heede, A, Matthews, M, and Mester, J. Effects of strength training on motor performance skills in children and adolescents: A meta-analysis. *Pediatr Exerc Sci* 23:186-206, 2011.

5. Beunen, GP, and Malina, RM. Growth and biological maturation: Relevance to athletic performance. In *The Child and Adolescent Athlete*. Bar-Or O, ed. Oxford: Blackwell Publishing, 3-17, 2005.

6. Beunen, GP, and Malina RM. Growth and physical performance relative to the timing of the adolescent spurt. *Exerc Sport Sci Rev* 16:503-540, 1988.

7. Carron, AV, and Bailey, DA. Strength development in boys from 10 through 16 years. *Monogr Soc Res Child Dev* 39:1-37, 1974.

8. Crone, EA, and Steinbeis, N. Neural perspectives on cognitive control development during childhood and adolescence. *Trends Cogn Sci* 21:205-215, 2017.

9. Delecluse C. Influence of strength training on sprint running performance: Current findings and implications for training. *Sports Med* 24:147-156, 1997.

10. Diamond, A. Executive functions. *Annu Rev Psychol* 64:135-168. 2013.

11. DiFiori, J.P. Evaluation of overuse injuries in children and adolescents. *Curr Sports Med Reports* 9:372-378, 2010.

12. Dotan, R, Mitchell, C, Cohen, R, Klentrou, P, Gabriel, D, and Falk, B. Child-adult differences in muscle activation: A review. *Pediatr Exerc Sci* 24:2-21, 2012.

13. Falk, B, Usselman, C, Dotan, R, Brunton, L, Klentrou, P, Shaw, J, and Gabriel, D. Child-adult differences in muscle strength and activation pattern during isometric elbow flexion and extension. *Appl Physiol Nutr Metab* 34:609-615, 2009.

14. Griffin, LY, Agel, J, Albohm, JM, Arendt, EA, Dick, RW, Garrett, WE, and Wojtys, EM. Noncontact anterior cruciate ligament injuries: Risk factors and prevention strategies. *J Am Acad Ortho Surg* 8:141-150, 2000.

15. Hewett, TE, Myer, GD, and Ford, KR. Decrease in neuromuscular control about the knee with maturation in female athletes. *J Bone Joint Surg Am* 86-A(8): 1601-1608, 2004.

16. Kerssemakers, SP, Fotiadou, AN, de Jonge, MC, Karantanas, AH, and Maas, M. Sport injuries in the paediatric and adolescent patient: A growing problem. *Pediatr Radiol* 39:471-484, 2009.

17. Koziel, SM, and Malina, RM. Modified maturity offset prediction equations: Validation in independent longitudinal boys and girls. *Sports Med* 48:221-236, 2018.

18. Lloyd, RS, Cronin, JB, Faigenbaum, AD, Haff, GG, Howard, R, Kraemer, WJ, and Oliver, JL. National Strength and Conditioning Association position statement on long-term athletic development. *J Strength Cond Res* 30:1491-1509, 2016.

19. Lloyd, RS, and Faigenbaum, AD. Age- and sex-related differences and their implications for resistance exercise. In: *Essentials of Strength and Conditioning*. 4th ed. Champaign, IL: Human Kinetics, 135-154, 2016.

20. Lloyd, RS, Read, P, Oliver, JL, Meyers, RW, Nimphius, S, and Jeffreys, I. Considerations for the development of agility during childhood and adolescence. *Strength Cond J* 35:2-11, 2013.

21. Lloyd, RS, and Oliver, JL. The youth physical development model: A new approach to long-term athletic development. *Strength and Cond J* 34:61-72, 2012.

22. Malina, RM, Bouchard, C, and Bar-Or, O. *Growth, Maturation, and Physical Activity*. Champaign, IL: Human Kinetics, 41-47, 2004.

23. Mandelbaum, BR, Silvers, HJ, Watanabe, DS, Knarr, JF, Thomas, SD, Griffin, LY, and Garrett, W. Effectiveness of a neuromuscular and proprioceptive training program in preventing anterior cruciate ligament injuries in female athletes: 2-year follow-up. *Am J Sports Med* 33:1003-1010, 2005.

24. Meylan, CMP, Cronin, JB, Oliver, JL, and Rumpf, MC. Sex related differences in explosive actions during late childhood. *J Strength Cond Res* 28:2097-2104, 2014.

25. Miller, AE, MacDougall, JD, Tarnopolsky, MA, and Sale, DG. Gender differences in strength and muscle fiber characteristics. *Eur J Appl Physiol Occup Physiol* 66:252-262, 1993.

26. Mirwald, RI, Baxter-Jones, ADG, Bailey, DA, and Buenen, GP. An assessment of maturity from anthropometric measurements. *Med Sci Sports Exerc* 34:689-694, 2002.

27. Miyaguchi, K, and Demura, S. Relationships between muscle power output using the stretch-shortening cycle eccentric maximum strength. *J Strength Cond Res* 22:1735-1741, 2008.

28. Myer, GD, Ford, KR, Divine, JG, Wall, EJ, Kahanov, L, and Hewett, TE. Longitudinal assessment of noncontact anterior cruciate ligament injury risk factors during maturation in a female athlete: A case report. *J Athl Train* 44:101-109, 2009.

29. Negrete, R, and Brophy, J. The relationship between isokinetic open and closed kinetic chain lower extremity strength and functional performance. *J Sport Rehab* 9:46-61, 2000.

30. Norrbrand, L, Fluckey JD, Pozzo, M, and Tesch, PA. Resistance training using eccentric overload induces early adaptations in muscle size. *Eur J Appl Physiol* 102:271-281, 2008.

31. O'Brien, TD, Reeves, ND, Baltzopoulos, V, Jones, DA, and Maganaris, CN. (2010). Muscle-tendon structure and dimensions in adults and children. *J Anat* 216(5), 631-642.

32. Philippaerts, RM, Vaeyens, R, Janssens, M, Van Renterghem, B, Matthys, D, Craen R, and Malina, RM. The relationship between peak height velocity and physical performance in youth soccer players. *J Sports Sci* 24:221-230, 2006.

33. Prencipe, A, Kesek, A, Cohen, J, Lamm, C, Lewis, MD, and Zelazo, PD. Development of hot and cool executive function during the transition to adolescence. *Psyc* 108:621-637, 2011.

34. Quatman, CE, Ford KR, Myer GD, Hewett, TE. Maturation Leads to Gender Differences in Landing Force and Vertical Jump Performance: A Longitudinal Study. *Am J Sports Med* 34:806-813, 2006.

35. Rabinowickz, T. The differentiated maturation of the cerebral cortex. In *Human Growth: A Comprehensive Treatise, Postnatal Growth: Neurobiology*. Vol. 2. Falkner, F, and Tanner, J, eds. New York, NY: Plenum, 385-410, 1986.

36. Rogol, AD, Clark, PA, and Roemmich, JN. Growth and puberty development in children and adolescents: Effects of diet and physical activity. *Am J Clin Nutri* 72:521-528, 2000.

37. Sheppard, JM, and Young, WB. Agility literature review: Classifications, training and testing. *J Sports Sci* 24:919-932, 2006.

38. Stracciolini, A, Myer, GD, and Faigenbaum, AD. Resistance training for pediatric female dancers. In *Prevention of Injuries in the Young Dancer*. Cham, Switzerland: Springer, 64-71, 2017.

39. Suchomel, TJ, Nimphius, S, and Stone, MH. The importance of muscular strength in athletic performance. *Sports Med* 46:1419-1449, 2016.

40. Teeple, JB, Lohman, TG, Misner, JE, Boileau, RA, and Massey, BH. Contribution of physical development and muscular strength to the motor performance capacity of 7 to 12 year old boys. *Br J Sports Med* 9:122-129, 1975.

41. Temfemo, A, Hugues, J, Chardon, K, Mandengue, SH, and Ahmaidi, S. Relationship between vertical jumping performance and anthropometric characteristics during growth in boys and girls. *Eur J of Pediatr* 168:457-464, 2009.

42. Tursz, A, and Crost, M. Sports-related injuries in children: A study of their characteristics, frequency, and severity, with comparison to other types of accidental injuries. *Am J Sports Med* 14:294-299, 1986.

43. Veldhius, JD, Roemmich, JN, Richmond, EJ, Rogol, AD, Lovejoy, JC, Sheffield-Moore, M, Mauras, N, and Bowers, C.Y. Endocrine control of body composition in infancy, childhood, and puberty. *Endocrine Reviews* 26:114-116, 2005.

44. Viru, A, Loko, J, Harro, M, Volver, A, Laaneaots, L, and Viru, M. Critical periods in the development of performance capacity during childhood and adolescence. *Eur J Phys Educ* 4:75-119, 1999.

45. Weyand, PG, Sternlight, DB, Bellizzi, MJ, and Wright, S. Faster top running speeds are achieved with greater ground forces not more rapid leg movements. *J Appl Physiol* 89:1991-1999, 2000.

46. Wisloff, U, Castagna, C, Helgerud, J, Jones, R, and Hoff, J. Strong correlation of maximal squat strength with sprint performance and vertical jump height in elite soccer players. *Br J Sports Med* 38:285-288, 2004.

47. Wojtys, EM, and Brower, AM. Anterior cruciate ligament injuries in the prepubescent and adolescent athlete: Clinical and research considerations. *J Athl Train* 45:509-512, 2010.

48. Wolf, JM, Cameron, KL, and Owens, BD. Impact of joint laxity and hypermobility on the musculoskeletal system. *J Am Acad Ortho Surg* 19:463-471, 2011.

49. Young, WB, James, R, and Montgomery, I. Is muscle power related to running speed with changes of direction? *J Sports Med Phys Fitness* 42:282-288, 2002.

Chapter 5

1. Atkinson, G, and Reilly, T. Circadian variation in sports performance. *Sports Med* 21:292-312, 1996.

2. Beck, AQ, Clasey, JL, Yates, JW, Koebke, NC, Palmer, TG, and Abel, MG. Relationship of physical fitness measures vs. occupational physical ability in campus law enforcement officers. *J Strength Cond Res* 29:2340-2350, 2015.

3. Chan, CK, Lee, JW, Fong, DT, Yung, PS, and Chan, KM. The difference of physical abilities between youth soccer player and professional soccer player: A training implication. *J Strength Cond Res* 25:S12, 2011.

4. Crawley, AA, Sherman, RA, Crawley, WR, and Cosio-Lima, LM. Physical fitness of police academy cadets: Baseline characteristics and changes during a 16-week academy. *J Strength Cond Res* 30:1416-1424, 2016.

5. Cronin, JB, and Templeton, RL. Timing light height affects sprint times. *J Strength Cond Res* 22:318-320, 2008.

6. Delaney, JA, Scott, TJ, Ballard, DA, Duthie, GM, Hickmans, JA, Lockie, RG, and Dascombe, BJ. Contributing factors to change-of-direction ability in professional rugby league players. *J Strength Cond Res* 29:2688-2696, 2015.

7. Delextrat, A, and Cohen, D. Strength, power, speed, and agility of women basketball players according to playing position. *J Strength Cond Res* 23:1974-1981, 2009.

8. Dupler, TL, Amonette, WE, Coleman, AE, Hoffman, JR, and Wenzel, T. Anthropometric and performance differences among high-school football players. *J Strength Cond Res* 24:1975-1982, 2010.

9. Farrow, D, Young, W, and Bruce, L. The development of a test of reactive agility for netball: A new methodology. *J Sci Med Sport* 8:52-60, 2005.

10. Gabbett, T, and Benton, D. Reactive agility of rugby league players. *J Sci Med Sport* 12:212-214, 2009.

11. Gabbett, T, Georgieff, B, Anderson, S, Cotton, B, Savovic, D, and Nicholson, L. Changes in skill and physical fitness following training in talent-identified volleyball players. *J Strength Cond Res* 20:29-35, 2006.

12. Gabbett, TJ. Performance changes following a field conditioning program in junior and senior rugby league players. *J Strength Cond Res* 20:215-221, 2006.

13. Gabbett, TJ, Kelly, JN, and Sheppard, JM. Speed, change of direction speed, and reactive agility of rugby league players. *J Strength Cond Res* 22:174-181, 2008.

14. Gains, GL, Swedenhjelm, AN, Mayhew, JL, Bird, HM, and Houser, JJ. Comparison of speed and agility performance of college football players on field turf and natural grass. *J Strength Cond Res* 24:2613-2617, 2010.

15. Girard, O, Brocherie, F, and Bishop, DJ. Sprint performance under heat stress: A review. *Scand J Med Sci Spor* 25:79-89, 2015.

16. Green, BS, Blake, C, and Caulfield, BM. A valid field test protocol of linear speed and agility in rugby union. *J Strength Cond Res* 25:1256-1262, 2010.

17. Guy, JH, Deakin, GB, Edwards, AM, Miller, CM, and Pyne, DB. Adaptation to hot environmental conditions: An exploration of the performance basis, procedures and future directions to optimise opportunities for elite athletes. *Sports Med* 45:303-311, 2015.

18. Haines, S, Baker, T, and Donaldson, M. Development of a physical performance assessment checklist for athletes who sustained a lower extremity injury in preparation for return to sport: A delphi study. *Int J Sports Phys Ther* 8:44-53, 2013.

19. Haugen, T, and Buchheit, M. Sprint running performance monitoring: Methodological and practical considerations. *Sports Med* 46:641-656, 2016.

20. Haugen, TA, Tonnessen, E, and Seiler, SK. The difference is in the start: Impact of timing and start procedure on sprint running performance. *J Strength Cond Res* 26:473-479, 2012.

21. Herda, TJ, and Cramer, JT. Bioenergetics of exercise and training. In *Essentials of Strength Training and Conditioning*. 4th ed. Haff, GG, and Triplett, NT, eds. Champaign, IL: Human Kinetics, 43-63, 2016.

22. Hetzler, RK, Stickley, CD, Lundquist, KM, and Kimura, IF. Reliability and accuracy of handheld stopwatches compared with electronic timing in measuring sprint performance. *J Strength Cond Res* 22:1969-1976, 2008.

23. Hoffman, JR. Athlete testing and program evaluation. In *NSCA's Guide to Program Design*. Hoffman, JR, ed. Champaign, IL: Human Kinetics, 23-49, 2012.

24. Iguchi, J, Yamada, Y, Ando, S, Fujisawa, Y, Hojo, T, Nishimura, K, Kuzuhara, K, Yuasa, Y, and Ichihashi, N. Physical and performance characteristics of Japanese Division 1 collegiate football players. *J Strength Cond Res* 25:3368-3377, 2011.

25. Jarvis, S, Sullivan, LO, Davies, B, Wiltshire, H, and Baker, JS. Interrelationships between measured running intensities and agility performance in subelite rugby union players. *Res Sports Med* 17:217-230, 2009.

26. Jeffriess, MD, Schultz, AB, McGann, TS, Callaghan, SJ, and Lockie, RG. Effects of preventative ankle taping on planned change-of-direction and reactive agility performance and ankle muscle activity in basketballers. *J Sports Sci Med* 14:864-876, 2015.

27. Keogh, JWL, Weber, CL, and Dalton, CT. Evaluation of anthropometric, physiological, and skill-related tests for talent identification in female field hockey. *Can J Appl Physiol* 28:397-409, 2003.

28. Kuzmits, FE, and Adams, AJ. The NFL combine: Does it predict performance in the National Football League? *J Strength Cond Res* 22:1721-1727, 2008.

29. Lockie, RG, Orjalo, AJ, Amran, VL, Davis, DL, Risso, FG, and Jalilvand, F. An introductory analysis as to the influence of lower-body power on multidirectional speed in collegiate female rugby players. *Sport Sci Rev* 25:113-134, 2016.

30. Lockie, RG, Birmingham-Babauta, SA, Stokes, JJ, Liu, TM, Risso, FG, Lazar, A, Giuliano, DV, Orjalo, AJ, Moreno, MR, Stage, AA, and Davis, DL. An analysis of collegiate club-sport female lacrosse players: Sport-specific field test performance and the influence of lacrosse stick carrying. *Int J Exerc Sci* 11:269-280, 2018.

31. Lockie, RG, Callaghan, SJ, Berry, SP, Cooke, ER, Jordan, CA, Luczo, TM, and Jeffriess, MD. Relationship between unilateral jumping ability and asymmetry on multidirectional speed in team-sport athletes. *J Strength Cond Res* 28:3557-3566, 2014.

32. Lockie, RG, Callaghan, SJ, and Jeffriess, MD. Analysis of specific speed testing for cricketers. *J Strength Cond Res* 27:2981-2988, 2013.

33. Lockie, RG, Callaghan, SJ, and Jeffriess, MD. Can the 505 change-of-direction speed test be used to monitor leg function following ankle sprains in team sport athletes? *J Aust Strength Cond* 23:10-16, 2015.

34. Lockie, RG, Callaghan, SJ, McGann, TS, and Jeffriess, MD. Ankle muscle function during preferred and non-preferred 45° directional cutting in semi-professional basketball players. *Int J Perform Anal Sport* 14:574-593, 2014.

35. Lockie, RG, Davis, DL, Birmingham-Babauta, SA, Beiley, MD, Hurley, JM, Stage, AA, Stokes, JJ, Tomita, TM, Torne, IA, and Lazar, A. Physiological characteristics of incoming freshmen field players in a men's Division I collegiate soccer team. *Sports* 4:34, 2016. doi:10.3390/sports4020034.

36. Lockie, RG, Jalilivand, F, Orjalo, AJ, Giuliano, DV, Moreno, MR, and Wright, GA. A methodological report: Adapting the 505 change-of-direction speed test specific to American football. *J Strength Cond Res* 31:539-547, 2017.

37. Lockie, RG, and Jalilvand, F. Reliability and criterion validity of the Arrowhead change-of-direction speed test for soccer. *FU Phys Ed Sport* 15:139-151, 2017.

38. Lockie, RG, Jalilvand, F, Moreno, MR, Orjalo, AJ, Risso, FG, and Nimphius, S. Yo-Yo Intermittent Recovery Test Level 2 and its relationship to other typical soccer field tests in female collegiate soccer players. *J Strength Cond Res* 31:2667-2677, 2017.

39. Lockie, RG, Jeffriess, MD, McGann, TS, Callaghan, SJ, and Schultz, AB. Planned and reactive agility performance in semi-professional and amateur basketball players. *Int J Sports Physiol Perf* 9:766-771, 2013.

40. Lockie, RG, Lazar, A, Orjalo, AJ, Davis, DL, Moreno, MR, Risso, FG, Hank, ME, Stone, RC, and Mosich, NW. Profiling of junior college football players and differences between position groups. *Sports* 4:41, 2016. doi:10.3390/sports4030041.

41. Lockie, RG, Liu, TM, Stage, AA, Lazar, A, Giuliano, DV, Hurley, JM, Torne, IA, Beiley, MD, Birmingham-Babauta, SA, Stokes, JJ, Risso, FG, Davis, DL, Moreno, MR, and Orjalo, AJ. Assessing repeated-sprint ability in Division I collegiate women soccer players. *J Strength Cond Res*, 2018. [e-pub ahead of print]. doi10.1519/jsc.0000000000002527.

42. Lockie, RG, Moreno, MR, Lazar, A, Orjalo, AJ, Giuliano, DV, Risso, FG, Davis, DL, Crelling, JB, Lockwood, JR, and Jalilvand, F. The physical and athletic performance characteristics of Division I collegiate female soccer players by position. *J Strength Cond Res* 32:334-343, 2018.

43. Lockie, RG, Risso, FG, Giuliano, DV, Orjalo, AJ, and Jalilvand, F. Practical fitness profiling using field test data for female elite-level collegiate soccer players: A case analysis of a Division I team. *Strength Cond J*, 2017. [e-pub ahead of print]. doi:10.1519/ssc.0000000000000343.

44. Lockie, RG, Schultz, AB, Callaghan, SJ, and Jeffriess, MD. Physiological profile of national-level junior American football players in Australia. *Serb J Sports Sci* 6:127-136, 2012.

45. Lockie, RG, Schultz, AB, Callaghan, SJ, and Jeffriess, MD. The effects of traditional and enforced stopping speed and agility training on multidirectional speed and athletic performance. *J Strength Cond Res* 28:1538-1551, 2014.

46. Lockie, RG, Schultz, AB, Callaghan, SJ, Jeffriess, MD, and Berry, SP. Reliability and validity of a new test of change-of-direction speed for field-based sports: the Change-of-Direction and Acceleration Test (CODAT). *J Sports Sci Med* 12:88-96, 2013.

47. Lockie, RG, Schultz, AB, Callaghan, SJ, Jordan, CA, Luczo, TM, and Jeffriess, MD. A preliminary investigation into the relationship between functional movement screen scores and athletic physical performance in female team sport athletes. *Biol Sport* 32:41-51, 2015.

48. Lockie, RG, Schultz, AB, Jordan, CA, Callaghan, SJ, Jeffriess, MD, and Luczo, TM. Can selected functional movement screen assessments be used to identify movement deficiencies that could affect multidirectional speed and jump performance? *J Strength Cond Res* 29:195-205, 2015.

49. Lockie, RG, Stage, AA, Stokes, JJ, Orjalo, AJ, Davis, DL, Giuliano, DV, Moreno, MR, Risso, FG, Lazar, A, Birmingham-Babauta, SA, and Tomita, TM. Relationships and predictive capabilities of jump assessments to soccer-specific field test performance in Division I collegiate players. *Sports* 4:56, 2016. doi:10.3390/sports4040056.

50. Lockie, RG, Stecyk, SD, Mock, SA, Crelling, JB, Lockwood, JR, and Jalilvand, F. A cross-sectional analysis of the characteristics of Division I collegiate female soccer field players across year of eligibility. *J Aust Strength Cond* 24:6-15, 2016.

51. Mayhew, JL, Houser, JJ, Briney, BB, Williams, TB, Piper, FC, and Brechue, WF. Comparison between hand and electronic timing of 40-yd dash performance in college football players. *J Strength Cond Res* 24:447-451, 2010.

52. McFarland, I, Dawes, JJ, Elder, CL, and Lockie, RG. Relationship of two vertical jumping tests to sprint and change of direction speed among male and female collegiate soccer players. *Sports* 4:11, 2016. doi:10.3390/sports4010011.

53. McGee, KJ, and Burkett, LN. The National Football League combine: A reliable predictor of draft status? *J Strength Cond Res* 17:6-11, 2003.

54. McGuigan, MR. Principles of Test Selection and Administration. In *Essentials of Strength Training and Conditioning*. 4th ed. Haff, GG, and Triplett, NT, eds. Champaign, IL: Human Kinetics, 249-258, 2016.

55. McGuigan, MR. Principles of Test Selection and Administration. In *Essentials of Strength Training and Conditioning*. 4th ed. Haff, GG, and Triplett, NT, eds. Champaign, IL: Human Kinetics, 249-258, 2016.

56. McGuigan, MR, Cormack, SJ, and Gill, ND. Strength and power profiling of athletes: Selecting tests and how to use the information for program design. *Strength Cond J* 35:7-14, 2013.

57. Moir, G, Button, C, Glaister, M, and Stone, MH. Influence of familiarization on the reliability of vertical jump and acceleration sprinting performance in physically active men. *J Strength Cond Res* 18:276-280, 2004.

58. Moreno, E. Developing quickness, Part II. *Strength Cond J* 17:38-39, 1995.

59. Nimphius, S, Callaghan, SJ, Bezodis, NE, and Lockie, RG. Change of direction and agility tests: Challenging our current measures of performance. *Strength Cond J* 40:26-38, 2018.

60. Nimphius, S, Callaghan, SJ, Spiteri, T, and Lockie, RG. Change of direction deficit: A more isolated measure of change of direction performance than total 505 time. *J Strength Cond Res* 30:3024-3032, 2016.

61. Nimphius, S, Geib, G, Spiteri, T, and Carlisle, D. "Change of direction" deficit measurement in Division I American football players. *J Aust Strength Cond* 21:115-117, 2013.

62. Nimphius, S, McGuigan, MR, and Newton, RU. Relationship between strength, power, speed, and change of direction performance of female softball players. *J Strength Cond Res* 24:885-895, 2010.

63. Nimphius, S, McGuigan, MR, and Newton, RU. Changes in muscle architecture and performance during a competitive season in female softball players. *J Strength Cond Res* 26:2655-2666, 2012.

64. Nuzzo, JL, Anning, JH, and Scharfenberg, JM. The reliability of three devices used for measuring vertical jump height. *J Strength Cond Res* 25:2580-2590, 2011.

65. Oliver, JL, and Meyers, RW. Reliability and generality of measures of acceleration, planned agility, and reactive agility. *Int J Sports Physiol Perf* 4:345-354, 2009.

66. Orr, R, Schram, B, and Pope, R. A comparison of military and law enforcement body armour. *Int J Environ Res Public Health* 15:339, 2018. doi:10.3390/ijerph15020339.

67. Paul, DJ, Gabbett, TJ, and Nassis, GP. Agility in team sports: Testing, training and factors affecting performance. *Sports Med* 46:421-442, 2016.

68. Risso, FG, Jalilvand, F, Orjalo, AJ, Moreno, MR, Davis, DL, Birmingham-Babauta, SA, Stokes, JJ, Stage, AA, Liu, TM, Giuliano, DV, Lazar, A, and Lockie, RG. Physiological characteristics of projected starters and non-starters in the field positions from a Division I women's soccer team. *Int J Exerc Sci* 10:568-579, 2017.

69. Robbins, DW. The National Football League (NFL) combine: Does normalized data better predict performance in the NFL draft? *J Strength Cond Res* 24:2888-2899, 2010.

70. Sassi, RH, Dardouri, W, Yahmed, MH, Gmada, N, Mahfoudhi, ME, and Gharbi, Z. Relative and absolute reliability of a modified agility T-test and its relationship with vertical jump and straight sprint. *J Strength Cond Res* 23:1644-1651, 2009.

71. Sayers, MGL. The influence of test distance on change of direction speed test results. *J Strength Cond Res* 29:2412-2416, 2015.

72. Sayers, SP, Harackiewicz, DV, Harman, EA, Frykman, PN, and Rosenstein, MT. Cross-validation of three jump power equations. *Med Sci Sports Exerc* 31:572-577, 1999.

73. Semenick, D. Tests and measurements: The T-test. *Natl Str Cond Assoc J* 12:36-37, 1990.

74. Sheppard, JM, and Young, WB. Agility literature review: Classifications, training and testing. *J Sports Sci* 24:919-932, 2006.

75. Sheppard, JM, Young, WB, Doyle, TL, Sheppard, TA, and Newton, RU. An evaluation of a new test of reactive agility and its relationship to sprint speed and change of direction speed. *J Sci Med Sport* 9:342-349, 2006.

76. Sierer, SP, Battaglini, CL, Mihalik, JP, Shields, EW, and Tomasini, NT. The National Football League Combine: Performance differences between drafted and non-drafted players entering the 2004 and 2005 drafts. *J Strength Cond Res* 22:6-12, 2008.

77. Spiteri, T, Nimphius, S, Hart, NH, Specos, C, Sheppard, JM, and Newton, RU. Contribution of strength characteristics to change of direction and agility performance in female basketball athletes. *J Strength Cond Res* 28:2415-2423, 2014.

78. Stanton, R, Hayman, M, Humphris, N, Borgelt, H, Fox, J, Del Vecchio, L, and Humphries, B. Validity of a smartphone-based application for determining sprinting performance. *J Sports Med*, 2016. doi:10.1155/2016/7476820.

79. Thomeé, R, Kaplan, Y, Kvist, J, Myklebust, G, Risberg, MA, Theisen, D, Tsepis, E, Werner, S, Wondrasch, B, and Witvrouw, E. Muscle strength and hop performance criteria prior to return to sports after ACL reconstruction. *Knee Surg Sports Traumatol Arthrosc* 19:1798-1805, 2011.

80. Thomeé, R, and Werner, S. Return to sport. *Knee Surg Sports Traumatol Arthrosc* 19:1795-1797, 2011.

81. Vallerand, RJ, and Losier, GF. An integrative analysis of intrinsic and extrinsic motivation in sport. *J Appl Sport Psychol* 11:142-169, 1999.

82. Vescovi, JD, Brown, TD, and Murray, TM. Positional characteristics of physical performance in Division I college female soccer players. *J Sports Med Phys Fitness* 46:221-226, 2006.

83. Vescovi, JD, and McGuigan, MR. Relationships between sprinting, agility, and jump ability in female athletes. *J Sports Sci* 26:97-107, 2008.

84. Whitting, JW, de Melker Worms, JL, Maurer, C, Nigg, SR, and Nigg, BM. Measuring lateral shuffle and side cut performance. *J Strength Cond Res* 27:3197-3203, 2013.

85. Wilkinson, M, Leedale-Brown, D, and Winter, EM. Validity of a squash-specific test of change-of-direction speed. *Int J Sports Physiol Perf* 4:176-185, 2009.

86. Woodman, TIM, and Hardy, LEW. The relative impact of cognitive anxiety and self-confidence upon sport performance: A meta-analysis. *J Sports Sci* 21:443-457, 2003.

87. Yap, CW, and Brown, LE. Development of speed, agility, and quickness for the female soccer athlete. *Strength Cond J* 22:9-12, 2000.

Chapter 6

1. Barnes, M, and Dawes, J, Plyometric, speed, and agility exercise technique and programming. In *Essentials of Tactical Strength and Conditioning*. Alvar, BA, Sell, K, and Deuster, PA, eds. Champaign IL: Human Kinetics, 387-390, 2016.

2. Dawes, J, and Lentz, D. Methods of developing power to improve acceleration for the non-track athlete. *Strength Cond J* 34(6):44-51, 2012.

3. Koski, S. ACL rehabilitation in injury prevention. *Athletic Therapy Today* 10(2): 40-44, 2005.

4. Potach, DH, and Chu, DA. Plyometric training. In *Essentials of Strength Training and Conditioning*. 4th ed. Haff, GG, and Triplett, NT, eds. Champaign IL: Human Kinetics, 474, 2016.

Chapter 7

1. Carlon, T. The importance of perceptual and decision-making factors of agility performance in open skilled sports: A review of the literature *J Aust Strength Cond* 20(4):82-88, 2012.

2. Henry, G, Dawson, B, Lay, B, and Young, W. Decision-making accuracy in reactive agility: Quantifying the costs of poor decisions. *J Strength Cond Res* 27(11):3190-3196, 2013.

3. Magrini, M, Dawes, J, Spaniol, F, and Roberts, A. Speed and agility training for baseball/softball. *Strength Cond J* 40(1):68-74, 2018.

4. Meir, R, Holding, R, Hetherington, J, and Rolfe, M. Impact of sport specific and generic visual stimulus on a reactive agility test while carrying a rugby ball. *J Aust Strength Cond* 21(1):45-49, 2013.

5. Nimphius, S, Callaghan, S, Bezodis, N, and Lockie, R. Change of direction and agility tests: Challenging our current measures of performance. *Strength Cond J* 40(1):26-38, 2018.

6. Oliver, JL, and Meyers, RW. Reliability and generality of measures of acceleration, planned agility, and reactive agility. *Int J Sports Physiol Perf* 4:345–354, 2009.

7. Scanlan, A, Tucker, P, and Dalbo, V. A comparison of linear speed, closed-skill agility, and open-skill agility qualities between backcourt and frontcourt adult semi-professional male basketball players. *J Strength Cond Res* 28(5):1319-1327, 2014.

8. Sheppard, J, and Young, W. Agility literature review: classifications, training and testing. *J Sports Sci* 24(9):919-932, 2006.

9. Sheppard, J, Dawes, J, Jeffreys, I, Spiteri, T, and Nimphius, S. Broadening the view of agility: A scientific review of the literature. *J Aust Strength Cond* 22(3):6-25, 2014.

10. Young, W. and Farrow, D. The importance of a sport-specific stimulus for training agility. *Strength Cond J* 35:39-43, 2013.

Chapter 8

1. Ericsson, K.A. *Peak: Secrets from the New Science of Expertise*. London: Random House, 2016.

2. Jeffreys, I. A motor development approach to enhancing agility: Part one. *Strength Cond J* 28(5):72-76, 2006.

3. Jeffreys, I. Warm-up revisited: The RAMP method of optimizing warm-ups. *Professional Strength and Conditioning* 6:12-18, 2007.

4. Jeffreys, I. A task-based approach to developing reactive agility. *Strength Cond J* 33(4):52-59, 2011.

5. Jeffreys, I. Agility training for team sports: Running the OODA loop. *Professional Strength and Conditioning* 42:15-21, 2016.

6. Jeffreys, I. *Gamespeed*. 2nd ed. Monterey, CA: Coaches Choice, 2017.

7. Jeffreys, I. RAMP warm-ups: More than simply short-term preparation. *Professional Strength and Conditioning* 44:17-23, 2017.

8. Jeffreys, I, Huggins, S, and Davies, N. Delivering a gamespeed-focused speed and agility development program in an English premier league soccer academy. *Strength Cond J* 40(3):23-32, 2018.

9. Lee, TD, Swinnen, S, and Serien, D. Cognitive effort and motor learning. *Quest* 46:328-344, 1994.

10. Schmidt, RA, and Lee, TD. *Motor Control and Learning: A Behavioural Emphasis*. Champaign, IL: Human Kinetics, 302-345, 2005.

11. Vickers, JN. *Perception, Cognition and Decision Training: The Quiet Eye in Action*. Champaign, IL: Human Kinetics, 164-184, 2007.

12. Wulf, G. *Attention and Motor Skill Learning*. Champaign, IL: Human Kinetics, 134, 2007.

13. Young, W. and Farrow, D. The importance of a sport-specific stimulus for training agility. *Strength Cond J* 25(2):39-43, 2016.

Chapter 9

Baseball and Softball

1. Magrini, M, Dawes, JJ, Spaniol, FJ, and Roberts, A. Speed and agility training for baseball and softball. *Strength and Cond J* 40(1):68-71, 2017.

Basketball

1. Drinkwater, EJ, Pyne, DB, and McKenna, MJ. Design and interpretation of anthropometric and fitness testing of basketball players. *Sports Med* 38(7):565-578, 2008.

2. Abdelkrim, B, El Fazaa, S, and El Ati, J. Time-motion analysis and physiological data of elite under-19-year-old basketball players during competition. *Br J Sports Med* 41(2):69-75, 2007.

3. McInnes, SE, Carlson, JS, Jones, CJ, and McKenna, MJ. The physiological load imposed on basketball players during competition. *J Sports Sci* 13(5):387-397, 1995.

4. Teixeira, AS, Arins, FB, De Lucas, RD, Carminatti, LJ, Dittrich, N, Nakamura, FY, and Guglielmo, LGA. Comparative effects of two interval shuttle-run training modes on physiological and performance adaptations in female professional futsal players. *J Strength Cond Res* 10:1519, 2017.

Combat Sports

1. Paul, DJ, and Akenhead, R. Agility training: A potential model for the reduction and rehabilitation of anterior cruciate ligament injury. *Strength Cond J* 40(1):98-105, 2018.
2. Tack, C. Evidence based-guidelines for strength and conditioning in martial arts. *Strength C J* 35(5):79-92, 2013.

Cricket

1. Draper, J, and Pyke, F. Turning speed: A valuable asset in cricket run making. *Sports Coach* 11:30-31, 1988.
2. Houghton, LA. Running between the wickets in cricket: What is the fastest technique? *International Journal of Sports Science and Coaching* 5:101-107, 2010.

Field Hockey

1. Buglione, A, Ruscello, B, Milia, R, Migliaccio, G, Granatelli, G, and D'Ottavio, S. Physical and physiological demands of elite and sub-elite field hockey players. *Int J Perform Anal Sport* 13:872-884, 2013.
2. Jeffreys, I. Motor learning—applications for agility, part 1. *Strength Cond J* 28(5):72-76, 2006.
3. Jeffreys, I. Motor learning—applications for agility, part 2. *Strength Cond J* 28(6):10-14, 2006.
4. Jennings, DH, Cormack, SJ, Coutts, AJ, and Aughey, RJ. International field hockey players perform more high-speed running than national-level counterparts. *J Strength C Res* 26:947-952, 2012.
5. Keogh, JW, Weber, CL, and Dalton, CT. Evaluation of anthropometric, physiological, and skill-related tests for talent identification in female field hockey. *Can J Appl Physiol* 28:397-409, 2003.
6. McManus, A, and Stevenson, M. Quantifying the physical demands in non-elite field hockey to develop training guidelines that minimise injury through adequate preparation. *J Sci Med Sport* 10:90, 2007.
7. Spencer, M, Bishop, D, Dawson, B, and Goodman, C. Physiological and metabolic responses of repeated-sprint activities: Specific to field-based team sports. *Sports Med* 35:1025-1044, 2005.
8. Spencer, M, Fitzsimons, M, Dawson, B, Bishop, D, and Goodman, C. Reliability of a repeated-sprint test for field-hockey. *J Sci Med Sport* 9:181-184, 2006.
9. Vescovi, JD. Locomotor, heart-rate, and metabolic power characteristics of youth women's field hockey: female athletes in motion (FAiM) Study. *Res Q Exerc Sport* 87:68-77, 2016.
10. Vescovi, JD, and McGuigan. MR. Relationships between sprinting, agility, and jump ability in female athletes. *J Sports Sci* 26:97-107, 2008.
11. Wdowski, MM, and Gittoes, MJ. Kinematic adaptations in sprint acceleration performances without and with the constraint of holding a field hockey stick. *Sports Biomech* 12:143-153, 2013.

Football (American or Gridiron)

1. Gleason, BH, Kramer, JB, and Stone, MH. Agility training for American football, *Strength and Cond J* 27(6):65-71, 2015.

Ice Hockey

1. Arshi, AR, Nabavi, H, Mehdizadeh, S, and Davids, K. An alternative approach to describing agility in sports through establishment of a relationship between velocity and radius of curvature. *J Sports Sci* 33(13):1349-1355, 2015.

2. Dawes, JJ. (2008). Creating open agility drills. *Strength Cond J* 30(5):54-55, 2008.

3. Dæhlin, TE, Haugen, OC, Haugerud, S, Hollan, I, Raastad, T, and Rønnestad, BR. (2017). Improvement of ice hockey players' on-ice sprint with combined plyometric and strength training. *Int J Sports Physiol Perf* 12(7):893-900, 2017.

4. Haukali, E, and Tjelta, LI. Correlation between "off-ice" variables and skating performance among young male ice hockey players. *International Journal of Applied Sports Sciences* 27(1):26-32, 2015.

5. Janot, JM, Beltz, NM, and Dalleck, LD. Multiple off-ice performance variables predict on-ice skating performance in male and female division III ice hockey players. *J Sports Sci Med* 14(3):522-529, 2015.

6. Serpell, BG, Young, WB, and Ford, M. Are the perceptual and decision-making components of agility trainable? A preliminary investigation. *J Strength Cond Res* 25(5):1240-1248, 2011.

7. Šimonek, J, Horička, P, and, Hianik, J. Differences in pre-planned agility and reactive agility performance in sport games. *Acta Gymnica* 46(2):68-73, 2016.

8. Veale, JP, Pearce, AJ, and Carlson, JS. Reliability and validity of a reactive agility test for Australian football. *Int J Sports Physiol Perf* 5(2):239-248, 2010.

9. Young, WB, Dawson, B, and Henry, GJ. Agility and change-of-direction speed are independent skills: implications for training for agility in invasion sports. *Int J Sports Sci Coach* 10(1):159-169, 2015.

Lacrosse

1. Gutowski, AE, and Rosene, JM. Preseason performance testing battery for men's lacrosse. *Strength Cond J* 33(2):16-22, 2011.

2. Richard, H, and Harald, T. Physiological profile differences of male Austrian lacrosse athletes: A comparison to US collegian lacrosse athletes. *Kinesiologia Slovenica* 23(3):18-31, 2017.

3. Sheppard, J, Dawes, JJ, Jeffreys, I, Spiteri, T, and Nimphius, S. Broadening the view of agility: A scientific review of the literature. *J Aust Strength Cond* 22(3):1-27, 2014.

Netball

1. Baker, D. Recent trends in high intensity aerobic training for field sports. *UK Strength and Conditioning Association* 22:3-8.

2. Davidson, A. and Trewartha, G. Understanding the physiological demands of netball: A time-motion investigation. *Int J Perform Anal Sport* 8:1117.

3. Fox, A, Spittle, M, Otago, L, and Saunders, N. Activity profiles of the Australian female netball team players during international competition: Implications for training practice. *J Sports Sci* 31:1588-1595, 2013.

4. Fox, A, Spittle, M, Otago, L, and Saunders, N. Offensive agility techniques performed during international netball competition. *Int J Sports Sci Coach* 9:543-552, 2014.

5. Hewit, JK. Assessing agility in netball players (Doctoral dissertation, Auckland University of Technology). 2011.

6. Hopper, A, Haff, E, Joyce, C, Lloyd, R, and Haff, GG. Neuromuscular training improves lower extremity biomechanics associated with knee injury during landing in 11-13 year old female netball athletes: A randomized control study. *Front Physiol* 8(883):1-13, 2017.

7. International Netball Federation. Conducting a training session. In: *INF Foundation Coaching Manual*. Manchester: INF; 24, 2012.

8. Mothersole, GA, Cronin, JP, and Harris, NK. Key prerequisite factors influencing landing forces in netball. *Strength Cond J* 35(2):47-54, 2013.

9. Steele, JR, and Chad, K. Relationship between movement patterns performed in match play and in training by skilled netball players. *Journal of Human Movement Studies* 20:2491278, 1991.

10. Thomas, C, Comfort, P, Jones, PA, and Dos'Santos, T. Strength and conditioning for netball: A needs analysis and training recommendations. *Strength Cond J* 39(4):10-21.

11. Young, C.M., Gastin, N.S., Mackey, L., and Dwyer, D.B. Player load in elite netball: Match, training, and positional comparisons. *Int J Sports Physiol Perform.* 11(8):1074-1079, 2016.

Soccer

1. Bangsbo J. The physiology of soccer—with special reference to intense intermittent exercise. *Acta Physiol Scand Suppl* 619:1-156, 1994.

2. Bangsbo J. Time and motion characteristics of competition soccer. *Science Football* 6:34-40, 1992.

3. Jeffreys, I. *Game Speed: Movement Training for Superior Sports Performance*. Monterey, CA: Coaches Choice, 2009.

4. Turner, A, and Stewart, PF. Strength and conditioning for soccer players. *Strength Cond J* 36(4):1-13, 2014.

Tennis

1. Kovacs, MS. A comparison of work/rest intervals in men's professional tennis. *Medicine and Science in Tennis* 9(3):10-11, 2004.

2. Kovacs, MS. Applied physiology of tennis performance. *Br J Sports Med* 40(5):381-386, 2006.

3. Kovacs, MS. Tennis physiology: Training the competitive athlete. *Sports Med* 37(3):1-11, 2007.

4. Kovacs, MS, Chandler, WB, and Chandler, TJ. *Tennis Training: Enhancing On-Court Performance*. Vista, CA: Racquet Tech, 2007.

5. Mero, A, and Komi, PV. Reaction time and electromyographic activity during a sprint start. *Eur J Appl Physiol* 61:73-80, 1990.

6. Roetert, EP, and Ellenbecker, TS. *Complete Conditioning for Tennis*. 2nd ed. Champaign, IL: Human Kinetics, 2007.

7. Roper, RL. Incorporating agility training and backward movement into a plyometric program. *Strength Cond J* 20(4):60-63, 1998.

8. Schmidt, RA, and Lee, TD. *Motor Control and Learning: A Behavioral Emphasis*. 3rd ed. Champaign, IL: Human Kinetics, 1999.

9. Weber, K, Pieper, S, and Exler, T. Characteristics and significance of running speed at the Australian Open 2006 for training and injury prevention. *Medicine and Science in Tennis*, 12(1):14-17, 2007.

10. Young, WB, McDowell, MH, and Scarlett, BJ. Specificity of sprint and agility training methods. *J. Strength Cond Res* 15(3):315-319, 2001.

Volleyball

1. Barnes, JL, Schilling, BK, Falvo, MJ, Weiss, LW, Creasy, AK, and Fry, AC. Relationship of jumping and agility performance in female volleyball athletes. *J Strength Cond Res* 21(4):1192-1196, 2007.

2. Gabbett, TJ. Do skill-based conditioning games offer a specific training stimulus for junior elite volleyball players? *J Strength Cond Res* 22:509-517, 2008.

3. Gadeken, SB. Off-season strength, power, and plyometric training for Kansas State volleyball. *Strength Cond J* 21(6):49-55, 1999.

4. Hedrick, A. Training for high level performance in women's collegiate volleyball: Part I training requirements. *Strength Cond J* 29(6):50-53, 2007.

5. Jaric, S, Ristanovic, D, and Corcos, D. The relationship between muscle kinetic parameters and kinematic variables in a complex movement. *Eur J Appl Physiol* 59:370-376, 1989.

6. Kukolj, M, Ropret, R, Ugarkovic, D, and Jaric, S. Anthropometric, strength, and power predictors of sprinting performance. *J Sports Med Phys Fitness* 39:120-122, 1999.

7. Mero, A, Luhtanen, P, Vitasalo, J, and Komi, P. Relationships between the maximum running velocity, muscle fiber characteristics, force production and force relaxation of sprinters. *Scandinavian Journal of Sports Science* 3:16-22, 1981.

8. Nesser, T, Latin, R, Berg, K, and Prentice, E. Physiological determinants of 40 meter sprint performance in young male athletes. *J Strength Cond Res* 10:263-267, 1996.

9. Sheppard, JM. and Gabbett, T. The development and evaluation of a repeated effort test for volleyball. Paper presented at the NSCA National Conference, Atlanta, Georgia, July 10-12, 2007.

10. Sheppard, JM, Gabbett, T, Taylor, KL, Dorman, J, Lebedew, AJ, and Borgeaud, R. Development of a repeated effort test for elite men's volleyball. *Int J Sports Physiol Perf* 2(3):292-304, 2007.

11. Young, W, and Farrow, DA. A review of agility: Practical applications for strength and conditioning. *Strength Cond J* 28(5):24-29, 2006.

Wrestling

1. Bompa, T, and Haff, G. *Periodization Theory and Methodology of Training.* 5th ed. Champaign, IL: Human Kinetics, 2009.

2. Brown, L, and Khamoui, A. Agility training. In *NSCA's Guide to Program Design.* Hoffman, J., ed. Champaign, IL: Human Kinetics, 161, 2012.

3. Chaabene, H, Negra, Y, Bouguezzi, R, Mkaouer, B, Franchini, E, Julio, U, and Hachana, Y. Physical and physiological attributes of wrestlers: An update. *J Strength Cond Res* 31:1411-1442, 2017.

4. Fernandez-Fernandez, J, Granacher, U, Sanz-Rivas, D, Marin, J, Hernandez-Davo, J, and Moya, M. Sequencing effects of neuromuscular training on physical fitness in youth elite tennis players. *J Strength Cond Res* 32:849-856, 2018.

5. Young, W, and Farrow, D. The importance of a sport-specific stimulus for training agility. *Strength Cond J* 35:39-43, 2013.

Index

Note: The italicized *f* and *t* following page numbers refer to figures and tables, respectively.

About the NSCA

The National Strength and Conditioning Association (NSCA) is the world's leading organization in the field of sport conditioning. Drawing on the resources and expertise of the most recognized professionals in strength training and conditioning, sport science, performance research, education, and sports medicine, the NSCA is the world's trusted source of knowledge and training guidelines for coaches and athletes. The NSCA provides the crucial link between the lab and the field.

About the Editor

Jay Dawes, PhD, CSCS,*D, NSCA-CPT,*D, FNSCA, is an associate professor of strength and conditioning and the program coordinator for the masters of science in strength and conditioning program at the University of Colorado in Colorado Springs. He has worked as an athletic performance coordinator, strength and performance coach, personal trainer, educator, and postrehabilitation specialist for more than 20 years. Jay also frequently coaches and provides sport science support to numerous elite and professional teams and law enforcement, fire, and military groups. Jay's primary research interests are improving and measuring performance for tactical athletes and first responders and enhancing athletic performance. He is certified by the NSCA as a certified strength and conditioning specialist with distinction and is an NSCA-certified personal trainer with distinction. Jay is also an NSCA tactical strength and conditioning facilitator, an American College of Sports Medicine clinical exercise specialist, and an Australian Strength and Conditioning Association level two strength and conditioning coach. Jay has been a fellow of the NSCA since 2009.

About the Contributors

Jason D. Barber, PA-C, MS, CSCS, TSAC-F, RSCC*D, USATF, USAW, is the high-performance coordinator for the U.S. Army's world class athlete program. He has trained athletes who have won multiple national and international competitions. More than 25 athletes he has placed in multiple summer, winter, Able, and Para Olympiads have won multiple gold, silver, and bronze medals. Previously, Jason has worked with athletes at every level from high school to professional as well as in the tactical environment. He has served in the U.S. Army for the past 27 years.

Simon Feros, PhD, is a lecturer of functional human anatomy and strength and conditioning sciences at Deakin University. His research focuses on explosive strength training and biomechanical adaptations underpinning sports performance, particularly in cricket fast bowling. Simon is a level two ASCA strength and conditioning coach and an ASCA PCAS intern strength and conditioning coach. He is owner and director of Bowlstrong, where he consults cricket fast bowlers to improve performance through explosive strength training and biomechanical interventions.

Jennifer Fields, MS, CSCS, is a PhD student and adjunct professor at George Mason University. She earned a BS in kinesiology from the University of Maryland and received her MS degree in health promotion and nutrition from American University. Jennifer has been a strength and conditioning professional since 2010, training collegiate, high school, and middle school athletes as well as individuals in the general population.

Javair Gillett, MS, CSCS, RSCC*D, is the head strength and conditioning coach for the Houston Rockets and oversees their sports science initiative as the director of athletic performance. Prior to joining the Rockets, Javair spent 14 years with the Detroit Tigers, 4 years in the minor leagues, and 10 years as their head strength and conditioning coach. He is certified as a registered strength and conditioning coach by the NSCA. Javair has an MS in human movement from A.T. Still University and completed his bachelor's degree at DePauw University, majoring in health and human performance with an emphasis in exercise science. Prior to joining the Tigers, Javair gained experience in the field working with the Orlando Magic during the 2002-2003 NBA season as well as at Indiana University (2001) and Pennsylvania State University (2000). He also lettered four seasons with DePauw University's baseball team and was given All-Conference honors two of those four years as well as All-American Honorable Mention his final season.

Erin E. Haff, MA, USAW-2, AWF-3, has more than 27 years of experience as a strength and conditioning coach for youth athletes through professional athletes. She has served as the head strength and conditioning coach for the West Coast Fever professional netball team in Perth, Western Australia. Additionally, she has provided strength training support for several youth resistance training studies designed to examine the impact of resistance training on netball performance. Prior to this, she served as the strength and conditioning coach for the Appalachian State University track and field team and for numerous high school sports teams. Along with her work as a strength coach, Erin has been an Australian national team coach for more than a dozen youth, junior, and senior international competitions in the sport of weightlifting as well as presenting for both Australia's Weightlifting Federation and Strength and Conditioning Association education programs.

Farzad Jalilvand, MS, CSCS,*D, RSCC, USAW, is the head strength and conditioning coach for Granada Hills Charter High School and is a strength and conditioning lecturer at California State University at Northridge in the department of kinesiology. Farzad completed his master's in exercise physiology at California State University at Northridge and has conducted research in soccer and team sport performance.

Ian Jeffreys, PhD, CSCS,*D, NSCA-CPT,*D, RSCC*E, FNSCA, is a professor of strength and conditioning at the University of South Wales, where he oversees the university's strength and conditioning provision. He is the proprietor and performance director of All-Pro Performance, based in Brecon, Wales. A highly experienced coach, author, and presenter, Ian has worked with athletes in a range of sports and at a range of abilities up to the international level. Ian has authored eight books and is the editor of the UKSCA journal *Professional Strength and Conditioning*. He is also on the editorial board for the NSCA's *Strength and Conditioning Journal* and the *Journal of Australian Strength and Conditioning*.

Margaret T. Jones, PhD, CSCS,*D, FNSCA, is a full professor of kinesiology and an affiliate of the Center for Sports Performance at George Mason University. Past experience includes 15 years at Springfield College as director of the strength and conditioning master's degree program and the director of strength and conditioning for intercollegiate athletics, where she supervised program design and implementation for 500 athletes from 24 sports. An active member of the NSCA since 1995, Margaret received the NSCA Educator of the Year Award in 2008 and became a fellow of the NSCA in 2012.

Logan Lentz Kell, MS, CSCS, is a partner with her father, Doug Lentz, in DKL Fitness and Performance LLC, a company devoted to providing information in training methodology for coaches and athletes of all ages and abilities. She earned a BS degree in exercise science from Southern Connecticut State University, where she was a full scholarship athlete, and received her MS degree in strength and conditioning from George Washington University in 2013.

Mark Kovacs, PhD, CSCS,*D, is a human performance expert who combines his academic, scientific, and training backgrounds in the fields of fitness, health, wellness, nutrition, sports, and executive performance. He received a PhD in exercise physiology from the University of Alabama and was the director of the Gatorade Sport Science Institute and the head of coaching education and sport science for the United States Tennis Association. Mark is the CEO of the Kovacs Institute and the executive director of the International Tennis Performance Association. He is a level two certified sprints coach through USA Track & Field.

Loren Landow, CSCS,*D, is the full-time head strength and conditioning coach for the Denver Broncos Football Organization and is owner and founder of Landow Performance in Centennial, Colorado. Loren has trained thousands of athletes of all ages and abilities, including more than 700 professional athletes competing in the NFL, NHL, MLB, UFC, WNBA, Pan Am, and World Jiu-Jitsu Championships  and in the Olympics. He has been a keynote speaker for the NSCA, ASCA, SPRINTZ, and the UKSCA, and he serves as a consultant for the University of Colorado Football Team, MLB Texas Rangers, USA Women's National Soccer Team, and the USA bobsled team. Loren serves on the board of directors for the exercise science program at Metro State University and the master's program for Setanta College in Ireland.

Doug Lentz, MS, CSCS,*D, RSCC*E, USAW, is the director of fitness and human performance for Summit Health in Chambersburg, Pennsylvania. He has been actively involved in the coaching and training of athletes of all ages and abilities for more than 35 years. Doug also serves as an adjunct professor at George Washington University, where he teaches a postgraduate course in power development for  sports performance. For more than 25 years, he has served the NSCA as the conferences and special programs coordinator; in this position, Doug has had the privilege of interacting with many of the top national and international minds in the field of sports and exercise science.

Robert Lockie, PhD, TSAC-F, is an assistant professor in strength and conditioning at California State University at Fullerton. He obtained his PhD from the University of Technology, Sydney, with research that focused on analyzing sprint techniques and strength and power capacities of field sport athletes. Robert has conducted research on linear speed, change-of-direction speed, and agility; strength and  conditioning; postactivation potentiation; and team sport analysis. More recently, he has completed research in the field of tactical strength and conditioning with a special emphasis on law enforcement, correctional, and firefighter populations, including both recruits and incumbent officers.

Mark Roozen, MEd, CSCS, NSCA-CPT, TSAC-F, FNSCA, is the owner and director of Coach Rozy Performance and has been in the strength, conditioning, and performance field for more than 30 years. Mark has worked with teams from high school to professional as a sports coach and a strength and performance coach. In addition to working in the NFL and training Olympic athletes, Mark has presented, authored, and consulted around the world for various sport and fitness groups and organizations.

Jeremy Sheppard, PhD, CSCS, RSCC*E, is the off-snow coach for Canada Snowboard's Slopestyle and Big Air programs and the director of performance for the Canadian Sport Institute Pacific. Prior to this, he was the manager of athletic development and sport science at the High-Performance Centre for Surfing Australia, and he has held positions at the Australian Institute of Sport, Australian Volleyball, and Queensland Academy of Sport. He is an adjunct senior lecturer for Edith Cowan University (Australia) and the University of Victoria (Canada).

Tania Spiteri, PhD, is the head of sport science at the World Basketball Academy. She received a PhD in biomechanics from Edith Cowan University and is a level two certified strength and conditioning coach with the Australian Strength and Conditioning Association. Tania is also an adjunct lecturer in exercise and sport science at Edith Cowan University.

Mark D. Stephenson, MS, ATC, CSCS,*D, TSAC-F,*D, is the director of player performance for the Detroit Lions (NFL). With more than 30 years of experience in a variety of settings, Mark has previously served in notable positions as the human performance manager for a special operations unit, head strength and conditioning coach for Colorado College men's hockey, director of tactical strength and conditioning for the NSCA, and head strength and conditioning coach for Providence College. Mark holds an undergraduate degree in exercise science and a master's in health science. He is a doctoral candidate in psychology with a specialty in sports and performance psychology. Mark is a certified strength and conditioning specialist, a certified athletic trainer, a certified sports psychology coach, and a certified professional in applied neuroscience.

David N. Suprak, PhD, ATC, CSCS, USAW-1, is a professor of kinesiology and physical education at Western Washington University, where he has worked since 2008. He has more than 15 years of experience designing and implementing strength and conditioning programs for collegiate teams and individuals of all skill levels. Before David's tenure at Western Washington University, he was an assistant professor of health sciences at the University of Colorado at Colorado Springs, a research and teaching assistant at the University of Oregon, and the head athletic trainer and athletic training education program director at Tabor College in Hillsboro, Kansas.

Contributors to the Previous Edition

Al Biancani, EdD, CSCS

Michael Doscher, MS, CSCS, RSCC*D

Todd Durkin, MA, CSCS

Greg Infantolino, CSCS, USAW

Jason Jones, MS, CSCS

Katie Krall, LMT, CSCS, NSCA-CPT, USAW

Mike Nitka, MEd, CSCS,*D, RSCC*E, FNSCA

Joel Raether, MEd, CSCS,*D, TSAC-F,*D

Mike Sanders, MEd, CSCS

David Sandler, MS, FNSCA